Latin America: Dependency or Interdependence?

A Conference Sponsored by the
American Enterprise Institute for Public Policy Research

Latin America: Dependency or Interdependence?

Edited by
Michael Novak and Michael P. Jackson

American Enterprise Institute for Public Policy Research
Washington, D.C.

Michael Novak holds the George Frederick Jewett Chair at AEI and is the author of numerous books, including *The Spirit of Democratic Capitalism* and *Freedom with Justice*. He is a founding editor of *This World* and of *Catholicism in Crisis*, he has served as head of the U.S. delegation to the UN Human Rights Commission, and he now serves on the Board for International Broadcasting, the private corporation governing Radio Free Europe and Radio Liberty. Michael P. Jackson is an assistant professor in the Department of Political Science at the University of Georgia, Athens. He was formerly a researcher in the Center for Religion, Philosophy, and Public Policy at the American Enterprise Institute.

Editor's Note

Several of the chapters that follow are based on oral delivery and derive from an edited manuscript. In their published form, they have retained the flavor of their original immediacy, in a form quite different from that of essays written out in advance.

Library of Congress Cataloging-in-Publication Data
Main entry under title:

Latin America, dependency or interdependence?

    1. Latin America—Economic conditions—1945-   —Addresses, essays, lectures. 2. Latin America—Dependency on foreign countries—Addresses, essays, lectures.
3. Investments, Foreign—Latin America—Addresses, essays, lectures. I. Novak, Michael. II. Jackson, Michael, 1954–
HC125.L3436 1985   337.8   85–20039
ISBN 0–8447–2258–8 (alk. paper)
ISBN 0–8447–2257–X (pbk. : alk. paper)

1 3 5 7 9 10 8 6 4 2

AEI Symposia 85D

Printed in the United States of America

Contents

Foreword

With the publication of this volume, the American Enterprise Institute continues to investigate the role of religion and morality in the formation of public policy.

A distinctive characteristic of AEI's approach has been the attempt to foster interaction among the various disciplines associated with public policy—economics, law, government, diplomacy, and the social sciences generally—in the belief that such interaction will lead to new insights and better modes of thought in the development of public policy. The papers and summaries presented here are from the sixth in a series of Summer Institutes sponsored by the Center for Religion, Philosophy, and Public Policy at AEI. The sixth Summer Institute was jointly sponsored by the University of Notre Dame and held at Airlie House in Warrenton, Virginia, from July 8 to July 11, 1984. It was enlivened by the energetic participation of some fifty persons from business, government, the church, and the academy.

Special thanks are due to the Rev. Oliver Williams, C.S.C., of the Department of Management at Notre Dame and to Michael Novak, resident scholar at AEI, for their help in planning and directing the proceedings.

WILLIAM J. BAROODY, JR.
President
American Enterprise Institute

Contributors

GUILLERMO O. CHAPMAN, JR., is the founder and chairman of the board of INDESA, a firm of economic and financial consultants. He has served as an economist in the Planning Office of the Presidency of the Republic of Panama and as a member of the Panamanian Canal Treaty Negotiating Mission. He holds an M.A. in economics and finance from Louisiana State University and has published many articles and essays on the Panamanian economy, on the Panama Canal, and on issues of social and economic development.

ROLANDO DUARTE, the brother of Salvadoran President José Napoleón Duarte, is a 1947 graduate of the University of Notre Dame and a resident of San Salvador, El Salvador. He has served as the dean of the Faculty of Economics at the Catholic University of San Salvador. In 1983 he was the Salvadoran representative at the International Rotary meeting in Canada. He is now engaged in private industry.

MICHAEL J. FRANCIS is chairman of the Department of Government at the University of Notre Dame and a fellow of the Kellogg Institute. He works in the area of international affairs with a special emphasis on Latin America. He received his Ph.D. from the University of Virginia and has held research grants from the Social Science Research Council and the University Consortium for World Order Studies. Dr. Francis is the author of *The Limits of Hegemony, The Victory of Allende,* and many articles in English and Spanish journals.

WILLIAM P. GLADE, JR., is the director of the Institute of Latin American Studies at the University of Texas at Austin. His Ph.D. in economics is from the University of Texas, and he has served on numerous public committees and associations related to Latin America. His books include *The Latin American Economies: A Study of Their Institutional Evolution* and *Latin American–U.S. Economic Interactions* (coeditor).

JERRY HAAR is associate professor of international business, Florida International University, and adjunct scholar of the American Enterprise Institute. He is also president of the Inter-American Management Group, Inc., and partner in Burkholder Wallender International. Since taking his Ph.D. from Columbia University, he has been director of Washington Programs for the Council for the Americas and has held several senior staff positions with the federal government, including service as a special assistant to two cabinet secretaries. Dr. Haar has written or co-written three books and a number of articles and has consulted for public and private organizations in the United States and abroad.

ARCHBISHOP MARCOS MCGRATH, C.S.C., is now the archbishop of Panama and has served as the dean of the Faculty of Theology at the University of Chile. He received his Ph.D. in theology from St. Thomas University in Rome, with additional studies at the Catholic Institute of Paris and in Germany. He was a member of the Vatican Council II and served on the steering committees of the Second and Third General Conferences of Latin American Bishops. A member of the Congregation of the Holy Cross, he has also served on several postconciliar Vatican bodies and is on the board of trustees of the University of Notre Dame.

RUSSELL E. MARKS, JR., was the first president of the Americas Society, Inc., a nonprofit organization that coordinates the activities of five affiliates: the Council of the Americas, the Center for Inter-American Relations, the Pan-American Society of the United States, the U.S. Business Committee on Jamaica, and Caribbean–Central American Action. He is a member of the Council on Foreign Relations. Mr. Marks received his B.A. from Princeton and was president of Phelps-Dodge International Corporation, which has manufacturing operations in fifteen countries in Latin America, Europe, Africa, and Asia. Earlier, he was associated with W. R. Grace as Latin American group vice-president.

THEODORE H. MORAN is Landegger Professor and director of the Program in International Business Diplomacy at the Georgetown University School of Business Administration. Formerly a member of the Policy Planning Staff of the Department of State, he has served as a consultant to corporations, governments, and multilateral agencies on investment strategy, international negotiations, and political risk assessment. Dr. Moran received his Ph.D. in government from Harvard. He has been a member of the Board or Advisory Committee of *International Organization, World Trade,* the Overseas Development Council, and the Americas Society. In addition to over thirty scholarly articles, Dr. Moran's publications include five books, of which *Multinational Corporations: The Political Economy of Foreign Direct Investment* (editor) is the most recent.

HOWARD J. WIARDA is a resident scholar and director of the Center for Hemispheric Studies at the American Enterprise Institute. Before joining AEI, he was a scholar at the Center for International Affairs at Harvard University and a visiting professor at MIT. Dr. Wiarda is also professor of political science and adjunct professor of comparative labor relations at the University of Massachusetts at Amherst. His recent books include *Politics and Social Change in Latin America, Latin American Politics and Development, The Continuing Struggle for Democracy in Latin America,* and *Ethnocentrism in Foreign Policy: Can We Understand the Third World?*

Introduction

Michael Novak and Michael P. Jackson

The aim of the Summer Institute of 1984 was to bring the question of the multinational corporations in Latin America down from the clouds of mythology and bump it against hard earth. To this end, the planning group for the conference—organized at the University of Notre Dame by the Rev. Oliver Williams, C.S.C., and professors Lee Tavis and Yusaku Furuhashi—arranged for a first-rank assemblage of lecturers and discussants.

The sequence of Summer Institutes, into which this sixth one made a natural fit, has as its general purpose to create a body of pioneering literature bridging the worlds of religion and economics. Thus, in 1978 the very first Summer Institute explored the most general topic: some theological concepts basic to both socialism and capitalism. The proceedings were later published under the title *Capitalism and Socialism: A Theological Inquiry.* Among its papers were some that have since become small classics, notably those by Irving Kristol and Seymour Martin Lipset. In 1979, the topic was those "mediating institutions" that fall between the state and the individual. The papers and edited discussion appeared as *Democracy and Mediating Structures,* among the latter of which were considered the church, the large business corporation, organized labor, and the family. The papers by Paul Johnson, Robert Lekachman, and James Luther Adams have since been especially often cited and reprinted. In 1980, the focus narrowed to one of these mediating structures, the corporation, and the resulting book, *The Corporation: A Theological Inquiry,* included Oscar Handlin's two brilliant papers on the history of the corporation in America, P. T. Bauer's much discussed essays on the third world, and several other papers, including one on such nonbusiness corporations as the foundation.

In 1981 and 1982, the Summer Institutes turned aside from this main line of inquiry to assume a broader perspective. They considered, respectively, the teachings of the Christian churches on the economy and the literary tradition and business. Major papers from these two institutes were published in *This World,* edited by Michael A. Scully in issues number One and Three.

By 1984, we were ready to resume the more specifically economic questions and so turned to the pressing problems of Latin America, and

1

particularly to the role therein of U.S. corporations and investments. The papers and edited transcripts of the discussions on that topic follow.

Although Howard J. Wiarda's presentation came at the end of the actual discussion, as a sort of summary, the editors have here placed it at the beginning because it serves as a splendid introduction. Professor Wiarda sees, more clearly than most, that the economies of Latin America, despite their variety, represent a virtually unique type. Although heavily statist, most are not (excepting Cuba and one or two others) Socialist. Although they respect private property and markets, they are by no means capitalist in the modern sense. The exact phrase for them is difficult to find: statist, feudal, corporatist, precapitalist, mercantilist. The influence upon them of the Latin Catholic traditions of the Holy Roman Empire is still quite powerful. In Latin America, such liberation theologians as Leonardo Boff have described their problem as "capitalism"; Wiarda's distinctions suggest that a more exact diagnosis is in order.

The other papers fall into three natural categories. Professors Theodore H. Moran, Michael Francis, William Glade, and Jerry Haar present state-of-the-art discussions about the connections between Latin American and other Western economies, with special attention to the multinational corporations and foreign investment. Professor Moran lays out an impressive case for a system of open trade and open investment, both to meet the necessities of Latin America (and other parts of the developing world) and for the long-term interests of the United States. The factual material he reports and the broad scholarship he introduces are of great assistance to the uninitiated; his references have abiding usefulness. His emphasis upon the constantly changing negotiating strength of host governments and multinational corporations is especially instructive.

Professor Francis, aiming his discussion at the skeptical, makes an intelligent case for a modified version of "dependency theory." His discussion is subtle, nuanced, and fair; without lingering upon them, he notes the weaknesses of that theory and takes care not to overstate his points.

Professor Glade brings to bear his broad scholarly familiarity with Latin America in a clear and dispassionate overview. One cannot speak wisely on the role of multinationals and foreign investment without broad and detailed knowledge of a complex economic situation. He notes how heavily the recent debt crisis, austerity programs, and other events have fallen upon small and moderate-sized domestic firms and how weighty the temptation is to hide an ever-wider range of economic enterprises behind the carapace of state protection. The state looms increasingly larger in Latin American economic thought and practice.

Jerry Haar, associate professor at Florida International University in Miami, discusses acute problems of private investment, tax policies, and institutions of economic growth. His list of practical suggestions for policy is provocative and stimulating.

The second group of papers includes those by participants from Latin America. Rolando Duarte, brother to President Napoleón Duarte, discusses not only some of the objective difficulties faced by policy makers who long to secure sustained development but also some of the passions and frustrations through which they must daily work their way.

Archbishop Marcos McGrath of Panama, one of the region's major ecclesiastical leaders, sets forth in an authoritative way the views, experiences, and teachings of the Latin American Conference of Bishops (CELAM). He puts the famous declaration of Medellín (1968) in context and explains its intent. His remarks exhibit a powerful instinct for concrete difficulties, as well as a sense of compassion and urgency.

Guillermo Chapman, also of Panama, a distinguished businessman and scholar, presents some of the historical and cultural realities that underlie attempts at economic development in the region. Mr. Chapman is an unusually good interpreter between North American and Latin American points of view.

In the final paper, Russell E. Marks, Jr., who has worked with American businesses in Latin America since 1953, adds a highly practical dimension to the discussion. In a plain-spoken and blunt style he discusses the economic—and political—turbulence of interdependence in the past thirty years. Recalling the high hopes of the early days, he evaluates disappointments and successes with candor and commonsense, not blanching from controversy.

The discussions that followed each of these representations were amazingly lively; some judged them the very best they had ever participated in. For reasons of space, the editors have, regrettably, had to limit themselves to only a few selections from each discussion. The humor and the personal dimensions of the interchanges were inevitably diminished by such cuts; much of the illumination at the conference flashed forth in discussion, as when one could feel restless puzzlement in the group, because of conflicting views, until someone hit upon the focusing point. These moments, given limitations of space, proved especially difficult to reproduce in print.

Finally, immense thanks are due to those at the University of Notre Dame who did nearly all the intellectual planning for the conference, choosing the presenters and the participants. Father Theodore M. Hesburgh, C.S.C., the distinguished president of Notre Dame, drew many participants simply by sending out the invitations in his name. The Rev. Oliver Williams, C.S.C., Lee Tavis, and Yusaku Furuhashi orchestrated the lectures and the good company assembled to discuss them. Mr. William Baroody, Jr., the president of the American Enterprise Institute, added to the occasion by his presence. Rowena Olegario managed the physical details of the conference with skill and grace. Scott Walter assisted the editors faithfully and intelligently.

Economic and Political Statism in Latin America

Howard J. Wiarda

My remarks address the general nature of the political economy of Latin America and also the place of foreign investment and perhaps domestic investment there. The presentation is not entirely pessimistic, though pessimism is much at large these days; it does serve to highlight from a new perspective the difficulties of relying on direct private investment in resolving Latin America's problems.

A Model of State Capitalism in Latin America

I would like to discuss a model of the Latin American political-economic systems. The model obviously applies more to some countries than others. My presentation is necessarily general and is intended as a heuristic device, not necessarily as a reflection of reality in any particular country. My use of the term "model" implies neither approval nor disapproval but rather how things are in that part of the world, and perhaps expresses some facts that we must face realistically.

The theme I want to develop is the following: that the political economy of Latin America conforms very poorly to any of the models with which we, from our background, training, intellectual life, and academic perspectives, have much familiarity. We are dealing with a system, I suggest, that at its heart is mercantilist, with various neo-feudal aspects, and perhaps can be defined as state-capitalist. In its basic features this system does not conform very closely to either the North American or Northwest European model of capitalism, or, in most of the countries of the area, to a Marxian model of socialism. Rather it represents a distinctive intermediary between these other two. Indeed that is how I want to define the state capitalism that prevails in Latin America: a system of national production and organization intermediate between that of liberal market capitalism where private interests dominate and where there is laissez faire in both the economic and the political realms, and a full-blown

4

command system where the state dominates in both economic and political affairs.[1]

The implication that might be drawn from these introductory remarks is that when we discuss or criticize capitalism in Latin America, we should be quite clear what precisely we have in mind. The form of capitalism that exists in Latin America, if it can be called that at all, is so much at variance with the familiar models of our own historical experience that it does not fit our usual categories. Furthermore, in studying or operating in these systems, academics and business people who go to Latin America often make major mistakes of assessment and interpretation; they do not know how to function effectively in that context because the form of capitalism there is quite unlike our own U.S. version.

Characteristics of the Region's Political Economy

Let me set forth a framework, a kind of systemization of characteristics, of what this mercantilist or state-capitalist system of political economy is all about.

First of all, if one looks at the percentage of GNP that is generated through the public sector, one finds that all the countries of Latin America have very large public sectors, with some very interesting differences. The state sector is so large, and its activities so extensive, that one comes to think of it not so much as a system like that of U.S. capitalism. But in most countries it is not socialist either. Rather, one must think of a continuum between capitalism and socialism. If one, so to speak, spaces out the various countries of the world on that continuum, one finds the United States at one end as the most laissez-faire economy. The figures that I have seen recently indicate that roughly 30 to 35 percent of our GNP is generated through the public sector. If one uses the measure of the percentage of capital generated through state-owned enterprises, then the figure for the United States is even lower—4.4 percent—making the United States far and away the least statist of the world's major economies.

At the other end of the continuum one finds the Soviet Union, with roughly 95 or 96 percent of GNP generated through the public sector. Other countries are strung out at various points between these two positions. Poland generates roughly 85 percent of its GNP through the public sector, allowing therefore for considerable small-scale farming and commercial enterprises that are still in private hands.

As one thinks, then, of a kind of scale or continuum between laissez faire and complete statism, the question then becomes, where does Latin America fit in this? It fits in an intermediary position, by and large, with virtually all the countries of the region spaced between the complete statist and the laissez-faire types. The form of state capitalism in Latin America is so distinct from,

5

so different from, the North American conception of laissez-faire or liberal capitalism that it is a quite different type of political economy with which we must grapple, not simply a slightly different version or pale imitation of the U.S. model of capitalism.

If one looks at the figures for the various countries of Latin America, one finds a wide range of percentages of state-generated GNP. It extends from about 35 to 40 percent (roughly equivalent to our own) in some of the lesser developed countries, Honduras or Guatemala, for example, to 50 or 55 percent in the Dominican Republic and to roughly 60 percent in Nicaragua. It further extends to about 65 or 70 percent in Mexico (with the nationalization of the banks and the various private concerns under the banks' domain) to about the same figure in Brazil, and to roughly 92 percent in Bolivia, according to the latest figures that I have seen. One could say that there is almost nothing left to nationalize in Bolivia.

The percentage of GNP generated through the public sector in Bolivia is higher than that of Poland or most of the Eastern European countries, yet we think of Bolivia as a capitalist country and the countries of Eastern Europe as socialist countries. As we examine these statistics about the percentage of GNP generated through the public sector, it becomes clear that we are dealing with a different form of capitalism in Latin America than we are used to dealing with in the United States. It is a type that I have chosen to define as a system of state capitalism or, if one thinks historically, perhaps an updated twentieth-century version of mercantilism. It is definitely not the system of laissez-faire capitalism one finds in the United States.

A second, related feature of these systems is the size of their bureaucracies, and here the figures more or less reflect the percentage of GNP in the public sector. That is, we are dealing with countries in which, by and large, 50, 60, or 65 percent of the gainfully employed work force in fact work for the state in one form or another. The state hence becomes one of the key hubs around which the national system revolves: employment, patronage, spoils, social status, career enhancement.[2]

Many have written about the heavy hand of bureaucracy in these countries, and if one looks at the percentage of the work force employed by the state, one again gets a certain sense that we are dealing with a system of economy, or maybe of political economy, that is quite different from our own. In the United States, where the number of persons who work for the state has been steadily rising since the 1930s, the percentage is still far below that of the Latin American bureaucracies. In Latin America the figures indicate that overwhelmingly the state is the largest employer, particularly of educated middle-class persons, almost all of whom look first to the state for employment and only second to private possibilities.

The figures also indicate that the state is, in the absence of very many effective social security or social assistance programs, de facto a large social

6

security agency. Sinecures, patronage, and nepotism are used to keep on the public payroll virtually the entire educated middle class and much of the organized working class as well, in this way providing the social services and levels of income support largely nonexistent through the social security system itself.

This phenomenon of large-scale public employment in Latin America also raises questions about the usefulness of certain prescriptions that economists often offer. One prescription has it that these state-owned enterprises ought to be returned to private hands because they are more profitable that way. Another suggests that the way to solve the economic crisis in the region, particularly the debt crises, is to impose such strict austerity programs that they force massive layoffs of personnel working in the state system. Such prescriptions may seem economically rational but the political costs would be immense, especially in the absence of any viable social safety net. No government in the area can afford to fire or lay off workers who are its own bases of patronage support and loyalty.

The third feature of these state-capitalist systems in Latin America involves close government control and regulation even of the fairly modest private sector that remains. In virtually all of the Latin American countries, even in those that call themselves capitalist, a vast range of government controls and regulations is in place that makes our own web of regulations in the United States seem very modest by comparison. These controls reach not only into what we would think of since the 1930s as more or less normal regulatory areas, but also include government control and regulation, in some countries and some economic sectors, of such basic areas of the economy as prices, wages, and production.

One finds throughout Latin America a mixed situation: the market sets prices and wages and determines production in some areas, while the state sets prices and wages and determines production in others. The state in Latin America thus not only owns a great deal and generates a very high share of the GNP, but has regulatory powers considerably more vast than those of the United States as well.

A fourth feature of these statist systems in Latin America is government suspicion of and regulation of investment, both foreign and domestic. I think this attitude is now changing. There was a great wave of romantic sentiment in Latin America and indeed some action toward the nationalizing of foreign firms in the late 1960s and early 1970s. There is still a strong thrust toward regulation of these firms, and the ancient suspicions of capitalism, especially emanating from foreign sources, remain. But we are now seeing in countries like Jamaica, for example, considerable national lamenting that Reynolds Aluminum is pulling out. In the Dominican Republic the firm that was long a kind of national phobia for Dominican politicians, the Gulf+Western Corporation, has also announced plans to sell its holdings, a move now being lamented, by left-wing and Marxist politicians as well as others. With the large multinationals pulling out, the jobs and capital they provided are being sorely missed.

The countries of Latin America are turning around to the extent that they would now welcome investment of virtually any sort, with some degree of control and regulation on their part, precisely at a time when American companies themselves are leaving the region as quickly as possible. I have some figures from the Chase Manhattan Bank that suggest that nowhere in all of Central America and the Caribbean is there an American company with more than 10 percent of its holdings there. Those who are old enough to remember some of the machinations of the giant Gulf+Western Corporation in the 1960s or maybe the United Fruit Company in the 1950s—those traditional bugaboos of Latin American politics—may be surprised by these figures. But we have to deal with a new reality: the multinational firms, rather than clamoring to enter either Central America and the Caribbean or, even more important, the South American countries, which are obviously bigger, have larger markets, and are thus more viable and attractive, are now in fact pulling their capital out of the region as rapidly as they can and are reinvesting it in Western Europe and in the Asian Pacific perimeter. We are seeing a rapid turnabout in the investment strategies of large corporations just when the actions of these companies are being closely scrutinized for the first time. Moreover, strong criticism of the multinationals is coming also at a time when the Latin Americans themselves are beginning to reverse their positions, in the sense that they (or at least their prudent and pragmatic leadership) would welcome almost any kind of investment capital, precisely because there is so much capital flight and disinvestment from the region at present.

A fifth characteristic has to do with state or government regulation of interest groups. That subject merits separate treatment by itself. Briefly stated, however, not only are we looking at political economies with limited space for the private marketplace, but also with limited space for private associational interest groups to operate. In various writings this kind of system has been called "corporatist."[3]

Most of the Latin American countries tend to have systems of limited pluralism, not necessarily the vast, hurly-burly interest-group struggle so familiar to us in the United States, with hundreds of thousands of groups and interests competing in the political marketplace. There may be only eight or nine major interests in many of the Latin American countries, and it should be emphasized that the term *interes* in Spanish means something different from the term "interest group" in the United States. The Spanish term usually has to do with a *corporate* body such as the Church or the Army, which is more than a mere interest group. Rather, these institutions constitute the backbone of culture and civilization, of politics and armed strength, inseparable from government and the state systems in these societies. That is quite different from our notion of interest group.

We have in Latin America not only a system of statism very strongly prevalent in the economic sphere but also a system of statism and corporatism very powerful in the political sphere as well. To organize not only a business in these countries but also a trade union is an enormously difficult process. One cannot simply go out in Latin America and organize an interest group and stage a march on the banks or other centers of power, as may happen in downtown Cambridge, Washington, Amherst, or wherever it is that interest groups organize in an ad hoc manner in this country. Rather, there is an entire and very elaborate system of licenses and permits in Latin America by which an aspiring group must satisfy state authorities before it can be duly recognized and receive its charter or before its legitimacy to function and carry out activities is recognized. Without such state recognition and the granting of "juridical personality," the group cannot bargain in the political process.

There is thus a close correlation between statism in the economic sphere and a high degree of statism, even authoritarianism, in the political sphere. Regulation of interest groups and of associability, as well as limits on the freedom of political groups to bargain politically, keep political statism, reflecting and reinforcing the economic statism, very powerful.

A sixth characteristic that we have begun to examine in a research program under way at AEI focuses on government-private cooperative ventures. These also exist in Latin America to an extent unknown in the United States; a careful examination of them would require more elaboration than can possibly be done here. The pattern is closer to that of the continental European countries than to the U.S. system.

There is not only a large degree of state ownership in the economies of these Latin American societies, but also a large degree of collaboration and cooperation in numerous joint ventures involving private capital and public capital. It is not unusual at all in Latin America these days for private capital to put up 50 percent for an investment project and state capital to put up the rest, or the ratio may be 51:49 or 49:51. The public sector in these countries is not only immense but also deeply involved in what we in the United States would think of as private sector activities. Public-private collaboration and joint ventures take all kinds of complex forms that largely do not exist as yet in this country. If one were looking for parallels, one would think perhaps of France, with its history of Colbertian, physiocratic statism, or perhaps of Italy, since both countries have long histories of state–private sector collaboration, and certainly not the laissez-faire, individualistic, private entrepreneurial capitalism of the United States. That again makes Latin American political economy quite different from that of the United States.

That brings us to a seventh characteristic of these systems—the inseparability of the private and the public domains. Those who have lived in Latin America and those who have taken Moral Philosophy 101 or 151 at Notre Dame and elsewhere know that the essential unity of the private and public spheres has a long history in Catholic political thought. In Latin America today the public and the private domains still get jumbled together in complex ways that we in this country often have difficulty comprehending. Part of this has to do, one suspects, with the historically fuzzy line between the private and the public weals, or the fact that "corruption" may mean something quite different from one society to another.

Those who grew up, let us say, in Mayor Daley's Chicago or in Boston or in other big cities with large political machines know that a chicken at Christmas time in return for a vote in November or five dollars to help a son in trouble, a man who was thrown in jail, or someone who needs money to buy a holiday dinner for his family at Christmas time or Easter is not thought of as corruption; rather it is viewed as normal operating procedure—a favor for a favor. In Latin America this form of patronage politics often operates at the level of national affairs and throughout the system. Carried over into the national political arena, where private and public domains are often inseparable, both politically and economically, one finds relatively little of what we would think of as entrepreneurial spirit. There is still that traditional Catholic hostility toward usury and investment, toward materialism and capitalism, which is present even today throughout the area. There is a certain resentment of the businessman as one who is not of noble calling, who is spending his time in demeaning pursuits rather than uplifting matters like poetry, perhaps, and other more "spiritual" and cultural pursuits.

Latin America therefore has a quite different system of political economy that we may call state capitalism. Michael Novak has written extensively about the *spirit* of democratic capitalism.[4] His writings and those of other scholars seem to indicate that the Latin American part of the world practices a form of capitalism, if it can be called that at all, quite distinct from that we are used to dealing with in the United States. If we are to make policy prescriptions regarding either the usefulness of that form of capitalism or the desirability of sweeping it away, we ought to make quite sure that we understand its nature.

Conclusions and Policy Implications

Let me draw some conclusions from this examination of economic and political statism in Latin America and in addition discuss certain implications for policy toward the region.

First, we have a set of societies—leaving aside for now national variations and immense differences between countries—in which there has been a long history of statism in the economy. This goes back, one supposes, to the Spanish medieval period; it was carried over into the New World and is reflected in a long history of mercantilism, statism, centralized bureaucracy, regulation, and quasi-feudalism, all of which are still alive throughout the area. Statism in Latin America has a long past in stark contrast to the United States.

Second, statism in the economy is closely related to statism in politics, and the two are connected in various complex ways. Again, Michael Novak has argued forcefully in various writings that freedom in the economic sphere is closely associated with freedom in the political sphere, and that these two complement each other and lie at the heart of the American political and economic experience. I suggest a corollary: statism in the economic sphere, which has been the dominant pattern in Latin America, is also related to statism in the political sphere, and those two are also equally intimately connected. This has major implications obviously for politics and economics in the region and indicates why Latin America is quite at variance with our own history and tradition in this regard. Authoritarianism, statism, semi-feudalism, top-down rule may well be endemic in Latin America in both the economic and the political spheres.

Third, I want to suggest in a provocative fashion that if one is dealing with economies in which there is such a high percentage of state ownership, the stakes involved in who commands the pinnacles of these pyramids tend to be greater than in our own society. If one travels to the American Midwest, one finds it makes little difference to most people whether Jerry Ford or Jimmy Carter won the 1976 election. Some of us care about these issues because jobs and patronage as well as ideology and politics hang on the outcome of the elections—we care, but most Americans do not, with considerable reason. The United States has a tradition of a weak, laissez-faire state, of limited economic resources located in the central government, of a society in which individual initiative is celebrated. In this country, the stakes for those who win control are still relatively modest.

In Latin America, however, the fact that the stakes are higher and that such a high percentage of the GNP is concentrated in state hands helps to explain why violence may also be endemic. The competition not only for control of the state system but for the patronage, spoils, jobs, and sinecures is intense. The licenses, the permits to open a business, and the favoritism and monopolies that flow down from control of the state pyramid mean that the stakes in that part of the world are obviously considerably higher, relatively speaking, than they are in our own. That helps explain something of the degree of competitiveness and indeed the violence that exists in some of these societies and the intense rivalries for control of the central pinnacles of the state system.

Fourth, the greater statism that one finds in Latin America grows not just out of history and culture and tradition, not just out of St. Thomas or out of Suárez, let us say, but also grows out of the present world situation and crisis. The experience of Latin America, as well as of our own country, is that statism tends to rise during times of economic crisis. The period of the 1930s in this society as well as in Latin America was characterized by immense expansion of state power, and it is clear that the same thing is happening at present throughout Latin America in the face of another economic crisis.

It is thus not just tradition and history that help explain the level of statism that exists in Latin America but, rather, the imperatives of an increasingly interdependent and crisis-prone economic world. The downturn in the world economy over the past five years forces the state to play a stronger role in the domestic economy of all of these countries, and the recent debt crisis again forces the state to play a greater role in the management of these national economies than it might otherwise have played. Trade and planning issues devolve further power upon the state, and social turmoil tends also to increase the coercive powers of the state.

In the present crisis, therefore, on the one hand we have the need for greater private investment there; indeed it is desirable both in our view and in the view of most Latin Americans. On the other hand, we have the likelihood of greater statism on the part of governments of the area simply because of the global economic situation in which they find themselves, a situation calling forth greater regulation and greater state involvement and intervention in their national economies.

A fifth conclusion has to do with IMF measures and the imposition of austerity programs in these regions. No one has any magic solutions for the debt crisis, or any ready solutions for Latin America's underdevelopment. But in the current debt situation, we have focused almost exclusively on the economic conditions involved—that is, the need to pay off the debts, the need to establish some degree of balance in the national accounts of these societies, the need for economic austerity.

We have largely ignored, though they are now becoming a matter of greater importance to us, the social and political implications of imposing IMF austerity measures, particularly in societies that are so heavily statist. In Latin America we are dealing not just with economic situations that need correcting; whole systems of national politics and national patronage are affected. In societies where the viability of the entire national system rests, to a major degree, upon patronage, the capacity to appoint to all those public sector positions not only friends and cronies of the regime in power but also its enemies is crucially important. That is, after all, the quickest and easiest way most astute Latin American politicians have found to ameliorate opposition: to put it on the public payroll. It neutralizes the opposition by giving it a stake in the very government it might otherwise oppose.

The imposition of too tough IMF austerity measures creates the very real possibility not only that economic crises will continue to occur but also that whole systems of politics and societies will become unraveled in the process. This is especially true in systems that are so heavily dependent on state-directed policies and patronage politics for their very survival. The patient will likely remain sick, and the doctor is likely to die in the process of administering the medicine.

Finally, let me suggest that if one is dealing with societies that are heavily statist to begin with, as I have suggested the Latin American societies are, then it is a relatively easy and quick step—and we want to think of the implications of this for policy as well as for investment—from a system of state capitalism to one of state socialism. All that is required really is a shift in the political leadership at the top. We saw that in Peru in 1968 when a new generation of young military leaders seized power and said that they wished to take their country in a new nationalistic and socialist direction. One can quarrel about what the effects, results, and final impact of that revolution in Peru have been, but of the fact there was a relatively quick and easy transition to a form of socialism there can be no doubt.

The transition to socialism in Nicaragua was immensely aided by the vast proportion of the national economy already in "state" hands when Somoza, who owned roughly 50 percent of it, fled the country. We consider the Somoza regime, if you will, either a version of quasi-feudalism on the one hand or almost state- or, let us say, family-capitalism on the other. But with so much of the wealth already "nationalized" or belonging to one family, when that family was overthrown half of the national economy was inherited by the state.

The other example is Portugal, a little outside of the Latin America frame of reference but relevant as well. That is, one of the reasons that the Portuguese revolution of 1974 became so radical so quickly was that, in nationalizing the banks immediately after the revolution, the Portuguese very soon discovered that they had nationalized de facto roughly 70 percent of their national economy. Suddenly, and somewhat unexpectedly, they had this huge windfall of an immense state sector on their hands that they then called socialism, whereas before it had been called capitalism, or "state capitalism."

What I am suggesting therefore is that the transition to, and the lines between, capitalism and socialism in Latin America (at least as measured in terms of state ownership) are often very blurry indeed. We can talk about different conceptions of socialism, and one can argue that it depends, also, on who benefits from the profits of those industries that are nationalized or under state control, and obviously that is a case that can be made. The transition from the one to the other can go very quickly. One of the key implications of this statement, therefore, is that in Latin America it is a very easy transition from state capitalism to state socialism that can occur almost overnight—as in fact it has in at least four or five of the countries of the region.

We need to be well informed, therefore, as to the precise nature of the state capitalist systems in Latin America, and the major political and economic implications of those systems. Understanding the Latin American political economy in this light not only enhances our general comprehension of the area but also has major implications for policy.[5]

I do not have any doubt that these statist systems of political economy in Latin America need to be thoroughly reformed to be made more efficient and viable. Before plunging headlong into such a reform, however, we need to know what we are doing. We need to encourage greater freedom in these economies, greater room for private initiative and private markets; but we must recognize that doing so too precipitously may wreck the fragile economies that do exist. Some of the state enterprises undoubtedly need to be rationalized, put in private hands, or both. Such changes must come gradually and carefully, though, so that entire national systems of patronage and politics are not destroyed and whole countries are not destabilized. We can similarly encourage the private sector in Latin America, but we must recognize that even in that area state permission is still required for the private sector or for individual businesses to operate. Whatever our wishes, the statist systems of Latin America will be with us for a long time to come.

Hence, we must proceed cautiously and prudently. We must understand Latin American realities. Too hasty reforms can easily result in the destabilization of the very Latin American systems we are trying to bolster.

Notes

1. Derived from William P. Glade, "Economic Policy-Making and the Structure of Corporatism in Latin America," Paper presented at the Sixth National Meeting of the Latin American Studies Association, Atlanta, Georgia, March 1976.

2. For a fascinating general discussion, see Michel Crozier, *The Bureaucratic Phenomenon* (Chicago: University of Chicago Press, 1964).

3. Howard J. Wiarda, *Corporatism and National Development in Latin America* (Boulder, Colo.: Westview Press, 1981).

4. Michael Novak, *The Spirit of Democratic Capitalism* (New York: Simon and Schuster, 1982).

5. AEI's Center for Hemispheric Studies is currently conducting a major new research project, "The State and Economic Development in Latin America," in which these themes and their implications are fully explored.

Multinational Corporations and Third World Investment

Theodore H. Moran

Introduction

The two most important issues in U.S.-Latin American relations at the moment are the debt crisis and the flow of trade. It is essential that the flow of trade remain open and free enough to allow the developing countries both to service the debt and to begin to grow internally again.

I address trade and the debt question only in the concluding section of this paper. My principal focus is a third issue: international investment and the ability of host governments in Latin America and the rest of the third world to "harness" or use multinational corporations. My motivation for choosing this topic is twofold: first, professional modesty, in that there are many other practitioners and experts at this conference who can discuss the details of debt and trade with more authority; second, professional immodesty, in that the research on which this paper is based may present a new and sufficiently unconventional (and even optimistic) view of relations between multinational companies and third world governments that this topic will more easily spark discussion and relieve gloom than an analysis focusing solely on debt or trade.

To balance my intense interest in the possibilities of using private direct investment as a vehicle for development (albeit an imperfect vehicle, and only one of many) in the difficult decade ahead, in the last section I address the topics of trade and debt as they relate to my findings about multinational corporate investment.

Multinational Corporations and Third World Governments: The Determinants of Bargaining Power

The Landegger Program in International Business Diplomacy at the Georgetown School of Foreign Service concentrates on the intersection between corporate strategy and public policy. The curriculum is designed to train students, managers, and government officials in the most effective conduct of the business-government relationship. In the context of third world development, our research has focused on the question of whether there has been a fundamental shift in the balance of bargaining power between multinational corporations (MNCs) and host governments in the third world.

The rhetoric on this issue is intense. The *dependencia* school in Latin America argues that multinational corporations are fundamentally exploitative and are growing more so; the Chicago school asserts that foreign investors are fundamentally beneficial and that any government intervention to exercise bargaining power is misguided and wrong.[1]

What does the evidence indicate about the strength of multinationals vis-à-vis host authorities in the third world and the exercise of negotiating power? A survey of investment agreements over the twenty-four years between 1960 and 1984 covering sectors from natural resources to manufacturing, indicates that, while the data are mixed, there does appear to be a trend in the direction of greater bargaining capability for the less-developed countries (LDCs).

What determines the relative strength of the two sides in the negotiations between multinationals and third world governments?[2] The primary determinant of MNC investment decisions is, of course, the economic attractiveness of a particular project, giving Latin American countries with large domestic markets, rapid growth, and ample resources an edge in attracting multinational companies on favorable terms. But, as I indicate later, once an investment project is successfully under way, even smaller and theoretically "weaker" states can negotiate favorable investment contracts as well—witness those of Jamaica and (outside of Latin America) Papua New Guinea.

Apart from the general economic attractiveness of the project, our research has shown that four factors are crucial in determining the bargaining strength between foreign investor and host country.[3] First is the size of the fixed investment. For some projects, such as nickel mines or oil fields, it is impossible to bring the operation into production without a commitment of at least $400–800 million (1983 dollars). In such cases, the investment agreement almost invariably favors the foreign corporation before the project comes on-line; but once the project is in operation (assuming it is successful), the corporation's investment becomes hostage to nationalistic pressures. The parent multinational cannot credibly threaten to withdraw, and there is a high probability that within six to eight years the agreement will be renegotiated to benefit the host authorities. In contrast, when smaller fixed investment is required there tend to be less dramatic renegotiations. Most industries dealing in natural resources (oil, natural gas, copper, nickel, and iron ore) require large fixed investments and exhibit the pattern of successful host-country renegotiation.[4] Some manufacturing ventures, however, (chemicals, petrochemicals, industrial machinery, and automotive assembly) are showing the same trend.

The second factor that determines the balance of bargaining power between MNCs and third world governments is technology—not high or low technology (as is widely thought), but the changeableness or the stability of the technology. (The separate issue of appropriate technology is discussed later.) Projects that use rapidly changing technology (for example, semiconductors, in which there is a revolutionary change every few years) provide terms much more favorable to foreign investors than projects in which the technology is relatively stable. For a growing number of projects both in natural resources and in manufacturing, however, the technology does not change rapidly, allowing a progressive tightening of terms by third world governments.

The third factor is the role played by marketing. When advertising and brand identification are important to the commercial success of a venture, foreign MNCs begin in a stronger bargaining position and maintain it longer than when a project's output is sold according to standard specifications. Thus, investors fabricating fine household products or cosmetics tend to enjoy more lucrative investment agreements than companies producing bulk textiles or undifferentiated office products. An increasing array of goods fall into the latter category, from petrochemical feedstocks to industrial equipment, electronic components, and many consumer durables.

Fourth, and perhaps most important in determining relative negotiating strength, is the degree of competition in the sector where the investment is being made.[5] Lack of competition means fewer alternatives for a host government to choose from; greater competition, whether among MNCs or between MNCs and local producers from the private sector or state agencies, means the possibility of playing one investor off against another. It is important to view the role of competition as a dynamic variable. In the 1960s, for example, General Motors (with sales greater than the GNP of most LDCs) was considered the exemplar of the emerging private sector superpower, able to put sovereignty "at bay" in the countries where it operated. With the reinvigoration of European automobile manufacturers and the spread of Japanese car companies, however, the strength of GM's bargaining position has eroded significantly. Increasing competition is evident as well in industries producing most natural resources, capital goods, heavy machinery, and consumer products, although the speed of dilution of oligopoly concentration varies greatly from industry to industry.

It should be noted that the ability of third world governments to tighten terms and to renegotiate investment agreements to their benefit also varies greatly according to the characteristics of the industry and the project. Consequently, a case-by-case evaluation of costs and benefits is much more useful in judging the contribution of MNCs to third world development than highly aggregate generalization across all sectors. (Most studies across sectors have been inconclusive.)[6]

A broader picture emerges as well: as long as MNC operations in the 1980s embody some combination of large fixed investment, stable technology, standardized marketing, and increasing competition, the bargaining position of the host government will grow stronger, and their agreements with MNCs will bring greater benefits (and fewer costs) to the third world. Most agreements regarding natural resource projects already exhibit these characteristics. It appears that a greater number of scale sized manufacturing ventures are coming to incorporate them as well. An example is the automobile industry. To be competitive, an automobile plant must produce at least 250,000 cars per year, requiring a fixed investment of more than $500 million. In the automobile industry, technology is relatively stable; marketing and advertising are becoming less important for smaller models with fewer annual design changes; and competition among GM, Ford, Volkswagen, Fiat, Toyota, Datsun, and the others is intense. These circumstances open the door to aggressive and effective host-country demands for the foreign corporations to contribute more vigorously to the economic objectives of the country.

Changing Host-Country Objectives

The preceding section paints a straightforward, but carefully circumscribed, picture of the growing bargaining strength of third world governments. To be sure, not all host governments are enjoying an equal increase of power because not all industries have exhibited an equal loss of strength: computer corporations, laser technology firms, brand-name food processors, offshore drilling service companies, to give but a few examples, are still able, frequently, to present their terms to local authorities on a take-it-or-leave-it basis. But an increasing number of natural resource and manufacturing investors cannot.

Where have host authorities been most successful in using their negotiating strength, and where have they been less successful? In natural resources it is possible to observe a regular and largely predictable pattern in MNC–host relations: investment agreements generally contain terms favorable to the foreign investors before they have made large commitments of capital; thereafter those terms are tightened (a process that is interrupted only when the host wants an expansion of operations or an extension of downstream processing from the foreign company).

The variable most affected by the tightening of terms is the tax rate, with 40–50 percent common at the beginning, rising after seven or eight years to an average of 60–70 percent (or as high as 96 percent in petroleum). Host countries also have made progress in enticing foreign corporations to smelt and refine a greater proportion of a resource locally. In the copper industry, for example, the capacity of third world smelters grew from less than 25 percent of output to more than 44 percent in 1983. In addition, local governments have trained their nationals to hold positions at all levels, including supervisory and executive positions. A final area of contention has been ownership structure, with the number of joint ventures (including those in which foreign investors occupy minority positions) increased greatly between 1965 and 1980. Although there have been postinvestment nationalizations in hard mineral industries (copper and iron ore), only in the petroleum industry have multinational natural resource companies been willing to relinquish equity entirely and to operate with a management or service contract (the exception being Anaconda, which constructed Sar Chesmeh in Iran during the period of the Shah on a management contract).

Greater Local Value-Added. In manufacturing, host-countries have improved their negotiating position most dramatically with regard to local value-added, the requirement that a specified amount of the final product be produced locally. For the first twenty years after the end of the Second World War, most manufacturing operations in the third world consisted of assembling components imported from the home country of the investor. Responding to domestic demands for greater employment, third world governments began in the 1960s to use their bargaining strength to insist on greater requirements for local content. In 1960, parts used in automobiles produced in Latin America, for example, equaled 30 percent of total value. By 1970, the local content had risen to 70 percent; and by 1980, local content in the Mexican automotive sector was approximately 60 percent, in Argentina 90 percent, in Brazil nearly 100 percent.

Increased Export Efforts. At the same time host countries are pushing for greater value-added locally, they are trying to use foreign multinationals as marketing vehicles for channelling products back to the home countries of the multinationals or to third country markets. In electronics, for example, Mexico, Taiwan, and Korea have used the distribution networks of MNCs assembling components locally to penetrate U.S. and European consumer markets. Contractual agreements allowing third world governments to use their countries as "export platforms" to break into the developed economies are relatively easy to negotiate with foreign multinationals, since such arrangements allow investors to build scale-sized plants and to reduce unit costs for local as well as export production.

The larger and more rapidly growing LDCs have created performance requirements demanding greater local content and access to external markets in an effort to make their countries the primary manufacturing centers of an MNC's products or components.

In both the natural resources and the manufacturing sectors MNCs have increasingly been required to employ host country nationals at all levels; in joint ventures, more than 50 percent of a sample of 180 U.S. MNC investments in the mid-1970s (the latest period for which data are available) had local partners. The MNCs' profit rates are much more difficult to judge; the examination of nominal tax levels is inconclusive, given the opportunities to use interaffiliate transactions (payments for licenses, royalties, and patents; transfer prices for goods and services) to vary the statement of profit. Since the first major exposés of transfer pricing abuses in Colombia in 1970 (when drug companies kept their local profit margins low by importing tetracycline at ten times the U.S. quotation), however, host-country efforts to scrutinize interaffiliate transactions have expanded substantially. They have been aided by growing cooperation with tax authorities in the industrial market countries, leading some observers to speculate about the expansion of information-sharing agreements in the 1980s.

Appropriate Technologies. In one area of particular sensitivity, however, progress has been slow, namely, the creation by MNCs of technologies appropriate for the more abundant labor resources of the third world.[7] When they move into third world markets, U.S., European, and to a certain extent, Japanese firms continue to employ technology developed in response to the factor proportions of the home country. The explanation for this is complex and points blame both at MNCs and at host-government policies.

First, the strongest influence on the development of new, more appropriate technologies is competition: the greater the competition at the local level, the more the technology used by an MNC in a host country will utilize labor instead of the capital-intensive processes of the home country. But the stimulation of competition at the local level requires painful host-country decisions, notably the lowering of import barriers, which creates pressure on national firms as well as on multinationals. Second, the largest pool of labor-intensive technology is in the second-hand equipment markets of the developed countries. Fearing that "second-hand" means "second best," however, many third world governments prohibit the importation of second-hand equipment. Third, many third world governments provide loans to preferred development projects at below-market rates. Ironically, this subsidizes capital-intensive rather than labor-intensive processes.

One interesting trend is the expansion of multinational investors from within the third world itself, notably from Korea, Taiwan, Malaysia, Singapore, India, Brazil, Mexico, and Argentina.[8] For example, of 360 foreign firms given promotion status in Thailand through the mid-1970s, ninety-three were from Taiwan, ten from Malaysia, five from Hong Kong, fifteen from India, and sixteen from Singapore. India has more than one hundred of its own MNCs (albeit of smaller average size than MNCs from the industrial market economies). Recent studies have found that these third world multinationals adapt technological processes to local circumstances more readily, and employ more labor intensive processes, than other MNCs. This could be a promising sign for the future, but still there are problems: the entrepreneurs most frequently associated with third world multinationals (Chinese and Indians in Southeast Asia or Africa, Argentinians in Paraguay, Brazilians in Bolivia) may handle large labor forces efficiently and cost-effectively, but they rarely earn local respect and affection in the process.

In addition, one must be cautious about how great an impact on third world employment problems even the most dramatic improvement in application of appropriate technology by foreign investors might have. In 1979, MNCs supplied work for approximately 4 million people in the third world. An increase of labor intensity in local operations by one-half would still produce no more than about 2 million additional jobs in the entire less-developed world, in which the United Nations estimates there are 680 million people who need work. The principal sources of growth in third world countries have been, and will remain, local rather than foreign in origin.[9]

What are the broader theoretical implications of the evidence presented here? The evolution of bargaining power between multinationals and third world governments offers a critical perspective on both of the predominant theories of foreign investment and third world development. The traditional Chicago school approach to foreign investment asserts that the activities of MNCs are harmonious with the desires of host authorities, that the firms if left to themselves will maximize local growth prospects, and that the best government intervention is the least government intervention. Yet the history of investment agreements over the past twenty years, as I have sketched it here, suggests that there is continuing struggle between foreign investors and host authorities, with the design of appropriate policies to harness multinational enterprises being an important strategy for helping the development process in the third world.

The *dependencia* or dependency approach to foreign investment, in contrast, suggests that investors and third world host-countries do not have common interests and that a greater number and spread of multinationals leads to greater domination and exploitation of the host countries. Yet the evidence examined here suggests that the greater the number and spread of MNCs the larger the opportunities for local governments to increase their bargaining power and autonomy.

The Reaction in the Developed Countries to
New Third World Objectives

However cautiously one interprets the evidence from the preceding section, and however guardedly one presents the results, the conclusion is nonetheless clear: a growing number of third world governments are learning to harness a growing number of multinational corporations to serve changing host-country objectives.[10] Moreover, as we move deeper into the 1980s, a clear set of priorities is emerging. In the 1960s, ownership was the principal focus of nationalistic demands by the host countries, with majority participation or complete nationalization a frequent outcome. In the 1970s, the profits of foreign investors were emphasized, with creeping tax rates the result. In the 1980s (beginning in the late 1970s), the overriding preoccupation has been with performance requirements, calling both for more value added locally and for more exports. In addition, the current debt crisis is reinforcing the drive to use multinational companies to raise the level of domestic employment and to raise earnings of foreign exchange. As the Latin American *dependencia* theorists began to recognize this evolution in the real world, their rhetoric began to lag; but they have been slow to accept the idea that third world governments can manipulate multinationals to their advantage. (As Hegel observed, Minerva's owl seldom flies before dusk.) The increased bargaining power of the third world has not gone unobserved, however, on the part of organized labor in the developed countries. Worker groups have mobilized industry support from companies squeezed by economic nationalism or threatened by imports from the areas that are manipulating international investors most effectively.

One of these groups, the Labor-Industry Coalition for International Trade (LICIT), has declared, for example, that "trade-related performance requirements—requiring minimum local content or export levels—now constitute one of the most serious trade policy problems facing the international trading community." [11] LICIT identified more than thirty-five countries (developed and developing) that regulate the activities of foreign affiliates with the aim of shifting investment, jobs, and production to the host country.

In the United States, both the executive branch and the Congress have responded to the appeals of such groups. In 1984 the U.S. trade representative, William Brock, promised that investment-related trade policies would be one of the highest priorities for GATT negotiation in the post–Tokyo Round period. The Congress is considering a series of domestic content bills and has threatened to end trade preferences for developing countries unless they abolish performance requirements. In Europe the reaction has been stronger still, with organized labor groups pushing the Vredeling proposal, which would give local workers and communities veto power over the decisions of international companies to move or expand their operations abroad.

Finally, foreign investment has become an issue in the chaos of American politics. Some partisans have argued that American firms be restricted from moving abroad too easily because outward investment undermines the U.S. industrial base and exports jobs; others have urged the U.S. government to encourage American companies' investments abroad with the same strong support that their competitors in Europe and Japan receive. The debate is complicated by the fact that many politicians (Republicans and Democrats) and organized labor want American firms kept at home, while other politicians of both parties and the international business community want to gear up

"USA Inc." to meet "Japan Inc." in competition throughout the world.

Does outward investment by American firms support the domestic econ-omy and create jobs or undermine the domestic economy and give away jobs? Determining the answer is trickier than it might seem. It requires determining, across large bodies of data, what would have happened if the investments had not been made in the first place.

The what-if-something-had-not-happened question can never, of course, be answered definitively. But to make a plausible assessment, we have com-pared the relative export performance of firms that did invest abroad with firms of similar characteristics that did not.[12] These characteristics include large size, high R&D, heavy advertising, and so forth. (The conventional methodology of corporate representatives—that is, to compare the export performance of firms that invest abroad with the national average for all manufacturing firms—is not a good test, since firm characteristics other than foreign investment might account for export performance.) It is also important to isolate the contribution of foreign operations to the level of exports by the parent.

Although the results varied from industry to industry, they showed a small positive correlation between exports and foreign investment as firms begin the process of investment, and a small negative correlation as firms increase their outward investment. In other words, a little bit of foreign investment tends to stimulate firms' exports a little, and a lot of foreign investment tends to depress firms' exports a little, when compared with the record of similar firms that do not engage in foreign investment at all. Our studies, and others like them, conclude that government regulation of outward investment by American firms through constraints designed to increase U.S. exports and U.S. jobs would produce slight gains, rather than large ones, under even the best of conditions. Moreover, the regulatory policy would have to be very selective and finely tuned to work, placing a tremendous burden on the judgment of even the most skillful Washington bureaucrats.[13] Further-more, any such policy could easily become counterproductive if it provoked retaliation.

These findings indicate that a policy of neutrality toward outward invest-ment, allowing comparative advantage to determine the investment decisions of American firms, makes better sense than a policy that either pushes MNCs abroad or keeps them at home by imposing artificial restraints. This is a conclusion based on the most effective defense of U.S. national interests, not an ideological conclusion based on political preference.

Other studies reinforce the conclusion that performance requirements by third world governments do not have a major impact on trade patterns that could be corrected by unilateral U.S. actions to keep multinationals at home. In 1983 the World Bank completed a study of seventy-four major investment decisions.[14] About half of the decisions (thirty-eight) were found to be subject to some form of foreign exchange balancing requirements. In contrast to the charge, however, that performance requirements are necessarily trade-distorting, the World Bank study found that in a number of cases the requirements merely speeded up the foreign firms' plans to develop local suppliers or to enter export markets. This finding indicates that the host-country policies did not necessarily violate the broad long-term structure of comparative advantage. Moreover, for cases in which the performance requirements did determine the country in which the investment was located, all were defensive in nature; that is, the firms accepted performance requirements in order to maintain access to the domestic market. In short, the "problem" of performance requirements was shown to be relatively limited and, in any case, the firms had little choice but to respond to the host-country demands or lose their position. If the multinational corporations were forced to stay at home, both export and overseas earnings would be lost, with producers, consumers, and workers in the home country all winding up worse off.

Nevertheless, contrary to what we have urged for the past three decades, we are now attempting to stop the third world from using multinational corporations to achieve export-led growth. The calls for restrictionism to keep multinational corporations from moving abroad with ease, and for protectionism to keep out the products they produce more cheaply abroad, are growing stronger in the name of defending U.S. interests.

The Future of the International Economic System

It is not hard to demonstrate, in the abstract, that an open approach to trade and investment produces lower prices, less inflation, greater choice among products, increased technological innovation and efficiency, and heightened competition among all the countries affected. Indeed, even workers have an interest in a liberal approach to trade and investment, since restrictions are seldom likely to result in a net increase in jobs: the number of jobs saved by protecting steel or copper is likely to be overshadowed by the number of jobs lost in industries for which high-priced steel or high-priced copper is an input.[15] The rub is that the jobs saved through protectionism toward trade or restrictionism toward investment are likely to be more concentrated geographically than the jobs maintained through a more open approach to trade and investment. Moreover, the workers whose jobs are saved through protectionism and restrictionism are more likely to be unionized and politically vocal.

The greatest danger at the present time is not that protectionism toward trade and restrictionism toward investment will result in losses in world economic efficiency. Rather, the greatest danger is the prospect of shaking an already fragile international economic system. During the three decades after the Second World War the United States identified its long-term interest with the maintenance of an international economic system open to relatively free flows of capital, goods, and services. Not only did this policy maximize global economic welfare, but it responded (however imperfectly) to American humanitarian concerns about promoting the development of poorer nations. Now, with the growing strength of third world states, the question is whether the United States continues to have as large an interest in preserving the open system.

The answer is that the United States has a larger stake than ever. Indeed, increasing interdependence between the North and the South is imposing new and more vital responsibilities on us.

Throughout the 1970s, the less-developed countries exhibited higher rates of growth than the developed countries. From 1970 to 1979 the developed countries had an average growth rate of 3.5 percent per year in comparison to 6.7 percent per year for the LDC oil exporters and 5.0 percent for the non-oil exporters, with Latin America doing better (6.2 percent per year) than all but the most dynamic states of Southeast Asia. The third world's share of global economic output rose from 12.5 percent in 1973 to 13.7 percent by the end of the decade. At the margin it claimed nearly one-third of the gains in global production in the same period. The North enjoyed a large benefit from this expansion in the third world. U.S. exports to developing countries rose rapidly and by 1980 accounted for 36 percent of all American exports—more than the total of Western European and Japanese markets combined.[16]

How was this third world growth generated? Contrary to the notion that many of the states eschewed exports in favor of imports, much of the dynamism of the LDCs came from export-led growth.[17] From 1975 to 1979, for example, American imports of industrial raw materials (excluding fuels) from the non-OPEC developing countries expanded by 67 percent, from $1.8 billion to $3.0 billion. The performance of the LDCs in exporting manufactured goods was even stronger. U.S. imports of manufactured products from the non-OPEC developing countries climbed by 188 percent in the same period, from $8 billion to $23 billion.

The dark side of this remarkable expansion was the massive build-up in debt of LDCs, from $177 billion in 1973 to $323 billion in 1979.[18] With the second oil-price shock of 1979, the growth of indebtedness accelerated, with bank lending expanding at an annual average rate of 20 percent to the second half of 1982 (when the debt crisis finally hit).

The situation has been made worse of course, by high interest rates in the United States. Approximately two-thirds of the external debt of the twenty-one largest LDC borrowers carries floating interest rates, with 80 percent dollar-denominated. After 1979 the interest payments of these twenty-one countries more than doubled, from 10 percent of exports to more than 20 percent of exports in 1982. For some countries (Argentina and Brazil, for example), interest payments have climbed to between 45 percent and 50 percent of total exports.

25

Since the onset of the debt crisis in August 1982, however, the largest debtor countries (Brazil and Mexico) have made remarkable improvements in their external accounts. In Latin America, for example, the seven major borrowers achieved a combined trade surplus of approximately $30 billion in 1983. Much of this success, however, has been achieved by reducing merchandise imports, with these seven principal debtors together cutting their imports 42 percent below 1981 levels.[19]

How much further can the international debt situation be improved by austerity alone? For several Latin American countries, according to Morgan Guaranty, the reduction in living standards rivals the conditions of the 1930s.[20] Not only does this situation threaten the social and political institutions of the countries, but it is eroding the capital stock and industrial base needed for renovation and recovery. Undoubtedly, the less-developed countries can make further improvements in the internal management of their own economies; but it is becoming equally clear that for the medium and longer term the LDCs must get back on the path of trade-led growth.

Thus, the rationale for keeping the international system relatively open springs not simply from traditional concerns about global efficiency and development for the poor. We must also be concerned about the impact of the South's recession on the economic health of the North (for the United States alone, from 1980 through 1983, exports to the third world fell $18.1 billion, 1.1 million export-generated jobs disappeared, and $14 billion in investment income was lost):[21] the health of the international financial system itself (by mid-1982 the exposure of nine of the largest commercial banks had reached 2.2 times their total capital); and ultimately, the preservation of social and political stability throughout the third world.

Notes

1. For the debate between *Dependencia* School and Chicago School perspectives on multinational corporations and development, see Fernando Henrique Cardoso and Enzo Faletto, *Dependencia and Development in Latin America* (Berkeley: University of California Press, 1979); Thomas J. Biersteker, *Distortion or Development: Contending Perspectives on the Multinational Corporation* (Cambridge, Mass.: MIT Press, 1978); Theodore H. Moran, "Multinational Corporations and Dependency: A Dialogue for Dependentistas and Non-Dependentistas," *International Organization*, vol. 32, no. 1 (Winter 1978); and Michael P. Todaro, *Economic Development in the Third World* (New York: Longman, 1981), pp. 402–4.

2. Raymond Vernon, *Sovereignty at Bay: The Multinational Spread of U.S. Enterprises* (New York: Basic Books, 1971); Theodore H. Moran, *Multinational Corporations and the Politics of Dependence: Copper in Chile* (Princeton, N.J.: Princeton University Press, 1974); David N. Smith and Louis T. Wells, Jr., *Negotiating Third World Mineral Agreements* (Cambridge, Mass.: Ballinger, 1975); C. Fred Bergsten, Thomas Horst, and Theodore H. Moran, *American Multinationals and American*

Interests (Washington, D.C.: The Brookings Institution, 1978); and Theodore H. Moran, ed., *Multinational Corporations: The Political Economy of Foreign Direct Investment* (Cambridge, Mass.: D.C. Heath, 1985).

3. Fariborz Ghadar, Stephen J. Kobrin, and Theodore H. Moran, *Managing International Political Risk: Strategies and Techniques* (Washington, D.C.: Landegger Program in International Business Diplomacy, Georgetown University School of Foreign Service, 1983).

4. Moran, *Multinational Corporations and the Politics of Dependence: Copper in Chile*; Franklin Tugwell, *The Politics of Oil in Venezuela* (Stanford, Calif.: Stanford University Press, 1975); Richard L. Skar, *Corporate Power in an African State: The Political Impact of Multinational Mining Companies in Zambia* (Berkeley: University of California Press, 1975); and Michael Shafer, "Capturing the Mineral Multinationals: Advantage or Disadvantage?" *International Organization*, vol. 37, no. 1 (Winter, 1983).

5. The phenomenon of host governments playing off "independents" versus "majors" in the extractive industries is well documented. More broadly, there appears to be a "burst phenomenon" of investors trying to match each other's behavior across the range of industrial groups. For the strategy of creating "oligopoly anxiety" between majors and independents in the petroleum and mineral sectors, see Theodore H. Moran, "The International Political Economy of Cuban Nickel Development," in Cole Blasier and Carmelo Mesa-Lago, eds., *Cuba in the World* (Pittsburgh, Penn.: University of Pittsburgh Press, 1979). For the "burst phenomenon" in manufacturing, see Fred T. Knickerbocker, *Oligopolistic Reaction and Multinational Enterprise* (Boston: Division of Research, Graduate School of Business Administration, Harvard University, 1973). For the possibility of declining rather than increasing competition, based on Latin American case studies see Richard Newfarmer, ed., *Profits, Progress, and Poverty: Case Studies of International Industry* (South Bend, Ind.: University of Notre Dame Press, 1984).

6. G. L. Reuber, with H. Crookell, M. Emerson, and G. Gallais-Hammond, *Private Foreign Investment in Development* (Oxford: Clarendon Press, 1973); C. Chase-Dunn, "The Effects of International Economic Dependence on Development and Inequality: A Cross-National Study," *American Sociological Review*, vol. 40 (December 1975); V. Bornschier, "Multinational Corporations and Economic Growth: A Cross-National Test of the Decapitalization Thesis," *Journal of Development Economics*, vol. 7 (June 1980).

7. Walter A. Chudson and Louis T. Wells, Jr., *The Acquisition of Technology from Multinational Corporations by Developing Countries* (New York: United Nations, 1974); D. J. C. Forsyth and R. F. Solomon, "Choice of Technology and Nationality of Ownership in Manufacturing in a Developing Country," *Oxford Economic Papers*, vol. 29 (July 1977); S. Lall, "Transnationals, Domestic Enterprises, and Industrial Structure in Host LDCs: A Survey," *Oxford Economic Papers*, vol. 30 (July 1978); B. S. Chung and C. H. Lee, "The Choice of Production Techniques by Foreign and Local Firms in Korea," *Economic Development and Cultural Change*, vol. 29 (October 1980); Steven W. Langdon, *Multinational Corporations in the Political Economy of Kenya* (London: Macmillan, 1981); Wayne A. Yeoman, *Selection of Production Processes for the Manufacturing Subsidiaries of U.S.-Based Multinational Corporations* (New York: Arno Press, 1976); and Louis T. Wells, "Economic Man and Engineering

Man: Choice in a Low-Wage Country," *Public Policy*, vol. 21 (Summer 1973).

8. See the contributions by Wells, Stephen Kobrin, and Carlos Diaz Alejandro in Tamir Agmon and Charles Kindleberger, eds., *Multinationals From Small Countries* (Cambridge, Mass.: MIT Press, 1977); and Louis T. Wells, Jr., "Small Scale Manufacturing as a Competitive Advantage," from *Third World Multinationals: The Rise of Foreign Investment from Developing Countries* (Cambridge, Mass.: MIT Press, 1983).

9. Michael B. Dolan and Brian Tomlin, "First World-Third World Linkages: External Relations and Economic Development," *International Organization*, (Winter 1980). Perhaps their most significant finding was that domestic economic policies on issues other than foreign investment were far more important in explaining the success or failure of development strategies than the level of penetration of multinational corporations per se.

10. This should not be seen as a zero-sum phenomenon. Many multinational corporations that allow themselves to be "harnessed," earn greater profits afterwards than they did before.

11. The Labor-Industry Coalition for International Trade, *Performance Requirements* (Washington, D.C.: LICIT, 1981).

12. C. Fred Bergsten, Thomas Horst, and Theodore H. Moran, *American Multinationals and American Interests*. See also R. E. Lipsey and M. Y. Weiss, "Foreign Production and Exports in Manufacturing Industries," *Review of Economics and Statistics*, vol. 63 (November, 1981).

13. See also Richard T. Frank and Richard T. Freeman, *Distributional Consequences of Direct Foreign Investment* (New York: Academic Press, 1978).

14. Stephen Guisinger, *Investment Incentives and Performance Requirements: A Comparative Analysis of Country Foreign Investment Strategies* (Washington, D.C.: World Bank, July 1983).

15. Cf. Alan V. Deardorff and Robert M. Stern, "American Labor's Stake in International Trade," in *Tariffs, Quotas, and Trade: The Politics of Protectionism* (San Francisco: Institute for Contemporary Studies, 1979).

16. For these figures, see John P. Lewis and Valeriana Kallab, eds., *U.S. Foreign Policy and The Third World: Agenda 1983* (New York: Praeger for the Overseas Development Council, 1983).

17. Roger D. Hansen et al., *U.S. Foreign Policy and the Third World: Agenda 1982* (New York: Praeger for the Overseas Development Council, 1982).

18. These figures came from Morgan Guaranty Trust, *World Financial Markets*, various issues, 1983–1984.

19. Morgan Guaranty Trust, *World Financial Markets*, February 1984.

20. Ibid.

21. Gabriel G. Manrique and Stuart K. Tucker, "The Costs to the U.S. of the Recession in the Developing Countries," Working Paper, Overseas Development Council, Washington, D.C., June 1984.

Discussion

COMMENT: We find that independent of the character of a regime, the negotiating posture really does not change because we are talking to the same people. The bureaucrats we talk to in Iran are the same bureaucrats that we talked to ten years ago. They are not the ones at the top; they were all wiped out. The ones that run the country, however, are still there. That continuity may explain one of Mr. Moran's points.

The other thing that we find is that, regardless of the economic conditions the negotiating power of a multinational does not improve. As an example, we might think that Mexico or Argentina, which have such terrible debt situations and are hungry for foreign investment, would soften their negotiating stance and change their long-term policies. Apparently they haven't.

One can talk to a president of a country, the minister of industry, or the finance minister, who will all admit they are a poor investment and appear to agree to do what is necessary, but this message never seems to get down to the negotiators.

A few years ago we negotiated in Delhi, where everything was done by hand. Ten thousand desks would all be absolutely piled with papers. We had to hire someone to carry our paper around. It was the only way we could possibly locate our paper. These countries deliberately generate red tape, just as our government does.

I believe these countries are in an "I'm going to wait you out" position, either because they want to wait out the banks or because they want to wait out the U.S. government. I don't see that the terms are changing very much.

COMMENT: Mr. Moran, in your analysis of the factors that influence negotiation, it seems to me you have left out some things. For instance, you did not factor in whether the investment that the multinational is bringing in represents a new entrance into the country for that multinational or whether it represents an expansion of an already existing business in the country. It seems to me that would affect negotiating strength. To clarify my point, let me cite Mexico. It is such a good example of restrictions imposed on new investment, as is common in the third world.

For years Mexico has had an investment law that has been applied to restrict the expansion of an already existing business, not only affecting new product lines but also new facilities, new plants, new locations—just about anything that a business needs to grow. If it were 100 percent foreign-owned or less than a majority owned by Mexicans, it had to receive permission from the Investment Commission to expand. In that situation, if a company wanted to bring a new product line into Mexico, let's say Pampers, and the company already had a business in Mexico selling detergents and was very large and prosperous, employing a lot of people. The Mexican government would say that if the company wants to sell Pampers in Mexico, it has to meet a series of conditions. The fact that the company is already there surely affects the negotiating position with the government of Mexico.

Specifically, though, I wanted to ask Mr. Moran about Ford in Mexico. Here is a country that has been hit by very bad economic problems, a deep recession, high debt, and high interest obligations. The only way it can begin to generate hard currency is by putting the brakes on its imports, with all that that entails. Into that market came Ford, which agreed to put $400 million into a plant in Mexico specifically to build for the export market. That occurred against a background of a Mexican decree which severely limited the variety of cars which could be produced. The attitude of the Mexican government was that Ford could take its offer or leave it.

This attitude runs contrary, it seems to me, to what we would expect. Indeed, Ford's agreement to follow that arbitrary law has strengthened the Mexican government in negotiating with multinationals in other industries. The best example I can cite on that score is the recent pharmaceutical decree that will virtually nationalize the foreign pharmaceutical industry in Mexico, if the decree is applied to the letter. Could you comment on that?

MR. MORAN: The Ford case is very interesting because it comes right at the time when General Motors is expanding a facility in this country with the Japanese. The United Auto Workers is putting a lot of pressure on Ford to try to expand its production here or to combine with the Japanese. The UAW is split; it is a bit schizophrenic about whether it wants to join up with the Japanese or keep the Japanese out. Yet Ford decided to expand enormously in Mexico.

Ford has decided to expand in spite of the Mexican automotive law, which I hear will be changed to a certain extent. As it now stands, it mandates all producers in the domestic market to export a certain percentage of what they produce domestically. The Mexicans have been very canny, unlike the Argentines and some others; they have not insisted that exports be a finished car or truck as in the Argentine case, but only a value. Thus they allow the companies to decide where comparative advantage lies and have the companies promise to generate a given amount of foreign exchange.

In this way, Mexico has become a very large supplier of automotive parts. Many parts and components that Detroit now uses are made in Mexico.

That means Mexican jobs in Monterey and not American jobs in Detroit, and in that sense the UAW is very anxious over this deal. This is an excellent example of a performance requirement, and it seems to reinforce your point: it comes right in the midst of the worst possible time for Mexico.

COMMENT: I have a difficult time in my job dealing with these governments when I hear others tell me how much power I am supposed to have in negotiations. I may have power, but somehow I am not able to exert it.

To comment a little more on the Mexican situation, it is evident by even the present economic situation of Mexico—high debt, difficulties in servicing that debt—that Mexico must do several things. One is to find sources of foreign capital that do not cause additional indebtedness. Mexico must also change the situation of the merchandise accounts or the balance of payments that generate foreign exchange surplus to be able to service the debt that it has already incurred.

It is evident that Mexico needs to attract private foreign capital. In general, the posture it has taken seems to be rational in view of its national interests. Let's take an extreme case. It is of little or no interest to Mexico for a foreign company to come into the country to buy out an existing Mexican producer, if that were even possible, because that sale adds nothing to the national economy. Obviously, foreigners will not be allowed to buy out existing Mexicans.

With respect to the Pampers case, I don't understand the rationale there. The policy does not seem very rational. What Mexico should attract, of course, is what it is attracting—firms that will establish themselves in Mexico, firms that will generate employment and foreign exchange. On the whole, I would say Mexico's policy is nationalistic, but nationalistic in the best national interest.

MR. MORAN: May I say the best evidence for your thesis would be the frustration of multinational negotiators. [Laughter]

COMMENT: The subject of codes of conduct is a subject near to my heart because I have been living with one for the past three years that applies to infant formula. While multinationals are not perfect and certainly should examine their internal practices, those who look to codes of conduct as panaceas to keep multinationals in line also have to realize that codes often have consequences the reverse of what were intended. For instance, in the infant formula code, one provision specifies the amount of supplies we can give to hospitals. In Africa we must now deny requests from Catholic hospitals for donations of infant formula that would save the lives of babies. We have to explain that the World Health Organization code requires us to give a certain amount for the full term of the baby, or else we are breaking the code. A lot of

31

foresight, then, is necessary to avoid the negative consequences of codes.

COMMENT: I would like to speak in defense of Mr. Moran's observations. I see a difference between marketing codes and negotiating codes. His point about codes was not that they allow us to wink at amorality, but rather that the codes themselves, for all their good intentions, might stand in the way of achieving greater fairness. Perhaps we could compare this process with the internal dynamics of a good marriage. Developing a code to regulate such domestic arrangements as who takes out the garbage and when, for example, strikes me as absurd.

I don't interpret what Mr. Moran is saying as winking at amorality. I see a deeper moral value at stake here: how people through interaction struggle toward reciprocity and mutuality.

MR. MORAN: My fear is that if we have codes governing some of the main issues at which the TNC Code aims—namely, ownership and renegotiation of contracts—we will have codes to which everything will be an exception. The Andean Pact is an example. The Colombians do not want to leave the Andean Pact, largely because it gives some access to the Venezuelan market. Although they do not want to leave the pact, almost every investment agreement makes some exception because they want to allow ownership here or not meddle with transfer pricing there, or because they believe they can get a better deal by allowing an exception.

Some of the moral decisions that I consider very important touch on empirical questions as well, and I don't know how to resolve them in my own mind.

One of the areas in which I do research concerns job generation, labor codes, and the whole issue of appropriate technology. I also explore the possibilities, if any, for convincing multinational corporations to develop effective labor-intensive techniques to be used in the third world. I mean effective from their point of view, so that they can take advantage of the labor abundance and turn it to a competitive advantage. As I look at the empirical data, I see that one of the main hindrances to developing labor-intensive technology is not the demand for higher wages but the labor regulations third world governments impose on multinationals. The companies want to be able to "adjust the size of the labor force," which means hiring and laying off people as necessary. If a company has a labor-intensive operation in textiles or microelectronics or whatever and that operation is subject to business cycle fluctuations, it must be able to hire and lay off workers; a layoff in the third world is the same as a layoff here—an agonizing human experience.

In those countries that have adopted the Italian-style approach—namely, making it almost impossible to lay somebody off once he has been hired—companies do not set up labor-intensive operations. Therefore, the countries with tight regulations do not have much labor-intensive production. In countries with loose regulations, manufacturers are changing their operations and using more labor. When they lay off workers, however, people return to their villages, for example, in Malaysia or in Sri Lanka, a situation generating ethical problems of its own. I see very serious ethical problems on both sides of this issue, and all of us have to struggle to find the best public policy in a circumstance like that.

COMMENT: Mr. Moran, you said something to the effect that the moral issue is not the gap between the rich and the poor, implying that the moral issue is the condition of the poor. I bring this up because Pope John Paul II and Pope Paul VI both said that the great scandal is the growing gap. As I read the evidence, however, that is not a moral matter at all, but an arithmetical matter. We can do nothing about that. No matter what we do, the gap will grow larger because the base is so different. In the case of Bangladesh and the United States, for example, if Bangladesh has a growth rate of 10 percent a year for the next ten years and the United States has a growth rate of 1 percent a year for the next ten years, the gap will still grow larger. At the end of ten years, the gap will be greater in per capita income.

What matters, though, is if the condition of the people ten years from now will be better. Of that, I am quite confident. By calling attention to the gap, we focus on the wrong moral point, the one about which we can do almost nothing. The condition of the poor is something we can do something about.

MR. MORAN: Although I am not qualified to interpret the pope's remarks, I have some observations that may be germane. I do not argue that it is morally irrelevant to look at the gap between rich and poor. My point was that we can believe and hope for and wish for and work for all of the improvements in harnessing the potential economic power of multinationals and still find that ten years from now the gap would be greater. Yet, we would still find a big success story. We could be proud of what had happened, even if the gap had increased.

One of the biggest ways in which the developed countries affect the fate of the third world is by the management of their own economies. If I thought that the United States or the OECD countries could generate a sustained 5 percent growth rate over the next five years, I would say a prayer of thanksgiving, just because of the beneficial effect on the third world. I wouldn't really care about the gap. The many good spillover effects on commodity prices, on demand for exports, and on reducing protectionism would all be so welcome that we would forget about the gap. We would just hope to sustain the pace and not fall back into high interest rates, stagflation, and recession.

COMMENT: Let me suggest one thing that perhaps the present pope does have in mind. In some of the documents that have been either written by him or generated under his guidance, a combination phrase "self-reliance and solidarity" recurs. What he seems to have in mind with solidarity, of course, is some emphasis on community and cooperation among communities. A less well-known theme of John Paul II is self-reliance. Maybe the kind of structural change he envisions is not massive redistribution or even a shrinking of the gap but an improved national economic status such as we have already seen with the Latin American countries that have become middle-income nations, where people are not as desperately poor as some Asian or African nations. Even more important, the structural changes in these countries, namely the beginning of some manufacturing as opposed to dependency on a single commodity, allows a nation to enter the world market on a somewhat different footing. Selling automobile parts rather than bananas may not make a difference in the short run, but it probably is a long-run structural change.

The papal literature on economics is becoming more and more sophisticated, starting from a preferential option for the poor and developing into the hard-headed realism about structures and negotiations that really will result in a better life for the poorest of the poor, regardless of gaps.

COMMENT: I spent a whole day wrestling with the question of the gap and what it will look like in fifty years. Let's assume a very optimistic 4 percent per capita growth rate in LDCs versus a 2 percent per capita growth rate in the developed countries over the next fifty years. As has already been pointed out, the arithmetic shows that the gap becomes just horrendous.

Now, you say that there is no way we could share. You say that if we start trying to share too much too soon, we will kill the goose that lays the golden egg. Frankly, I would like to see some creativity in addressing the dilemma of how we should share, assuming we could reach a consensus in the developed world that we should. I don't think that the basis has to be guilt, but rather how could we share without killing the goose, the free enterprise system?

MR. MORAN: The harder question to me is, How do we avoid killing the growth? I am thinking, in particular, about killing the growth in the third world. So many sharing programs, agricultural programs, for example, are destructive in the final analysis. In Bengal, such a program began with the greatest desire to help feed Bengalese and ended up crushing Bengali agriculture and corrupting officials.

COMMENT: I would like to speak to the question of structural change. I was very surprised that no one has yet mentioned the document on the development of a new international economic order, which was put forth a number of years ago by Latin America and disdained and rejected by the West. It suggested a great many structural changes in the international economic order that perhaps deserve more consideration than they have been given.

The thrust of those documents was not that the Western countries should deprive themselves of anything, but that they should take from their continued growth. As the well-to-do in the United States contribute to the welfare of the people through various programs, so international programs should be developed that, in effect, are supported by taxing the countries with continued growth. A program of international taxation and redistribution would certainly be a fundamental structural change in the world order, yet we have given very little thought to such a possibility, partly because national sovereignty stands in the way. Such proposals have been made, and we could easily think of others if we put our minds to it. We could imagine a world community in which giving up some of our national sovereignty would result in an eventual closing of the gap and a fulfillment of obligations across borders, which we are loathe to consider.

MR. MORAN: I can't forbear saying before we end our discussion that it is extremely easy to imagine such a plan but very hard to imagine it working.

Latin America: Debt, Destruction, and Development

William P. Glade, Jr.

Although remarks on the diversity of the Latin American countries may be commonplace, this diversity must be acknowledged as a preface to any serious discussion of the economic circumstances of the region. Both economic problems and economic possibilities differ from country to country. For convenience, therefore, we shall sort out the economies of Latin America and the Caribbean under three distinct but intersecting sets of cases to correspond to three of the overriding problems of the area.

Debt: Roll Out the Consols

With the partial exception of Colombia, the more important economies of the region are, as is well known, all caught up in a crisis associated with high levels of external debt. The plight of these countries has, for the past two years or so, done much to shake the confidence of the international banking system. In some ways the predicament of Brazil, Mexico, Argentina, Peru, Venezuela, and Chile seems even more fraught with risks than was the case in Poland, Romania, and Yugoslavia, which were in the debtors' pillory only a short while before. The debt difficulty is scarcely less acute in some of the small countries, too: in an advanced one like Costa Rica, in more backward Bolivia, and in Ecuador, which lies somewhere in between Costa Rica and Bolivia in level of development. These, like such countries as Nigeria, Sudan, Indonesia, Zaire, and Tanzania, have also managed to get deep in debt, but since they are less conspicuous in the profile of arrearages and stretch-outs, we shall not consider them here.

External debt crises are hardly new in Latin America's history. From soon after independence to the Great Depression, with its massive defaulting, the region recurrently ran into these problems. The postwar expansion started promisingly on the basis of the large external reserves accumulated during World War II, with a debt service ratio of only 6 percent in 1956. Borrowing soon began to rise, however, though largely through official credits on concessionary terms. By 1964, when the total external debt of less developed countries (LDCs) stood around $38 billion (about the nominal size of today's Argentine debt alone), the debt service ratio had already risen to 15 percent—enough to prompt moderate concern, if not outright anxiety. Despite some acknowledgment of a need for caution, the region's external debt continued to creep upwards. In the 1970s the financial picture began to change dramatically.

For three of the debt-plagued countries—Mexico, Venezuela, and Ecuador—the problem emerged in part from a splurge of public and private overspending when the oil shocks of 1974 and 1979 brought substantial windfall gains to these countries. Equally ill-fated were the assessments of foreign lenders of the prospects for continued prosperity in these oil-exporting countries. For most of the other debtor countries, a significant factor was the sharp rise in the cost of imported fuels and petroleum derivatives, although this demand itself resulted from remarkable success in development. Thanks to the impressive development momentum that had been built up in the 1960s and 1970s, a growing industrial plant, higher per capita incomes, and thriving internal commerce (with its corresponding claim on transport systems) all rested on access to petroleum from abroad, which became ever more costly.

Three other adversities conspired to bring the debtor countries to the bar of fiscal and monetary judgment: the global inflation of the late 1970s (which made a great many other Latin American imports much more expensive), the global recession of the early 1980s (which cut deeply into the current export earnings of Latin America), and the run-up in interest rates on borrowed funds. Entrapped in this financial Bermuda Triangle, the Latin American countries eventually faced a choice of spiraling debt or an end to growth. The convergence of these and other trends, such as the shortfall in agricultural output in countries where the development of that sector had been long disregarded, thrust Latin America into its most severe economic crisis since the 1930s. The main wonder is that it took so long for the creditworthiness of most of the countries to come under a cloud. Although 20 percent was the maximum debt service level that was long considered prudent, by late 1982 the debt service burden reached 58 percent of export income for Mexico, 67 percent for Brazil, and 78 percent for Argentina.[1]

For the time being, relief has come only from roll-over of debts, but no one believes that the restructuring plans cobbled together so far offer the slightest promise for the long haul. Interest rates may eventually repeat their recent rise. Recession in the advanced countries will sooner or later return to deal a further blow to Latin American export earnings, quite possibly coinciding with maturity bunching in the region's foreign debt. And banks outside the money centers show a growing disinclination to increase their Latin American exposure through repeated short-term bail-outs. Protectionism in the advanced industrial countries shows no signs of abating, so Latin American exporters of manufactures are likely to face tariff or quota penalties precisely in the degree that they are successful. We have already seen this happen in relation to Brazil and Mexico, for instance, in spite of our substantial financial stake in those two countries.

A related, but more subtle, risk has been the growing inclination in the United States to require reciprocity in trade liberalization. If we press in this direction—say, on domestic content legislation—we are virtually halting trade concessions to Latin America and giving considerable support to the protectionist camp in the United States. Few, if any, Latin American countries will be in a position to lift their controls on foreign trade, even if they were so minded, while wrestling with the chronic balance-of-payments problems of the foreseeable future. We may see more trade intervention, rather than less, in Latin American countries if they try to relax the debt burden on foreign trade through a reactivation of regional integration.

Moreover, the risk mounts that the delicate fabric of domestic politics, often subject to stress even in the best of times, will unravel in many countries if economic life is confined for too long. Should the roll-over of debt roll right into another global recession, political upheaval becomes a virtual certainty. Even now it is hard to spot a recovery in Latin American exports strong enough to (1) service and amortize the accumulated debt, (2) restore the aggregate growth rate to its former level, and (3) make up for the decline in foreign financing. These factors hover all too visibly over the Latin American investment scene, creating an uncertainty that can only inhibit both domestic and foreign capital formation in the region. (The developments in Mexico in 1982 virtually ensure a leak of that nation's capital, as soon as circumstances permit, on a scale much larger than in decades past.) This uncertainty, in turn, seems sure to trouble the economic performance of the region for years to come, over and beyond the balance-of-payments constrictions. Although an expectation of greater stability in the debt situation might somewhat alleviate the problem, the negative investment climate will deter foreign capital inflows, no matter what official welcome may be proffered in the effort to substitute equity financing for borrowing.

It is easy to succumb so fully to the vision of banking catastrophe that other important elements are not seen. In the long run, however, these elements are far more consequential than the current financial crunch. For one thing, Latin America's foreign bankers may have been excessively optimistic, but they were not hallucinating when they channelled increased resources to the countries to our south. The newsletter of a major money-center bank, for example, ran an article in November 1980 headlined "Latin American Investment Outlook Bright." The opening sentences catch the spirit of the whole article: "The nations of Latin America and the Caribbean are undoubtedly among the world's most promising markets for investments in the coming decades. Their aggregate economic growth rate is expected to continue rapid, and they possess large and expanding domestic markets, elements that have historically proven to be prime magnets for direct foreign investment." Later the essay relates that "indications are that the 1980s will see the pattern [of the 1970s] repeated, with Latin America and the Caribbean recording average annual GDP growth of 5 percent–6 percent."

To be sure, by the latter half of 1980 there was a dawning realization—reflected, for example, in the September 1980 issue of *World Financial Markets* put out by Morgan Guaranty Trust—that a greater banking exposure in some countries might be imprudent. With the benefit of a few more months of observation, the Economic Commission for Latin America took a more cautious position in its "Estudio Económico de América Latina 1980" (September 1981) but, even so, anticipated a deceleration of growth rather than what actually came to pass. Around 1960, the potential supply of funds available to Latin America may have exceeded its capacity to absorb them; by 1980, however, the economic landscape in the major countries differed greatly, not least in the evident growth of bankable investment projects.

Population growth continues to be a problem in some of the more important Latin American economies, as it is throughout most of the region. For example, Central America, the weakest economic area, had a population of some 12 million at the end of World War II and now has to provide for around 39 million. Worse yet, high demographic growth rates, despite some moderation in recent years, still prevail, as the 1982 figures indicate: Costa Rica 2.6 percent, El Salvador 3.1 percent, Guatemala 2.9 percent, Honduras 3.2 percent, and Nicaragua 2.4 percent. Among the large economies only Argentina and Chile can take much comfort from their demographic situation. Mexico (2.8 percent), Brazil (2.5 percent), Colombia (2.1 percent), Peru (2.1 percent), and Venezuela (2.7 percent) all continue to experience dismayingly high increases. Nevertheless Latin America's human capital—the amount and diversity of labor, managerial, and technical skills—vastly exceeds the endowment of only a quarter century ago. Entrepreneurial skills, in both the private and the public sectors, have increased through experience. Organizational capability and the amount and quality of economic information are notably improved. The maturation of physical and organizational infrastructure, the widening of urban markets, and the obvious rise in standards of living (including improvements in social indicators) all point to an impressive record of accomplishments.

The size of debt is itself a further measure of the material progress. In a region with a high import coefficient, the capital inflows of the past two decades financed a rate of growth much higher than could have been achieved on a pay-as-you-go basis. Official financing, particularly on concessionary terms, dropped off as a share of total capital flows. The major countries, in fact, rose above their status of the 1960s when they had qualified for the more generous terms now being reserved for the "poorest of the poor." More reliance was placed on foreign equity capital, which capitalized on the investment opportunities generated by the broadening and deepening industrial structure. By the 1970s, the leading Latin American economies had improved so much that they could rely even more on bank loans than on the kind of external financing they had in the 1960s. Although financing appears in retrospect to have been unbalanced, the heavy use of loan capital was probably necessary to hold foreign ownership to politically acceptable levels.

Two very different cases illustrate just how far the main Latin American economies had come by the end of the 1970s. Chile had developed its industrial structure in an almost classical version of the protectionist and other interventionist policies of *étatisme*. The manufacturing industries it cultivated before Allende came to office were hothouse plants *par excellence*. Buffeted by the extreme disorder of the Unidad Popular episode and then by a wrenching redirection of national economic policy after the military *coup d'état*, the Chilean industrial sector should, by all rights, have vanished. Industrial employment at the end of the 1970s nevertheless constituted about the same percentage of the employed labor force as at the end of the 1960s—remarkable testimony to the resiliency of the sector in the face of great adversity, although a perverse exchange rate policy nearly ruined the sector in the 1980s. Brazilian industrial accomplishment is so well known that only one aspect need be cited to drive the point home: the new capacity of Brazil to export industrial services. By 1982, for instance, Brazilian firms had exported industrial services of one sort or another to Algeria, Angola, Argentina, Bolivia, Canada, Chile, Colombia, Costa Rica, Dominican Republic, Ecuador, Egypt, El Salvador, West Germany, France, Guatemala, Haiti, Honduras, Iran, Iraq, the Ivory Coast, Mauritania, Mexico, Mozambique, Nigeria, Panama, and nine other countries farther down the alphabet.

In recent years, Brazil has probably made the most headway in policy management, though by the late 1960s several countries had adopted such corrective measures in industrial policy as lowering tariffs, shifting to more realistic exchange rates, simplifying export administration, and rationalizing the automotive industry. Because of these changes and the general maturation of Latin American industrial enterprise, Latin America will probably take a more prominent global role in fields like textiles, shoes, steel, chemicals, automobiles, and even electronics.

In short, behind the account book problems of refinancing lie substantial real assets that put Latin America in the vanguard of the third world. Much uncertainty surrounds the question of how these resources can be put back on the path of growth. As the crash of 1929 and the dislocation of the 1930s taught us, however, life not only can continue after a crisis but also can be richly satisfying. Because of its higher income levels and the increasing complexity and sophistication of its industrial sector, Latin America will in time figure in the U.S. external sector as much as it did in the past—and probably more so, thanks to the global relocation of manufacturing production that has been under way for some time.

Sooner or later the lawyers, accountants, and politicians will figure out the best way to disguise the default that has—strictly speaking—already begun. The Commodity Credit Corporation's payments to banks and the use of the reserve backing for housing loans are a sure sign of this dénouement. Similar signs are the rush into extended grace periods and the extraordinary leniency with which interest obligations have been treated. Clearly, the search is on for palliatives.

Some private sector debt may, for example, be converted into equity, although a transfer of national interests to foreign hands on anything remotely approximating the outstanding loan liability would be politically ticklish. Foreign investment has long been exploited as an issue by the political left in most countries—with enormous exaggeration of its size, cost, and impact (for example, on consumerism). With a characteristic ambivalence on the subject, the local private sector, particularly middle and smaller sized firms, has been circumspect at best in refuting such allegations. The feelings of both groups would of course be intensified by a massive conversion of private debt into foreign-held equity.

Only slightly more promising is a second possible expedient: some public sector debt may be transformed into shareholdings in joint ventures spun out of reorganized state enterprises. An important policy development of the past ten years has been the inclination to require parastatal firms to aim for commercially sound operating criteria. As a variant, in Mexico it was proposed that some of the industrial equity the government acquired in the banking nationalization be used to scale down the debt obligation; such returned companies would face an uncertain future, however, because of the price controls that have forced their decapitalization in a number of cases. A similar problem affects the conversion of many other parastatal enterprises into joint ventures: the new concerns may inherit redundancy in the work force, insufficient capitalization, and contractual or other obligations to suppliers and customers that can be changed only with difficulty.

Another part of the debt may even be repaid, however gradually—and yet another part handled through the bail-outs known, discreetly, as official financing. Yet, for all practical purposes, the alternatives for much of the rest are either writing it off, writing it down through public sector grants in aid (that is, subsidies to bankers), or, at best, converting it into a permanent obligation with market value that, like that of the British consol, fluctuates with the interest rate. If, on the other hand, lending institutions press for eventual full repayment, or if protectionist interests succeed in keeping out Latin American manufacturing exports, then the practical outcome will more probably be that of the old Russian consols.

The U.S. national interest in the debt is by no means identical to that of the banks. While averting a wave of failures of major lending institutions is, to be sure, in the public interest, banks should in principle have to accept protracted periods of depressed earnings as a consequence of miscalculations

41

and unforeseen circumstantial changes, just as other industries do. Meanwhile U.S. exporters to Latin America (especially exporters of investment goods), importers of nontraditional Latin American export products, and investors with subsidiaries and affiliates located there all share an interest in eliminating the mistakes of the past and in reactivating Latin American economic expansion as soon as possible. Firms must sometimes write off technology that has not been fully depreciated to make way in the accounts for new growth-conducive technology; by the same token, it would be foolish to let obsolete financial arrangements stand in the way of a resumption of regional economic progress. Moreover, from the standpoint of U.S. national security, the cost of a continuing financial imbroglio could be incalculable.

Preoccupation with the debt issue, besides obscuring the sizable real-resource assets of Latin America, presents another risk: it diverts attention from issues that in the long run may be no less consequential. Latin American inattention to agriculture is one of these issues. After entrenched latifundiary interests blocked reform programs for decades, agricultural modernization paradoxically fell victim to the relative eclipse of political influence of those interests. In the past quarter-century or so, urban demands have grown too strong to be denied and have brought about policies counterproductive to agriculture while absorbing the lion's share of social investment. Neglect of the rural sector will have to end, for a number of reasons, so that in the next decade or so, most of the industrially advanced countries of Latin America will need to give priority to agricultural development.

How can the United States relate constructively to this policy realignment? Our own experience in agribusiness may not be altogether relevant, because agrarian modernization in Latin America may have macroeconomic consequences—such as its effect on employment generation, on improved income distribution, and on domestic market breadth—almost as important as its impact on production and on import structure. Our development, based on ample supplies of land and capital and on comparative labor scarcity, may provide fewer answers than, say, the recent Taiwanese experience. Land tenure questions have abated somewhat since the early 1960s, at least partly because of restrictions on popular political expression prevailing over much of the continent in recent years. If the policy framework for the agricultural sector were more satisfactory, and ecologically more sound than that pursued by Brazil in Amazonia, the U.S. public and private sectors would have a golden opportunity to devise innovative programs exemplifying the social responsibility and creativity of private enterprise.

A second major problem area concerns the state sector and its relation both to private enterprise and to the accumulation process. One might suppose IMF stabilization policies would curtail the parastatal enterprises that abound in Latin America and foster privatization. Such a curtailment would seem to follow from the need to reduce the public sector borrowing requirement by reining in the deficit-generating operations of public enterprises—and perhaps from a political reaction as well by an electorate that has been put through the wringer by the misguided government policies of the past. In the view of foreign, or at least U.S. business interests, Latin American governments in addition to learning the virtues of private enterprise should welcome foreign equity capital more warmly since the risks of overextended credit positions have been brought home so sharply.

This view, I believe, misreads the Latin American policy experience and its enduring state-centered orientation. The credit crunch and market shrinkage brought on by austerity programs have generally fallen more heavily on domestic private firms than on state enterprises; as a result, even in Chile intervention has been extended in the form of rescue operations designed to salvage ailing private firms.[2] Given the fragility of domestic economic interests in times of crisis, the impetus to shelter national interests behind the carapace of state power will probably be even stronger than before. If domestic economic setbacks are contrasted with the vigorous recovery of foreign firms, highlighted by foreign takeovers of domestic assets at distressed prices, all the old xenophobic misgivings about dependency are sure to be evoked with renewed fervor. This tendency will become all the more pronounced as the deepening of industrial structure in import-substitution pushes investment into technically more complex fields dominated by multinational capital. For better or for worse, intervention has long been commonly accepted as the palladium of national integrity, and it is likely to continue to be so conceived in the future. What this means, in all probability, is that, increasingly, foreign capital will be admitted mainly in association with public capital and domestic private capital, along the lines of Brazil's *tri-pe* arrangement, and that the international sourcing networks of multinational firms will be enlisted even more than heretofore to move nontraditional Latin American exports abroad. In the case of the new Ford engine plant in Mexico, for example, 85 percent of the output is destined for the U.S. market.

Institutional barriers and conditions could also impede the state's divesting itself of any considerable portion of its industrial and other assets. At a time when the domestic economy is strapped, conditions are hardly propitious for selling parastatal companies to national investors. Without an extended transition period to rehabilitate government-owned firms through management contracts and the like, these companies probably cannot be made salable and transferred to private status anyhow. To the extent that an overriding aim of privatization is to shrink the public sector deficit, an additional complication presents itself: the most likely candidates for disposition are the ones with operating profits. For the government to shed these, while it retains the deficit-causing enterprises, would simply increase the public sector borrowing requirement.

Finally, the state sector may conceivably be amplified from yet another

43

source, in spite of current expectations that it should contract. Parastatal firms, from Europe as well as in Latin America, may well be able to increase their investment and to expand their market share since they, more readily than private companies, can accept several years of relatively low (or possibly negative) earnings on their capital. They also, at least indirectly, stand some chance of sharing in any new flow of official credit to the region.

To be sure, there are other problems, such as a revival of the badly flagging regional integration efforts, on the policy agenda of the more industrially advanced countries. The demonstrated capacity of these nations to get this far along the development road, however, establishes a presumption that the journey can be resumed, though not necessarily in the fast lane, if the debt issue can be expeditiously laid to rest.

Destruction: Accumulation Amid Disinvestment

Toward a second set of nations, one must be less sanguine. It is sobering to reflect on how recently the prospects for Central America appeared bright. Although the region has long exemplified the underdeveloped banana-republic stereotype, the Central American Common Market (CACM), established in 1961, seemed, the most successful modern integration scheme outside Western Europe before it began to unravel with the Honduras/El Salvador war of 1969. Even for a few years thereafter—despite continuing violence in Guatemala and the onset of terrorism in El Salvador—hope was not abandoned that the CACM could somehow be put back on track.

Intraregional trade flows were thriving, growing from around $30 million (in U.S. currency) when the CACM was set up to almost $300 million in 1970. As foreign capital poured in, most of the countries achieved a quite respectable economic performance at the macro level. The annual rate of per capita growth for 1960–1972, for example, averaged 2.8 percent in Costa Rica, 2.0 percent in El Salvador, 2.2 percent in Guatemala, 1.4 percent in Honduras, and 4.0 percent in Nicaragua. As a barometer of these conditions, U.S. investment in Central America rose from $307 million (in U.S. currency) in 1955 to $620 million in 1969. Significantly, Central America was in those days mainly of interest to U.S. business; it was not yet popular among the revolution groupies on U.S. campuses.

With dismaying rapidity events took a turn for the worse. By the end of the 1970s, a civil war had destroyed much of the physical capital of Nicaragua, and terrorism and guerrilla warfare began to decapitalize El Salvador and, to a lesser extent, Guatemala. In the latter two countries, as well as in Honduras and Costa Rica, the destabilization fostered by Nicaragua and Cuba and the general climate of fear and foreboding began to stimulate the export of capital and deter new capital inflows. The collapse of the CACM brought further dislocation to an industry that had grown up on intraregional trade. It remained for the oil shocks, global inflation, high interest rates, and, after 1980, global recession to precipitate the worst economic setback since the 1930s. Indeed, because the region's economies had become much more broadly integrated into the world trading system, the situation may have become even worse than at the time of the Great Depression. From 1980 to 1982, per capita product fell in U.S. dollars, from $1,538 to $1,310 in Costa Rica, stagnated at about $1,040 in El Salvador, and dropped from $1,208 to $1,110 in Guatemala and from $654 to $610 in Honduras. In Nicaragua the per capita income rose from $916 to $934 between those two years but remained below the level reached in 1970.

The development approach of the Bipartisan Commission headed by Henry Kissinger has much to recommend it, especially its focus on human resources development, on labor-intensive infrastructure, on institution building and reform and its proposed revival of intraregional trading, export development, and small business and agricultural development. Commendable, too, is the establishment of a Central American Development Organization as a central coordinating mechanism for planning and assistance—an updated CIAP, as it were. The roots of the strategy in the Alliance for Progress are unmistakable and all to the good. No later U.S. administration has remotely matched the vision and logic of the concerted development program of that era.

At the same time, there are good reasons to be cautious in assessing the probabilities of success. First, the region historically seems unusually resistant to social progress. President Eisenhower expected Guatemala, for example, to become a "Free World Showcase" following the overthrow of the Arbenz government, but there are surely few who would want to lay claim to such a showcase at any time since. The reform accomplishments of the later Alliance for Progress were modest, at best, not only in Guatemala but also in El Salvador and Nicaragua. In the early 1970s an AID program conceived as an imaginative model for the rehabilitation of the Guatemalan peasant sector proved to be a nonstarter, again because of the intransigence of local interests. In spite of the backwardness of politics and social policy outside Costa Rica and some social improvement in Honduras, the region did experience economic expansion, but the countries would never have arrived at their present predicament if only economic growth had been required. In the dimensions crucial to stabilizing the social and political environment, two of the countries show a notably blank record, while a third, Honduras appears only relatively hopeful on the social side.

What is worse, we have little experience in conducting a successful development program amid civil war like that prevailing in El Salvador and hovering just beneath the surface in Guatemala. In addition, Honduras and especially Costa Rica have also begun to experience the early stirrings of subversion and strife. Good as it is, the Kissinger Commission's plan affords little hope of either arresting local capital flight or attracting significant new private investment from abroad, at least for the first years of its operation. Capital destruction will almost certainly continue to be a preferred weapon of the revolutionaries, unless the Sandinistas, Cubans, and Russians can somehow be persuaded to cease their destabilization campaign. Consequently, the infusion of the prospective aid funds appears likely to be offset by new leakages of capital out of the region, with very little gain in real capital formation.

A variety of factors, then, conspire to darken the outlook for Central America, not the least being the vacillation of the U.S. Congress in responding to the recommendations of the Bipartisan Commission. We cannot be sure how to produce a genuine political will to bring about reform and how to build an effective consensus for that end. We should not overestimate the administrative capability of most of the states for dealing with social reconstruction in peace, much less in extreme adversity. In the almost four decades of foreign assistance programs, we have not yet reached firm conclusions on how capital (including human capital) can be accumulated and retained in a region when circumstances impel it to escape. If there *is* to be a hope that satisfactory growth and social progress can somehow be engineered for Central America, economics has, at this point, little or nothing to say about the matter.

Development—within Limits

The third set of countries are the island states of the Caribbean and Belize, for whose benefit the Caribbean Basin Initiative (CBI) was chiefly designed. Less economically advanced than the big debtor group, these are smaller but generally more prosperous than the second set that we just examined, except for Haiti and a few microstates. They are also less politically troubled, for the time being, thanks to the success of the Grenada operation and to who-knows-what combination of factors in the case of Haiti.

Given that literacy levels, health levels, and standards of living are generally higher—again with the notable exception of Haiti—than they are in Central America, the development problem would in some ways seem to be simplified. Since domestic tranquillity is a further boon, the design of the CBI passed in January 1984 has a certain persuasive logic. Who could quarrel with capitalizing on the strong comparative advantage of the islands in the field of tourism, or with the policies that aim at facilitating their development as export platforms for manufacturing operations? It is to be hoped that the export-led growth that has done so much for the Asian Gang of Four—South Korea, Taiwan, Hong Kong, and Singapore—will prove no less efficacious closer to our shores.

Nonetheless, there are at least five reservations to temper expectations, quite apart from the possibility that protectionist interests in the United States may yet reduce the free trade envisaged by the original version of the CBI. Congress may talk about the need for hemispheric progress and solidarity, but such has been the recent record that it would probably never even have occurred to Diogenes to visit that institution as he made the rounds on his quest.

With regard to the first cautionary note, insufficient attention seems to be directed to the untapped opportunity in deep sea fishing and fish farming, and to exploring the possibilities of other maritime resources—at least as an integral part of a development scheme devised for the benefit of island economies whose main natural resource base may be offshore. Although these resources are less important to the Dominican Republic, with its relatively large land base, and possibly Jamaica, they can scarcely be left out of the scheme of reckoning for most others. National development is not just a Holiday Inn, however useful tourism may be as a foreign exchange earner, and in most instances the land resources are insufficient to support other development options.

Second, the parastatal sector is clearly here to stay in most of the Caribbean economies. Since its management bears directly on resource use in the public sector and indirectly on the productivity of the private sector as well, the quality of that management would seem to warrant a greater priority than the private enterprise focus the CBI design has accorded it. This, in turn, leads to a third reservation.

With regard to private enterprise, foreign firms are better positioned to initiate new export-related business undertakings than are most domestic companies. Accordingly, unless the entrepreneurial capabilities and support systems of national business are deliberately programmed to increase, foreigners—who are its chief exponents—will come to be perceived as the chief beneficiaries of the CBI. Not only U.S. companies are involved here; Asian firms may be trying to penetrate the Caribbean in order to consolidate their export platform for the U.S. market, and European firms could follow suit. But whether the enterprises are American, Asian, or European, they could easily look invasive if they capture the gains of the CBI. Such a development outcome would hardly be acceptable in this day and age.

A fourth doubt stems from the fact that the Caribbean is not alone in the export promotion business. While other areas may not enjoy quite the same duty-free access to the U.S. market (though assembly plants along the northern Mexican border do in part), lower costs and a variety of special inducements still make the established Asian export economies formidable competitors for the Caribbean. Moreover, a giant new competitor, China, is already gearing up for major export expansion, and its way of handling wages and other industrial costs may give it an unbeatable market edge in many product lines.

Finally, it is evident that the CBI draws much of its inspiration from the

Operation Bootstrap strategy of Puerto Rico, which brought considerable benefit to the inhabitants of that island. Yet, the number of jobs created by Operation Bootstrap has been disappointing even after some three decades of operation, though Puerto Rico has had far more subsidy than is envisaged in the CBI, with considerable out-migration to the mainland (and emigrant remittances and access to the U.S. welfare system), and still other advantages—such as inclusion in the U.S. monetary system, a stable and favorable business environment, and virtually unlimited duty-free access to the U.S. market. Official unemployment figures never dropped below 10 percent and rose during the 1970s, to reach 20 percent in 1977. Whatever else it may be, in other words, the CBI cannot be expected to serve as a quick fix for the problems brewing in the Caribbean and, given the inconstancy of U.S. presidential commitments to hemispheric development programs, it may not last beyond the present administration.

An Envoi, of Sorts

Of the three sets of countries discussed in this article, those whose problems have loomed largest on the financial pages may be the ones most likely to find a way out. The immediacy of such matters as debt repayment schedules does not permit their difficulty to be ignored indefinitely—or allow it to outlive the short attention span of the U.S. Congress, as may well happen to the third group of economies. One way or another, the problem will have to be resolved, and the nonbanking stakes may be too high for a resolution unfavorable to Latin American development. Further, unlike the case of the middle set of countries, the political situation here seems less problematic and military considerations are not yet germane to the probable economic outcome.

No major Latin American country faces an easy economic future or a rosy political and social prospect. On the contrary, the future looks hard indeed for Chile and Peru, uncertain though moderately hopeful for Argentina and Brazil, and only just a bit more assured for Venezuela and Colombia. Even Mexico is likely to find more *picante* in its political stew than it has been accustomed to digesting since Plutarco Elias Calles left office. Yet these more developed economies look well worth a gamble compared with the small Caribbean states, subjected to inexorable population pressure in a context of limited resources, and the truly pitiable Central American states.

For the second and third sets of countries, the prospects are more perplexing, despite the much smaller scale of the resources involved. Nations of the third set appear better positioned for progress, but may for that reason slip from view sooner than the Central American states and hence from a concerted and sustained attack upon their problems. Should a Manley government return to power in Jamaica or the centrist administration of the Dominican Republic give way to a less desirable one on either the left or the right, whatever political support remains in the United States for making a serious effort to overcome the problems of the Caribbean economies would probably evaporate.

Although interest will probably not soon wane in Central America because of a sudden outbreak of peace, the U.S. Congress may indeed fall between the two stools posited by the Kissinger Commission: neither abandoning the region to its fate outright (and thereby saving considerable resources in the short run), nor doing enough to turn the drift of events decisively around. One recalls with nostalgia the days lauded by Gilbert and Sullivan when legislative "statesmen did not itch to interfere in matters which they did not understand." Perhaps there is grim comfort only in the fact that, should Central America go down the drain, it will do so because of problems of such long standing that, if blame is to be distributed, it can be allocated in a fully bipartisan way—assuming any outside force could have saved the region from itself in the first place.

Notes

1. Through refinancing of its short-term debt, Latin America was able to reduce its debt service from 54 percent in 1982 to 44 percent in 1983, but there is doubt about how much more can be expected in this direction for the year ahead.

2. The Continental Bank case, not to mention earlier efforts to save Chrysler, Lockheed, and Conrail, should increase our understanding of the factors considered by Latin American governments in these cases. There the pressure to intervene is often even stronger since government-owned industrial development banks are among the major creditors of the firms heading into receivership.

Discussion

QUESTION: In the past fifteen or twenty years places like Singapore, Taiwan, South Korea, and Hong Kong have experienced strong development; they seem to have done it themselves. On the other hand, your remarks appear to suggest that we will do something to help the Caribbean and the Latin American countries.

What are the factors that contributed to the development of the Asian areas that are missing in Latin America?

MR. GLADE: If we have learned anything at all over the years, it is that we can do very little for Latin America or for that matter to Latin America. At times our hubris is matched by the paranoia in Latin America, but we really are not very influential in the region, for good or for bad.

What ultimately happens there results from things that go on within Latin America itself. The Caribbean Basin Initiative, the Bipartisan Commission program, and so forth are only contributions. Clearly, whatever is done in the long run will have to be done in Latin America by the people there.

That is where the success story is, too: most of the capital formation and the investment in the region have been made by the people themselves through their own business firms, in their own sectors, and through their own savings. Foreign investment, of course, has made a tremendously important contribution: critical technological, managerial, and technical inputs, and so forth. But the major portion of capital formation in Latin America, even with all the aid, foreign investment, and borrowing, has been internal domestic capital formation.

As you suggest in your question, there is a difference between the Latin American experience and that of Korea, Taiwan, Singapore, and particularly Hong Kong. I cannot explain that difference because I don't know much about the Asian experience. But I think it's an extremely interesting question.

QUESTION: I see two main differences between the Latin American experience and the East Asian experience. At the human and social value level, the East Asians stress hard labor, the work ethic, frugality, a belief in self-improvement through education, and savings. At the level of economic policy, East Asia is the reverse picture of Latin America. While we Latin Americans tend to have overvalued rates of exchange and subsidized real rates of interest and import-substitution-based strategies, East Asians have exactly the opposite: a manufactured-exports led strategy with low tariffs in general, realistic ex change rates, and realistic interest rates.

My question refers to Puerto Rico. Do you see a basic difference between Puerto Rico and the East Asian countries? What would happen in the rest of the Caribbean, given the unique status of Puerto Rico.

MR. GLADE: Puerto Rico's relationship with the United States enables it to send people abroad to relieve some of its unemployment problems temporarily, an option not open to Jamaica, Barbados, or the other islands. Puerto Rico relies very heavily on immigrant remittances, massive social security and other subsidies, and welfare through the special arrangement with the United States.

Puerto Rico has also been able to offer a greater security in the business environment than any of the independent states are likely to be able to offer. Although, of course, there are liabilities, I believe those have been more than offset by some of the other relationships and the macroeconomic effects of U.S. expenditures in Puerto Rico, as well as by access to our welfare system. Puerto Rico, therefore, enjoys unusual advantages despite its high rates.

QUESTION: I have a brief comment about Taiwan before I pose my question. Several years ago Taiwan was between 90 and 95 percent self-capitalized, a setting quite different from any of the Latin American countries. The problem of external debt does not exist in the same terms.

Dr. Glade, when you were talking about some of the real assets of Latin America, you mentioned human capital, the development of certain kinds of skills, and organizational ability, flexibility, and versatility in industrialization. You also said that these were major factors in some of the improvement in Latin America. What were the factors behind success in those economically advanced countries?

MR. GLADE: I think it's largely historical experience. Those countries became industrialized somewhat earlier than other third world countries. The policies of the postwar period began to take shape as pragmatic adaptations to the conditions of the 1930s and early 1940s, the economic dislocations of that period. Most of the major states in Latin America, then, were beginning to look for inwardly oriented development policies even in the 1930s.

By now they have had about fifty years experience with conscious development promotion, at first on an ad hoc basis, but later on a much more systematic and sustained basis. Latin America, then, has enjoyed a continuity of experience in the design and management of development programs.

To be sure, these development programs have had shortcomings. Many have been failures. But out of the experiments with development has come a certain amount of experience and knowledge that serves the region well today. The major measure of Latin America's success is simply the development of Latin America. It began to invest in education in the 1950s and even more in the 1960s and thereafter, so that on top of the actual on-the-job learning that developed skills, there has been a remarkable proliferation of institutions of higher learning, specialized training, research, and so forth. The area is really far richer, more sophisticated than other third world areas, excepting maybe the "gang of four" in Asia.

The United States contributed a great deal, too, over the years with the early Point Four programs of the 1950s. Then of course the Alliance for Progress in the 1960s was a massive concerted development effort that put a lot of resources into institution building, varied scholarship programs, and training.

These efforts and the rise of U.S. and other foreign investment there, creating more highly skilled positions for the employment of Latin American nationals in the region itself, have resulted in a very impressive cumulative buildup. Even things that could be judged unsuccessful, then, had their elements of success. For instance, the Alliance for Progress was built on conscious development planning. The various participating countries were supposed to draw up development plans as the basis for providing external resources to them. We all know that these plans often were no more than paper plans. The French have sometimes made a distinction between the plan *imperatif* (Soviet-style planning, imperative planning) and what they use in France, the plan *indicatif* (indicative planning). Well, if that's true, Latin American planning was the plan *decoratif* in many cases. [Laughter.]

Even so, preparation of the plans helped mobilize economic information. Statistics were gathered. Economic intelligence that did not exist previously was brought together, and even though all of us who work with Latin American data know their shortcomings, they are better in many cases than no data at all.

As a byproduct of an effort that seemed like a failure, a lot more information about economic and social variables exists today than existed thirty years ago. The buildup of experience is increasingly reflected in the success, for example, of Brazil as Brazilian firms began to prosper in a variety of export markets. The foreign office in Brazil developed skill in scouting out export and investment opportunities. Whether all this will make the Latin Americans as clever as the Asians, I don't know.

QUESTION: Perhaps we have missed an element in comparing the gang of four with Latin America. As I understand it, the approach of the governments of Singapore, Hong Kong, Korea, and Taiwan in developing their economies has essentially been to recognize that their major resource is people and to structure the development of their economies around that resource. That's why these countries export shoes, clothing, and anything that takes handwork. By and large, Latin American countries have invested their borrowed money in large capital-intensive industries: the oil industry in Mexico, cement manufacture in Mexico, and the oil industry in Venezuela. In Ecuador and Peru, the money went into infrastructure. Over the past ten or twelve years Latin Americans have taken these vast resources and devoted them to building up industries that by and large do not use people.

If that analysis is correct, and if Latin America is to solve its own problems, the governments in Latin America must make radical changes in how they manage their economies. Perhaps they could open their borders to more foreign investment, something I would like to see. It need not be that, however. For example, one of the most interesting investment markets in the world today is Korea, but you cannot go into Korea and own the company 100 percent. You must go into Korea as a joint venture. One of the most exciting and undeveloped markets in the world is mainland China, and yet, except in the rarest case, you cannot go into mainland China with 100 percent ownership; you must go in with a minority.

The issue of offshore ownership does not seem to me to presage the future direction of Latin American development: the future lies in how those countries use their vast resource, their people.

MR. GLADE: There is truth in what you say. Many promotion policies that Latin America has pursued to accelerate development have had an unintended effect: tilting the balance in favor of capital against labor in the production factor mix. The low-interest loans on capital investment have subsidized capital-intensive development. Generally, where differential exchange rates on imports have been used, the preferential exchange rate applied to the importation of capital equipment. Encouragement of investment, then, has had the unintended effect of also tilting it in a capital-intensive direction. Moreover, many social programs have been financed not through taxes on net profits, but through taxes on payrolls. This system has, of course, inflated the cost of labor and tended to bias the decision still further.

In addition, many anti-employment policies were built into the whole policy structure in Latin America and remain today in many countries. It would be very hard to do away with some of them, because they have been incorporated into institutions.

Paradoxically, however, these capital-intensive industries are, in a few cases, those in which the nontraditional export opportunities are developing: steel, petrochemicals, automobiles, automotive components, and in Brazil aircraft and munitions. So some of the more capital-intensive lines of production are, contrary to what we might have expected, precisely some of the fields in which exports are growing most rapidly.

One of the advantages, though, of the debt problem is that policy makers have to be more concerned, more conscious than ever before of the need to increase export earnings. That recognition will lead to more selective policies of the sort mentioned.

QUESTION: If we assume that the trajectory of human capital development needs to remain on the upswing to solve some of the massive problems of the region and that the Catholic church with its enormous influence will have something to do with the way that human capital develops, how would you assess what has been described as a dramatic shift to the left among certain Roman Catholic elites in Latin America? Leadership elites and intellectual elites, in their views of political economy, believe that it is precisely the market-centered, enterprise-centered, entrepreneurial values that you and others have celebrated here that are the problem rather than the solution.

How do you see that conflict sorting out over the next ten years?

MR. GLADE: It is always very difficult, to speak of the church in Latin America as having a predominating influence. Certainly during the 1950s and 1960s some elements in the Roman Catholic church, and to some extent in other churches as well in Latin America, moved to the left. But this change was part of the general shift in the intellectual climate as a whole. University communities, too, moved drastically to the left. Liberation theology attempts, in essence, to reconcile Marxism as a method of social analysis with various theological dimensions.

Although I'm not qualified to judge whether the attempt was successful, one can see how the Latin American reality was structured in a way that seems to confirm the validity of a Marxist analysis. It is easy to see class warfare or class distinctions, even when the actual data show some Marxian analysis to be quite misleading.

I have an impression, however, that Marxism is much stronger in some countries than in others. It is virtually absent in some Latin American countries. And it is very much a minority point of view even in some of the more important countries. More than anything, Marxism represents an intellectual, moral criticism of an order that was perceived as unduly resistant to social change and improvement, an indictment that is quite clearly truer of some countries than of others.

Guatemala is a notorious case in point. When a left-leaning, Communist-influenced regime was thrown out in the 1950s, President Eisenhower declared that Guatemala would become a free world showcase. It didn't, and the Alliance for Progress didn't make much headway there either, nor did an imaginatively conceived AID program in the 1970s. This country has almost seemed to follow a script written by Marxists who would like to show the resistance of the social, economic, and political structure to change and improvement.

54

Nevertheless, even in a country that seems made-to-order to confirm Marxist analysis, we find statistics that show, in spite of all the shortcomings, life expectancy rates, literacy rates, and infant mortality rates all moving in positive directions. Rates like that do not change in this magnitude without reasonably broad improvement. Clearly segments of the population other than the elites are benefiting.

One liberation theology reading of all this experience is very critical of development and interprets even what many of us would view as improvements as malevolent changes. Other currents in the church today, either traditional or postliberation, are, however, perhaps more centrist, if not more on the right in their political orientation.

QUESTION: Mr. Glade, in your presentation I was impressed by the fact that you blamed no one for Latin America's economic difficulties. Yet in many of the descriptions that come out of Latin America, the United States bears a great deal of the blame, and therefore many people feel that the United States has some obligation to help remedy the situation. Your comments, however, imply that the Latin American countries have to extricate themselves from their own mess.

Do you think the United States historically bears any blame for the conditions in Latin America, and do we have any obligation to help remedy conditions there because of that?

MR. GLADE: I don't have much to say about that. Guilt is a useful concept in child rearing, but not in social analysis. It is a fact of life that some Latin Americans tend to ascribe blame to the United States for many of their ills: either we are not importing enough or we are importing too much and making them more dependent; either we are not sending enough money to meet the needs or we are sending so much that we increase their dependency. It is a useful game for political purposes in Latin America. Except for explaining some of the political dynamics, this concept of guilt really helps us very little in understanding economic relationships.

QUESTION: Is there a way to crack through the misinformation and ideological misinterpretation and supply some analysis that reasonable people in Latin America, even though they share these perceptions and resentments, can grasp? Is it at least possible to gain a second hearing for the Alliance for Progress strategy?

MR. GLADE: Yes. I think things will probably work out in that direction. There's not much that we can do. Those perceptions are deeply ingrained in Latin America—the tendency to place virtually all blame on the United States for anything that happens or to blame the United States in league with domestic interest groups of one sort or another. This is an old game. It's built into the

55

political culture of the region, and its roots go farther than that, if we wanted to probe more profoundly.

Offsetting this tendency is the real growth of the region, however. You could say the Alliance for Progress was a failure, as any human enterprise is a failure, but it was also a success. Regardless of the degree of success of any development effort, though, Latin America has enjoyed aggregate growth rates well above the historical norm for the world for a much longer period of time. Indeed, one of the things that has made this current economic crisis so traumatic in Latin America is that it is almost unprecedented. We have to go back fifty years to the Great Depression before finding anything at all comparable in the way of economic setbacks. Since the 1930s Latin American countries have grown at rates on average higher than the West achieved in the same growth period and higher than any of the Western European economies achieved in earlier stages of their industrial development. Almost all the empirical indicators suggest that the region has done rather well, maintaining high aggregate growth rates and increases in per capita income. Other social indicators—increased literacy and programs in public health, for example—have been good in spite of the problems. I believe that as evidence of broad progress becomes incontrovertible and forces people to admit it into their view of reality, they may gain more self-confidence and be able to approach the rest of the world, particularly the United States, less fearfully.

In the case of Brazil, the government that came into power in 1964 was ostensibly committed to greater market orientation. What happened, in fact, was that the Brazilian state has increased enormously since 1964, creating very strong public enterprises and instituting controls on investment across the board. On the one hand, these can be assessed negatively because some of these policies have had fairly counterproductive effects at the micro level. On the other hand, at the macro level they have given the Brazilians a sense that they are in control of their economy. Today they are less fearful of foreign investment, of foreign capital coming in, than countries less in control of their economic destinies. As these controls develop, even though they may be unpalatable and subject to criticism in many cases, I think they will probably give the Latin American electorate more confidence that it controls the situation and that it has less to fear from external relations, unless those controls do such economic damage that they slow the growth rate, as in Argentina, and precipitate collapse.

Another factor is that Latin American external relations have become more varied. The countries relate more to the rest of the world and not exclusively to the United States any longer. This is the case economically: more foreign capital now than before comes from parts of the world other than the United States. To some extent these countries have succeeded in diversifying their export markets, lessening their dependence on the United States. The import sources have also become more diversified. As we lower our profile in

Latin America, the simple evolution of these economic relationships will help people reassess the nature of external relations in general and the external relations with the United States in particular.

Moreover, in some countries the critical left has begun to rethink some of its positions. So far as I can tell, this probably started in Venezuela, a country that had almost no democratic tradition to fall back on, but that somehow succeeded in establishing a more or less democratic electoral system. The guerrilla movement gained momentum in the early 1960s there, influenced by Castro, as part of a general political development in Latin America. And the movement was frankly a failure. It was not put down by U.S. aid; it was put down by the Venezuelan government and has achieved virtually no significant support in the Venezuelan electorate. The Marxist thinkers associated with the guerrilla movement learned from experience: they saw that their diagnosis of the situation was clearly in error, and they rethought their ideology, their strategy, and their mode of action and reentered the political system. The verbiage remains much the same, but I see a more sophisticated, and perhaps in the long run a more useful, criticism by the Venezuelan left compared with the kind of dogmatic, knee-jerk phrases of the past.

A bit of that attitude is present in Chile. Thoughtful Chileans of the left have come increasingly to appreciate that Allende's downfall was not engineered by the United States, although it was, predictably, first attributed to U.S. intervention through the CIA. Obviously, we applauded and celebrated Allende's collapse and would not stand in its way, but Chilean intellectuals and others of the left appear to be reassessing this experience and seeing that it failed internally. From our point of view, this perception has two benefits. First, the left must try to devise a more realistic, more valid criticism and reading of reality. Second, it is encouraged to come up with more constructive proposals for social, economic, and political change. Gradually, we see, at least in some countries, a changing formulation of ideology and political analysis on the left itself. Although at least in our lifetime the left is not likely to become aficionados of the United States, perhaps relations will become a bit easier than would have been possible before.

Private Investment, Taxes, and Economic Growth

Jerry Haar

Last month in Cartagena, Colombia, the finance and foreign ministers of eleven Latin American countries issued a manifesto—the "Cartagena Consensus"—calling on creditor and debtor countries, commercial banks, and multilateral lending institutions to work together to alleviate debt problems. The officials cited the monetary policies of the industrialized nations and their resulting high interest rates, as responsible for the debt crisis. They proposed, among other things, that:

1. interest charges of commercial banks be tied to the real cost of funds rather than to administered rates such as the U.S. prime rate and the London Inter-bank Offered Rate (LIBOR) and that spreads be narrowed to the "minimum," loan fees abolished, repayment periods lengthened, and interest payments suspended during debt renegotiations

2. creditors cease demanding that governments guarantee private sector debt

3. repayment of debt be limited to a "reasonable" percentage of export earnings

4. International Monetary Fund (IMF) programs deemphasize austerity measures and focus, instead, on countries' needs for real economic growth

5. the multilateral lending institutions such as the World Bank, the International Finance Corporation (IFC), the IMF, and the Inter-American Development ment Bank receive an increase in funding

6. industrial nations take "immediate and drastic action" to reduce interest rates and institute "temporary mechanisms" (for example, compensatory financing) to protect debtors from any interest rate increases

It is doubtful that the Cartagena group will be able to fashion from this rhetoric a concrete plan of action; and it is even more doubtful that commercial banks, industrial nation governments, and multilateral financial agencies will respond in a significant way to the group's proposals.

Nevertheless, the Cartagena meeting marked a milestone in the Latin

58

American debt crisis. The meeting was important not because of the Cartagena Consensus, but because of a less publicized, yet potentially far-reaching development—the acknowledgment of Latin American government officials that they must take steps to liberalize foreign investment rules, institute tax reform, and reassess their strategies (not to mention theories) for economic growth.

Ironically, it was Andean Pact officials who were among the most vocal proponents of liberalizing foreign investment regulations. (The investment rules of these nations—Venuzuela, Colombia, Peru, Ecuador, Bolivia—particularly decision 24, have been especially onerous for foreign investors.) It remains to be seen, however, whether meaningful changes will occur in investment, tax, and economic development policies throughout Latin America. (In the past, the gap between rhetoric and reality has been enormous.) Within the context of debt and adjustment, a discussion of recent economic research findings is useful in deliberations over changes in policy.

The Debt Problem

The roots of the international debt crisis may be found in the inflationary pressures that began to accelerate throughout the world in the 1960s. Indeed, increasing economic and social development (particularly large-scale infrastructure, urban renewal, public housing projects, and social programs in education, health, and welfare) were overly stimulative. The first oil shock (1973) enabled lending institutions to recycle large amounts of "petrodollars" to non-oil-producing developing nations. Even the heaviest demands for capital were accommodated in an inflationary environment, at low or negative real interest rates. The less-developed countries (LDCs) were under no pressure to pursue economic readjustment measures; instead they expanded their programs of high-cost import substitution, public works, and subsidization of industry and agriculture. Internal capital requirements forced further external borrowing, and both oil-exporting as well as oil-importing nations placed tremendous pressure on the international financial system.

It was the second oil shock (1979) that actually triggered the Latin American debt crisis in August 1982. Rampant inflation worldwide prompted the industrial nations, led by the United States, to contain monetary growth. In October 1979, the U.S. Federal Reserve Board, in a dramatic shift of policy, instituted strict monetary controls as a means of rapidly bringing down the rate of inflation. The shock treatment hit LDCs particularly hard, since much of their accumulated debt was short-term, pegged to floating interest rates; in addition, a significant decline in the price of commodities—coffee, sugar, and metals, to name but a few—produced a major slump in export earnings. As debt-service costs grew and the value of the U.S. dollar soared in foreign exchange markets, LDCs were especially vulnerable to the effects of the ensuing global recession.

Latin America has accumulated the largest external debt. In 1983 global long-term and short-term debt equaled $651.2 billion, with $294.4 billion (45.2 percent) from Latin American nations. The debt estimate for 1984 is $693.3 billion worldwide, of which 44.8 percent is Latin America's share.[1] The largest Latin American debtors in 1983 were Brazil ($93.1 billion), Mexico ($89.8 billion), Argentina ($45.3 billion), and Venezuela ($36.1 billion).[2] These four countries account for nearly 90 percent of Latin America's external debt, two thirds of which is owed to commercial banks; of that amount, 85 percent is owed by Argentina, Brazil, Mexico, and Venezuela.

Although it has become fashionable in many circles to castigate the banks for imprudent lending policies during the last decade—and surely there have been more than a few instances where loans should not have been made—it is indisputable that at the time the loans were made the principal debtors (Argentina, Brazil, and Mexico) were good credit risks. To illustrate, Brazil's real gross national product increased at an average annual rate of almost 9 percent from 1970 to 1979. Mexico's annual growth rate was 6.4 percent. In exports, Argentina experienced an average annual growth rate of 10.7 percent; Brazil, 9.1 percent, and Mexico, 10.9 percent.[3]

Adjustment Issues

Today Latin American debtor nations are struggling with comprehensive economic adjustment programs—some voluntarily imposed, most involuntarily imposed (by the IMF, for example). Painful though it has been and will continue to be, the debtor nations must get their economies on "sound, sustainable, non-inflationary growth paths."[4] Spending and development projects must be curtailed to levels that can be financed to a greater degree from domestic savings, supplemented by lower and more sustainable levels of foreign borrowing.

In carrying out adjustment programs, the debtor nations must confront endemic impediments to economic health:
- rigid overvalued exchange rates
- costly subsidies
- nonmarket-determined consumer and producer prices
- inefficient state enterprises
- uncontrolled government spending and large fiscal deficits
- inefficient tax systems
- excessive and inflationary monetary growth
- interest-rate controls that discourage savings and distort investment flows
- disincentives to private sector development

In its assessment of developing nations' implementation of comprehensive adjustment programs, International Monetary Fund officials conclude that austerity and reform measures do bring about economic improvement:

> The experience of developing countries in the 1980s suggests that those countries that have more consistently applied restraints in monetary, credit, and fiscal policies and have been able to maintain or improve their international competitiveness have also had greater success in managing their current account positions and in maintaining or improving their economic growth.[5]

Although it is debatable whether deficits induce monetary expansion and inflation—Korea and Japan both have large fiscal deficits—excessive levels of external debt, in an environment of low savings and high taxation, can impair capital investment, erode competitiveness, and lower the overall rate of economic growth. Consequently, the cornerstone of the IMF's fiscal policy regime is debt reduction. Tables 1 and 2 show the magnitude of the deficit problem in the developing countries.

Although non-oil developing countries strived to increase revenue and decrease expenditures in relation to the gross domestic product (GDP) last year, their progress in this area was not significant. This year may not be much different, in light of the following:

• the social and political tensions resulting from recession and austerity will lead governments to maintain or slightly increase selected public spending to buy tranquility among the poor and the lower middle class

• reduction and phase-out of food, fuel, and housing subsidies may have to be slowed for the same reason

• government attempts to divest selected parastatal companies—all money losers most likely—will probably fail because of lack of interest and capital within the local private sector

• a number of major capital projects, launched before the debt crisis, are too far along to scrap, halt, or even slow down

• increases in taxation of private enterprise would further diminish the possibility of an eventual recovery of the local productive sector and of a subsequent increase in private investment

As for other indicators of economic adjustment, the IMF reported excessive credit and monetary expansion in 1983 among Western Hemisphere nations—particularly Argentina, Brazil, and Mexico. On the positive side, these three nations implemented exchange-rate policies that depreciated the nominal effective rates (Argentina and Brazil, 47 percent; Mexico, 39 percent) in order to neutralize the negative effect of high inflation on their competitiveness.[6] Additional economic adjustments made by non-oil developing nations included raising interest rates charged by financial institutions, thereby aligning them more closely with current inflation rates; easing price controls on goods

TABLE 1

DEFICITS FOR ALL DEVELOPING COUNTRIES, CURRENT AND PROJECTED,
1982–1995

	Total deficits in billions of current dollars		Annual growth (%)		
	1982	1995	1979–80	1980–82	1982–95
Current-account balance	−118.2	−276.2	17.2	41.7	6.7
Net capital flows	85.2	294.2	20.4	2.2	10.0
official development assistance	23.9	81.2	17.9	−1.0	9.9
official nonconcessional loans	11.0	42.0	24.5	5.6	10.9
private loans	35.0	109.6	22.3	−0.4	9.2
private direct investment	15.3	61.4	18.6	12.5	11.3
Use of reserves and other capital	33.0	−18.0	n.a.	n.a.	n.a.
Debt outstanding	548.0	1,996.8	19.9	13.7	10.5
official	199.0	809.8	16.5	12.5	11.4
private	349.0	1,187.0	22.3	14.3	9.9
Deflator	95.7	213.8	10.3	−1.6	6.4

NOTE: n.a. = not available.

SOURCE: Group of Thirty, Foreign Direct Investment 1973–1987 (New York: Group of Thirty, 1984), p. 10.

and services to reflect costs; and reducing or eliminating subsidies. (As pointed out earlier, social and political tensions are increasing in Latin America—note the food riots in the Dominican Republic, Peru, and Brazil within the past six months. Consequently, it is possible that subsidies or price controls will be reinstated, and that governments will be reluctant to hold back wage increases.)

Perhaps the greatest gains in economic adjustment made by the non-oil developing countries have been in their balance of payments—specifically, a reduction of nearly 50 percent in their current-account deficits between 1981 and 1983 (from $109 billion to $56 billion). Although this feat was accomplished largely through a $60 billion cut in imports (other accounts varied slightly, and exports fell by $7 billion), the achievement is noteworthy nonetheless. Among Western Hemisphere nations, Brazil and Mexico reduced their current-account deficits most dramatically: Brazil, from an $11.7 billion deficit in 1981 to a $7.7 billion deficit in 1983; and Mexico from a $12.5 billion deficit to a $5.5 billion surplus.[7]

TABLE 2

PROJECTED CHANGE IN THE SOURCE OF THE DEFICIT, 1982–1995
(percentage of GNP)

	1982	1995
Resource gap	3.7	1.6
Current-account deficit	5.0	2.5
Net capital flows	3.6	2.9
Debt service	4.7	3.5
Interest payments	2.1	1.5

SOURCE: Group of Thirty, Foreign Direct Investment 1973–1987 (New York: Group of Thirty, 1984), p. 10.

Improvement in the current-account position via import compression is, however, a partial, remedial, and short-term prescription for balance-of-payments difficulties. It cannot mask the folly of high-cost import-substitution policies, nor can it be a substitute for a vigorous, market-oriented export-promotion policy:

> An import substitution strategy, by its very nature, increases the role of government in managing the economy. It introduces price distortions in the production process. It also discourages realignment of the exchange rate in response to balance-of-payments disequilibria. Import substitution frequently is administered through a system of tariffs, or more often, quantitative restrictions regulated by complex import-licensing systems.
>
> Governments control (or sometimes prohibit) the flow of goods through allocations of import licenses and foreign exchange. Domestic production fostered by such protection is not internationally competitive, and exporters using the domestically produced item are forced to purchase it at a higher price. Consequently, to enable the exporter to compete in the international marketplace, the government must subsidize exports in some way to compensate for price distortions.[8]

Price readjustment through currency realignment subsequently becomes less viable as a policy option, as national governments manipulate the exchange rate to sustain a low price level for needed imported capital goods. The outcome is an overvalued exchange rate, creating a disincentive to export and an incentive to import, and leading to trade restrictions and capital controls.

Statistical survey data and empirical research findings confirm the economic wisdom of market-oriented export promotion strategies. The most striking contrast occurs between Latin American and Asian debtor countries:

exports as a percentage of nominal GNP from Asian nations were twice that of Latin American debtor countries.[9] Even Brazil with its elaborate system of export subsidies (Befiex and Finex, for example), which have subjected that nation to countless countervailing duty cases in the United States, has failed to build a strong, diversified, and competitive export sector. Quantitative evidence reveals that:

> On balance, despite some generous export incentives, the Brazilian incentive system overall still appears to favor the domestic market and to discriminate against exports. The increase in the anti-export bias of economic policies is indeed a partial explanation for the decline of Brazilian export growth observed after the mid-1970's.[10]

Export-oriented growth policies can be especially beneficial to countries wracked by recession and high debt-service payments. Such policies increase the utilization of plant and equipment (often operating far below capacity), foster diversification across and within sectors of the economy, and generate much-needed hard-currency earnings.

An additional benefit of an export promotion strategy is increased employment, particularly in the manufacturing sector. This is validated by research findings on alternative trade strategies and employment sponsored by the National Bureau of Economic Research (NBER). The ten-country study employed rigorous econometric methodology, and explored links between a developing country's policies toward international trade and its ability to create sufficient employment for its population.[11] The results of the NBER project confirm the efficacy of the Heckscher-Ohlin-Samuelson model of international trade, with respect to labor supply and labor market conditions—namely, that export promotion generates significantly more employment growth than does an import substitution strategy. The four Latin American nations included in the study (Brazil, Chile, Colombia, and Uruguay) mirror the general findings: export promotion policies increase manufacturing output, generate a greater demand for labor, produce a significant increase in labor-intensive employment, and achieve more egalitarian effects on income distribution than import-competing production.

The export–employment link is of critical importance in light of recession, austerity, and the social and political tensions that have accompanied the implementation of economic adjustment programs.

The Private Sector and Economic Growth

Private enterprise in Latin America, both local and multinational, has been ravaged by the effects of recession, external debt, and economic adjustment regimes. Generally speaking, the impact on local firms has been especially severe, since they lack the resources and organizational structure (that is, the institutional "safety net") that the multinational's parent company can provide. When one considers the official bias in favor of the public sector and a pattern of increasing government encroachment, it becomes clear that private enterprise in Latin America is in a fight for survival.

Private sector–government relations have changed over the past thirty years, with an increasing trend toward public ownership, government regulation, central planning, and welfare state policies.[12] Reinforced by nationalist and socialist ideologies (among these the dependency theories of Prebisch, Sunkel, and Cardoso), government intervention in the economies of the third world has produced marked increases in the public consumption share of GNP; public ownership of economic activities beyond infrastructure, encompassing extractive industries, manufacturing, financing, and international trade and commerce; government investment expenditure (typically more than half of national capital formation); and regulation of private economic activity via money, credit, and exchange controls, licensing systems, price controls, wage rates, and marketing systems.[13]

While the endless philosophical and ideological debates rage over private versus public investment, recent economic research findings conclusively demonstrate that private enterprise is the most efficient mechanism for achieving economic development.

Some Empirical Evidence: Investment. Often problems of modeling and measurement have inhibited research on private investment in less developed countries.[14] These methodological obstacles have been successfully dealt with, however, in a number of recent studies on the role of private investment in less-developed countries.[15] Although the research designs, methods, and techniques differed in each study, all of the results supported the superior utility of the private enterprise system.

The vital importance of private investment both to long-term development and to the design of short-term stabilization programs in less-developed nations is manifested in the research findings of Mario Blejer and Mohsin Khan. Their study analyzed bank data for a group of twenty-four developing countries. In examining the average ratios of total investment to GDP, the researchers noted considerable variation from country to country—from 12 percent for Haiti to 36 percent for Singapore. They also found a relationship between the average investment/income ratio and the level of development. Countries with high average per capita income or nominal GDP in U.S. dollars deflated by population (Argentina, Venezuela, Trinidad and Tobago, and Singapore) had the highest average investment/income rates. Lower-income LDCs such as Bolivia, Haiti, and Sri Lanka had a smaller average ratio of investment to income. In addition, higher rates of investment are associated with higher rates of growth. During the period 1971–1979, private investment's share of total gross investment varied from over 75 percent in some LDCs (Brazil, Colombia, Guatemala, Barbados, Trinidad and Tobago, Thailand, Singapore, and Korea) to less than 50 percent in Bolivia, Chile, and Haiti.

The data yield two major empirical findings. First, countries with a higher proportion of private direct investment to total investment tend to have a higher ratio of total investment to income. (See figure 1.) Public policies that accord the private sector a greater role in investment have succeeded in increasing the overall level of savings and therefore, of aggregate investment. Clearly, the public sector can "crowd out" private sector investment if it claims scarce resources (physical or financial) that could otherwise be used by the private sector, or if its marketable output competes with privately produced output. Private sector investment is further depressed by public sector project financing, since taxation, issuance of public debt, and inflation-producing monetary policies produce disincentives to invest.

The second finding is that countries with a larger proportion of private investment to total investment tend to have higher rates of economic growth. The availability of financing and the level of public sector investment are critically important factors affecting private investment. Unlike the developed nations, where funds are readily available and the major impediment to investment is the high cost of borrowing, LDCs face their greatest impediment in the lack of available financial resources. Rates of return on investment in the LDCs are usually quite high, while the real interest rates for loan funds are kept artificially low by the government. It is not surprising, therefore, that with limited total financing, due to price-mechanism distortions, shortages emerge in the level of available bank financing, creating a great disadvantage for the private investor.

The financing of private investment in LDCs is generally limited to the use of retained profits, bank credit, and foreign loans, with bank credit being the most important. Increasing real credit to the private sector will stimulate private investment; rolling over bank loans can lengthen the maturity of the debt; and foreign financing clearly expands the pool of financing savings.

The importance of bank credit, the principal instrument of monetary policy in LDCs, cannot be overemphasized. Keith Marsden, in his twenty-nation study on links between taxes and economic growth, found that nations that provide their private sector wider access to credit realize more rapid growth than their paired counterparts. Statistical analyses revealed that an increase in the share of the private sector of 10 percentage points caused the GDP growth rate to increase by 0.41 percent. This coefficient, significant at the 1 percent level, explained 27 percent of the inter-country growth variance.

As far as public sector investment is concerned, Blejer and Khan found that under certain conditions government investment in infrastructure and the provision of public goods can, in fact, complement private investment. Public investment in private enterprise can increase the demand for private output

FIGURE 1

RATIOS OF PRIVATE INVESTMENT TO TOTAL INVESTMENT AND TOTAL
INVESTMENT TO INCOME, 1971–1979

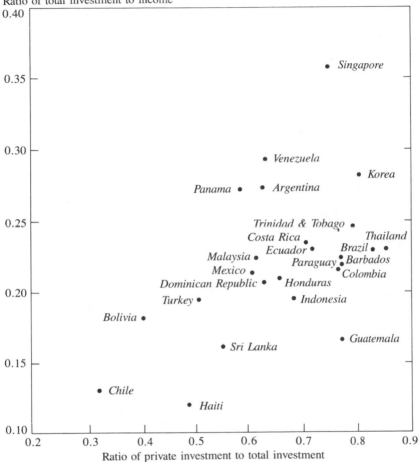

SOURCE: Blejer and Khan treatment of IMF data.

through greater demand for inputs and ancillary services, and can boost the aggregate amount of available resources by expanding total output and savings. It is therefore important to keep in mind that any assessment of the effect of public sector investment on private investment must gauge the extent to which infrastructural investment projects linked to private enterprise nullify the crowding-out effect from other types of public investment. For the most part, long-term, infrastructural investment can have a positive effect on private capital formation, whereas short-term public investment tends to crowd it out.

In light of the current IMF adjustment programs undertaken (or about to

67

be undertaken) by a number of LDC debtor nations, policy makers must be made aware of the potential danger of austerity measures to private capital formation. The zealous implementation of a monetary policy designed to reduce the rate of inflation rapidly and to cut the fiscal deficit deeply can hurl a nation into a severe recession and cause irreparable harm to the private sector as an institution. (This holds true, as well, for the industrialized nations of the West, including the United States.) Contraction in monetary growth can lead to a reduction in economic growth, unless the government takes measures to ensure that the flow of real credit to the private sector is not cut back. In addition, if the aggregate amount of foreign financing to less-developed countries is curtailed, larger government sector borrowing will diminish the amount available for the private sector.

Sound economic management, therefore, dictates that policies designed to reduce the fiscal deficit target public investment not related to infrastructure projects that are linked to the private sector. In that way, capital, labor, land, and technology slated for use by the government would be released, to be utilized by the private sector.

Some Empirical Evidence: Taxation. Unquestionably, the most convincing and comprehensive policy research on taxation and its relationship to economic growth has been carried out by Keith Marsden.[16] Analyzing data from twenty nations representing practically the entire spectrum of world incomes, he found substantially higher real rates of GDP growth among countries that placed a lower effective average tax burden on their citizens. The average annual rate of growth of GDP was 7.3 percent in the low-tax group and 1.1 percent in the high-tax group.

One finding that will be particularly disturbing to those with a socialist perspective on economics and social class is that in low-tax countries higher rates of economic growth produced a significant increase in the standard of living of all classes. An expansion of the tax base (a result of a supply-side tax approach) was associated with growth and resulted in increased revenues, which financed a more rapid expansion of expenditures for health, social services, education, nutrition, and defense. (It should be pointed out that neither the prudence nor the merit of specific government program expenditures is relevant here.) Most important, available data on income distribution refute the argument that high-tax countries possess a more equitable distribution than low-tax ones.

Marsden found that the structure, complexity, and efficiency of the tax system can be significant:

> A country with a higher tax/GDP ratio but a favorable tax structure may outperform a country with a lower overall tax level that discourages growth-promoting activities or imposes an excessive burden on the most productive or innovative segments of the population.[17]

Using regression analysis, based largely upon tax/GDP ratios, significant negative effects were found between taxes and economic growth. An increase of 1 percent in the tax/GDP ratio was associated with a decline in the economic growth rate of 0.36 percent. Differences in the overall tax burden explained 45 percent of the intercountry variance in GDP growth.

Lower-income countries were affected more greatly than higher-income nations with respect to tax fluctuation. A 1 percent increase in the tax/GDP ratio reduced GDP growth by 0.75 percent when tax was the only independent variable taken into consideration. Taxation clearly affects growth by influencing the main factors of production (increasing or decreasing their net returns) and total factor productivity (the efficiency of resource utilization).

That the level of taxation affects investment is supported by the findings of Blejer and Khan, which in turn complement Landau's work on government expenditures and economic growth. Low-tax countries experienced average annual growth of gross domestic investment of 8.9 percent compared with a 0.8 percent decline in high-tax countries. Furthermore, an increase in the total tax ratio of one percentage point was associated with a 0.66 percent reduction of the rate of growth of investment. The strongest deterrent to investment seemed to be corporate taxes.

Recent research findings on U.S. taxes reveal similar findings: reductions in corporate and personal income taxes can, indeed, increase the tax base. James Gwartney and Richard Stroup analyzed 1982 Internal Revenue Service data and found that taxable income is not invariant to changes in tax rates. Declining tax rates boost take-home pay, motivating taxpayers to earn more and to avoid tax shelters, which generate comparatively less tax saving. The researchers point out, however, that the so-called supply-side cuts in marginal tax rates did little more than correct for bracket creep and higher social security taxes. Moreover, they claim that by providing more rapid depreciation allowances, the 1981 legislation actually increased the attractiveness of tax-shelter investments. Were it not for writeoffs for rapid depreciation and imminent tax increases supported by Congress, the tax base in the upper brackets, they assert, would most likely have grown by an even larger amount. They conclude: far from suggesting that marginal tax rates were cut too much, the data indicate the potential of still lower marginal rates—in essence, tax rates should be reduced more dramatically.[18]

Returning to Marsden's study, regression analyses of export growth found that taxes on foreign trade negatively affected the growth of that sector, whereas tax relief for exporters increased foreign and domestic sources of capital. Tax alleviation and tax incentives facilitated export growth in low-income countries, particularly in labor-intensive manufactures. An extremely positive result was the accelerated transfer of surplus labor from agriculture into growth areas such as industry and services. Productivity also was raised: the results identified a reduction in the tax/GDP ratio of 1 percentage point with an increase in labor productivity of 0.28 percent.

The two major conclusions are that lower taxes result in higher after-tax returns to savings, investment, work, and innovation, boosting the total supply of these factors of production and increasing total output; and low-tax countries have provided fiscal incentives that have steered resources from less productive to more productive sectors and activities, thereby increasing the efficiency of resource utilization.

State Enterprises. Any discussion of private investment would be remiss without a few words about state enterprises. During the past twenty years there has been a marked increase in state ownership (this includes home-grown public companies as well as nationalized local private firms and multinational subsidiaries).

The phenomenon is one of worldwide dimension[19] and includes aerospace, steel, aluminum, shipbuilding, automobile manufacturing, electronics, computers, office equipment, pharmaceuticals, telecommunications, petrochemicals, and air transportation. In Western Europe, half the industrial sector is state-owned. To illustrate, President Mitterrand of France took control of 80 percent of the country's steel industry in 1982 and purchased five other key industrial groups. Even in Great Britain, Prime Minister Margaret Thatcher—an ardent supporter of private enterprise—has failed to dismantle nationalized companies completely: the majority state-owned enterprises remain under public control and are expanding into new technologies.[20]

Destatization is making little headway, despite economic findings demonstrating that the private sector makes more efficient use of financial resources:

> The private sector tends to have more experienced management, greater competitive stimulus, more entrepreneurial drive and stronger work incentives and motivations. Public enterprises are subject to tighter political constraints and pressures from sectional interest groups. They are also used for political patronage. They frequently set social objectives—such as preserving employment and restraining rises in the cost of living—which are difficult to reconcile with efficiency. They are rarely allowed to go out of business, even if their products and obsolete plants are incurring huge losses. Red tape and excessive bureaucracy sometimes undermine the effectiveness of government services. And a large public sector often coincides with greater controls over private sector decisions through licensing, rationing and regulations. Such interventions tend to distort incentives and bring about a misuse or misallocation of resources in the economy as a whole.[21]

Government enterprises directly or indirectly constrain the private sector's access to credit. First, the government may own a large percentage of productive assets and be responsible for a high share of total employment and GDP. Thus public sector requirements for short-term credit for working capital could be substantial just to keep its operations running. Second, the government may need to borrow on a still larger scale to cover deficits on its current or capital expenditure accounts.

One study found that an increase in the central government deficit of 1 percent of GDP was associated with a decline in the rate of growth of GDP of 0.61 percent.[22]

Three factors may account for this. First, substantial government borrowing crowds out the private investors by raising interest rates. Second, deficit financing tends to be used to prop up loss-making public enterprises with low economic returns. Third, deficits may reflect heavy government expenditure on free or subsidized services.[23]

In Latin America, state enterprises are omnipresent, and it is unlikely that their power, authority, or resource base will be altered significantly. In Mexico, the government's 1982 expropriation of the banks gave the government much more than control of the nation's financial institutions. Because Mexican banks were used as holding companies, nearly 450 nonbanking private firms also were expropriated.

Thus, in nationalizing the banks, these companies—representing a diverse cross section of Mexican business—became overnight partners with the federal government.[24] Trend data reveal that in 1970 there were only eighty-four government enterprises. This number grew to 760 by 1982. Over the same period, total public spending as a percentage of gross national product rose from 23 percent to 46 percent.

By 1982, public capital formation in Mexico reached 45 percent of total capital formation—three times that of the United States—and all the country's major industries were under government control. Nowhere in Latin America, however, is the state sector as massive as in Brazil, where public expenditures, including those of state-owned companies, approach 50 percent of GDP. From the Vargas era of the 1930s to the present, the state has maintained a dominant role in the nation's economy.

Although it is true that the Brazilian government has implemented belt-tightening measures for the state sector, the 1984 budget provides an 88 percent increase in investment (the total investment figure exceeds $10.7 billion—a tidy sum). As indicated in table 3, some twenty-eight giant corporations account for all but 3 percent of Brazil's total investment.

It would be incorrect to say that the Brazilian government has not attempted to deal with problems resulting from the large state role in the economy. In 1979 President Figueiredo created a special ministry to debureaucratize the government. Among the general objectives of the program were: strengthening the free enterprise system; containing the indiscriminate growth of state-owned enterprises; and, where feasible, selling off public enterprises to the private sector.

Nevertheless, it would be erroneous to assume that the government is sincere in its commitment to privatize major enterprises within the state sector. As Dennis Mahar points out:

TABLE 3
BRAZILIAN STATE FIRMS' EXPENDITURES AND INVESTMENTS, 1983–1984
(billions of cruzeiros)

Firm	Spending			Investments		
	1983	1984	% change	1983	1984	% change
Cobra	56,282	120,446	114	250	2,204	782
Cobal	341,855	782,935	132	3,757	4,760	27
ECT	217,496	526,005	142	8,554	20,294	137
Serpro	99,211	243,008	145	3,712	8,834	138
Caralba	193,705	537,906	178	30,000	3,421	−89
Mafersa	36,425	72,764	100	808	3,333	312
Usimec	66,194	166,497	152	219	514	135
Codevasf	55,843	87,435	57	39,404	51,310	30
DNOCS	94,777	91,440	−4	76,844	49,479	−36
DNOS	59,007	65,211	11	52,425	43,444	−17
Engepron	30,501	111,897	267	20	169	745
Itaipu	612,752	1,533,893	150	363,874	559,068	54
Fostertil	101,330	248,186	145	1,012	2,405	138
Lloydbras	178,275	483,106	171	12,043	78,620	553
DNER	586,612	1,038,246	77	322,261	482,977	50
EBTU	161,408	764,334	374	87	148	70
Embraer	171,073	347,290	103	20,159	48,909	143
Infraero	289,503	789,309	173	510	760	49
Telebras	1,434,471	3,562,821	148	525,691	1,213,294	131
Aceslia	318,145	791,931	149	16,657	40,702	144
CNA	51,749	112,887	118	6,975	2,452	−65
Siderbras	3,126,730	7,566,613	142	418,303	316,838	−24
Eletrobras	2,929,874	6,746,827	130	788,101	1,397,677	77
CVRD	1,082,903	2,530,892	134	352,269	847,933	141
Nuclebras	383,147	1,074,135	180	225,017	454,326	102
Petrobras	9,654,595	28,005,100	190	1,507,573	3,582,939	138
Portobras	363,301	716,274	97	95,623	134,680	40
RFFSA	994,449	2,700,805	172	251,984	577,541	129
Other	4,236,497	5,592,009	32	264,281	347,415	31
Total	27,928,111	67,410,291	141	5,388,412	10,276,447	91

SOURCE: *Business Latin America*, January 11,1984.

By excluding from the list to be privatized state monopolies, firms linked to national security, firms supplying inputs of strategic importance and enterprises established to prevent foreign domination, the government is presumably removing from consideration most, if not all, of the largest public enterprises in the utilities (e.g., Electrobras, Telebras, Purnas), transportation (e.g., Federal Railroad Network—RFFSA) and basic industry (e.g., Petrobras, CVRD, CSN) sectors. In terms of invested capital, such large firms probably account for 80–90% of all state-owned enterprises. Even if the government were inclined to divest itself of its largest firms, it seems highly unlikely that the Brazilian private sector would be able to amass the huge financial resources necessary to purchase them.[25]

There is little prospect that the governments of individual Latin American nations will make significant efforts to divest themselves of state-owned companies.

The Condition of Foreign Direct Investment

Foreign direct investment (FDI) plays a vital role in trade, commerce, and economic development. For developing countries, it is not only a critically important source of capital, technology, and know-how, but a catalyst for international economic integration through the world trading system.

Size and Trends. The world stock of foreign direct investment is approximately $500–550 billion; the U.S. share is roughly half. During the last decade, global FDI flows increased 55 percent in real terms. Interestingly, from 1977 to 1982, a period that included three years of recession, FDI continued rising. There are various explanations for this: (1) implementation of previously planned investment activities; (2) falling demand in the home country; and (3) tariff and nontariff barriers to promote host-country manufacturing as an alternative to importation.[26]

From 1982 to 1983, U.S. assets overseas increased by $49.3 billion to $887.5 billion.[27] In light of the 1984 projected U.S. trade deficit of $131 billion, it is interesting that overseas affiliates of U.S. companies account for approximately 40 percent of U.S. exports.[28]

It is estimated that 35 percent of FDI flows to less-developed nations. While the amount may seem small in terms of total FDI flows, it nevertheless constitutes large inflows for the developing nations.

A recent survey (1984) of a representative sample of major international firms has projected a 25 percent increase in real terms in FDI during the 1973–1987 period.[29] Although this is a slowing down from the pace of the two preceding five-year periods, the growth is substantial nonetheless—especially coming after a decade during which an increasing volume of international bank lending eclipsed foreign direct investment.

Among the pertinent survey findings are:

• The main influence on FDI decisions is access to the host country's domestic market; moreover, this factor is gaining even greater importance in business planning and decision making.

• During the past decade subsidiaries of multinational companies have had to become more independent. Consequently, they have become less reliant on financing provided by parent companies and more on retained earnings of subsidiaries, debt, and equity issues in the host countries.

• A significant portion of future FDI will be in high technology, agribusiness, services (for example, financial), and energy-related industry.

• The climate for foreign investment has deteriorated more in Latin America than elsewhere because of increasing government controls, arbitrary intervention, and nationalism.

Business Environment. One would think that the high debtor countries of the developing world would take dramatic steps to court foreign direct investment as a highly attractive alternative to bank financing. After all, no fixed interest payments are attached to private direct investment as they are to bank lending; earnings are repatriated only if the investment is profitable; if technology and managerial skills can be transferred to the developing nation; if real jobs (as opposed to public employment) are created; if new sectors are developed (manufacturing exports for example); and if local enterprises can become suppliers to multinational firms and even gain access to new markets and distribution channels in developed as well as developing nations. No shift in financing has actually taken place, however:

> Unfortunately, there exists no consensus in debtor developing countries today that private direct investment can play a positive and important role in helping to resolve the debt problem. Too often, developing countries remain wed to the prejudices and policies of the past that were based on the assumption that foreign direct investment is a source of economic exploitation and a direct threat to national sovereignty.[30]

Given the growing power of the state in Latin America, recession, debt, IMF austerity programs, high unemployment, inflation, and high interest rates in the industrial countries, it should not be surprising that a scapegoat had to be found—it was: the multinational corporation. Speaking out against discriminatory policies toward foreign investors, Brazilian Senator Roberto Campos (a former minister of finance) chastised a number of his colleagues in a Senate speech:

> To fear this paper tiger, the multinationals, is the true 'Banana Republic' syndrome. The government controls all the basic inputs— petroleum, electricity, telecommunications, railroad transport, credit and imports. Three technocrats—one controlling prices, another controlling credit at the Central Bank and a third controlling CACEX (the Brazilian Foreign Trade Authority)—could bring any of the great multinationals to a state of agony in a few weeks.[31]

Regrettably, Latin American governments, for the most part, remain ambivalent toward foreign direct investment. They want, in essence, what Senator Campos calls "foreign investments without foreign investors."

It would be an understatement to say that the general condition of multinational firms in third world debtor countries is not good. These firms have been and continue to be subjected to uncontrollable inflation, shrinking markets, blocked funds, uncontrolled debts, price controls, sharp currency devaluations, ownership restrictions, local content and export requirements, discriminatory technology and labor laws, and bureaucratic interference. No doubt a great many of these firms would like to divest; they are, however, too heavily committed financially to afford to do so. Some multinationals, though, have decided to cut their losses—witness the exit of Revlon, Campbell Soup, and Sears, Roebuck & Co. from Brazil.

The effects of currency devaluations—especially the large ones in Mexico, Argentina, and Venezuela—have hit multinational subsidiaries particularly hard, especially those that borrow hard currencies.

Moreover, local borrowing by corporations is either extraordinarily expensive or simply not permitted. Furthermore, even if subsidiaries have the cash for repatriation of dividends or royalties, exchange controls on central bank "priority lists" impede corporate access to foreign exchange. While barter is a viable alternative for the repatriation of hard currency, few corporations are familiar with the complexities or the potential uses of barter transactions.

The export loss for multinational corporations has been tremendous. To illustrate, Latin American importation of goods fell 28 percent in 1983 following a 21 percent decrease a year earlier. U.S. exports to Latin America in 1983 were $16 billion less than in 1981—a 40 percent drop (and a loss of 400,000 jobs). Farm machinery, energy equipment, and other capital goods produced in the United States for sale to Latin America have been affected most severely.

In 1983 the Council of the Americas undertook a survey of a representative sample of companies to gauge the impact of the continuing economic crisis in Latin America on the investment, trade, and financing flows of U.S. firms to Argentina, Brazil, Mexico, and Venezuela.[32] The overall findings were as follows:

Investment
- Overall, 1983 dollar earnings would be sharply reduced from prior years.
- Dividend remittances would be down in 1983, in some cases sharply.
- As of mid-1983, dollar equity invested in the four countries had dropped in three countries and was flat in the other.

Trade
- A major shift to secured trade terms with third parties had taken place.

75

- Barter, countertrade, and the like were starting, with more expected in 1984.

Finance

- Of dollar borrowing by subsidiaries, about 10 percent was owed to parent companies, with 48 percent of that past due. The rest was owed chiefly to banks, with 6 percent past due.
- Some companies said they would continue indefinitely to finance fully their local affiliates, but others reported having reached their limits, and still others were approaching theirs.

Greater access by their subsidiaries to foreign exchange, as well as liberalization of price controls, were cited by the firms as the principal host-country policy changes needed to maintain their investing, financing, and trading activities.

Policy Considerations

While it is not possible in this space to present a comprehensive list and discussion of policy considerations, a few summary comments are in order.

The present debt crisis is not merely a problem of liquidity, but one of structural economic proportions. Consequently, it cannot be resolved within a short time frame; patchwork remedies and cosmetic changes will be of little help.

Although there is little that Latin American nations can do about the U.S. prime rate or bumper crops of their key agricultural exports, it is indeed within their control to develop and implement policies that will stimulate savings, investment, productivity, and economic growth:

- *Economic adjustment.* Latin American nations must confront and alleviate structural impediments to economic health (nonmarket consumer and producer prices, for example). In the implementation of economic adjustment programs, as in body-building, the maxim holds true: "no pain, no gain." But a voluntarily imposed austerity program, which will produce the same positive aggregate economic results as an involuntarily imposed one (that is, via the IMF), is clearly preferable, since it considers the extraordinarily important social and political variables that the latter neglects. Governments must face up to their responsibility to cut public spending, phase out costly subsidies, and pursue reasonable and coherent monetary and credit policies.
- *Trade promotion.* If there is any salutary effect of high interest rates in the United States, it is the "sponge effect," bringing goods, services, and investments from overseas. The United States is purchasing an increasing amount of Latin America's exportable output, causing policy makers to reassess the role of exports in economic growth. Studies show that employment and income-distribution benefits from export-related industry are very signifi-

cant, and that Latin American nations (including Brazil, Mexico, Colombia, and Argentina) have exporting capacity and market opportunities far beyond what they presently use. (Ignorance of actual and potential market opportunities is one of the greatest impediments to export earnings among Latin American nations.) It would behoove policy makers in these countries to consider tax and investment incentives (particularly in agribusiness, light manufacturing, intermediate technology, services, and assembly operations) for the export sector while keeping their own markets open to ensure consumer choice and competitiveness within local industry as well as to avoid protectionist retaliation from their trading partners.

• *Restarting the productive sector.* Both local and multinational firms in Latin America have been ravaged by the effects of recession, debt, and high interest rates. Drastically reduced earnings, employee layoffs, and bankruptcies have been widespread. National governments have done little, however, to aid the private sector: interest payments on sovereign debt, imports and financial resources for state companies, subsidies, and public spending requirements all take precedence over the needs of the private sector. Moreover, little effort has been made on the part of Latin American governments to lessen the regulatory burden on business; in a number of instances the burden has actually been increased.

If Latin American nations are serious about promoting real economic growth with a thriving private sector in the vanguard, they must: reduce public consumption, decrease government investment expenditures, curtail the expansion of state enterprises, and divest of these companies wherever politically feasible. In addition, governments should deregulate or at least ease the regulation of money, credit, exchange rates, price controls, wage rates, licensing systems, and trade performance requirements. In tax policy, real reduction in rates should take place, with the greatest reduction going to the most productive sectors and income groups; tax codes should be simplified and the efficiency of tax collection improved substantially; and tax incentives should be structured to promote investment, savings, cost-effective technology, and hard-currency earnings.

• *Foreign direct investment.* A structurally sound, healthy, and growing host-country economy is one of the most important, if not the most important, factors in investment decision making. The considerations necessary to revitalize the productive sector clearly are relevant to multinational companies as well. To illustrate, many multinational firms have supplier relationships with domestic companies; given their interdependence, each is genuinely concerned about the other's financial health. In the areas of taxation, investment, and regulatory policy, Latin American nations should take firm measures to ease the burden on multinational companies. For example, the typical manufacturer's tax load in Argentina, Brazil, Mexico, and Venezuela varies from 42 percent to 52 percent—an incredible tax burden in view of the depressed demand for capital goods worldwide, not to mention the increasing costs of international business operations in an environment of exchange rate volatility. In investment policy, Latin American nations would gain much by revamping their profit remittance laws, as well as those dealing with copyrights, patents, and trademarks. Brazil's profit remittance law, for example, limits remittances to 12 percent, naively assuming that invested capital/net profit ratios do not vary greatly from industry to industry; this limit, therefore, severely discriminates against service firms and high-risk enterprises such as mineral exploration.[33]

As far as regulation of business is concerned, the burden carried by multinationals is actually being increased by governments in a number of instances. To illustrate, Mexico's drive to develop and implement sector-specific legislation, as was recently done in the pharmaceutical sector, threatens the survival of many multinational firms. In both Mexico and Colombia, for example, companies such as Pfizer—the pioneer of Feldene, a remarkable antiarthritic drug—lack the copyright and patent protection to operate successfully. In Mexico, European pharmaceutical "pirates" acquired and sold the active ingredients of Feldene to Quimsa, a Mexican drug company, resulting in Pfizer's being cut out of the market after it had spent $2.5 million on literature, symposia, and samples to introduce Mexican physicians to the new product. In Colombia, the same drug, was acquired by firms that market it at a government-approved "international price"—far below Pfizer's cost of manufacturing the product, thereby shutting the firm out of the market. In short, Latin American governments would do well to improve the business environment in their countries—not so much for fear that multinationals might begin to divest in greater numbers, but for concern that parent-company strategic and financial planners might choose other countries or other regions (including the home country) for future business development.

It would be naive to assume that Latin American governments will move quickly to transform many of the policy recommendations I have presented here into specific plans and actions. Nevertheless, it is possible, even in the current economic milieu, to make real and lasting progress.

The implementation of a sound program of economic adjustment, export promotion, private sector renewal, and enticements for foreign direct investment would assuredly steer Latin America down the path of economic recovery, growth, and development.

Notes

1. International Monetary Fund, *World Economic Outlook* (Washington, D.C.: International Monetary Fund, 1984).

2. Morgan Guaranty Trust, *Morgan International Data* (New York: Morgan Guaranty Trust, 1984).

3. Robert Solomon, "The Debtor Nations Aren't Deadbeats," *Washington Post*, October 20, 1983.

4. Testimony of Marc E. Leland, assistant secretary of the treasury for international affairs, before the subcommittees on Western Hemisphere Affairs, and International Economic Policy and Trade of the Foreign Affairs Committee, U.S. House of Representatives, Washington, D.C., July 21, 1983.

5. *World Economic Outlook*, p. 50.

6. Ibid., p. 53.

7. Merrill Lynch Economics, *Latin American Quarterly* (March 1984).

8. William E. Brock, "Trade and Debt: The Vital Linkage," *Foreign Affairs* (Summer 1984), p. 1040.

9. Morgan Guaranty Trust, *World Financial Markets* (New York: Morgan Guaranty Trust, 1983).

10. William G. Tyler, "Changing Perspectives on Brazil's International Economic Relations," (Paper delivered at the Conference on Trade, Investment, and Public Policy in Latin America: Trends and Prospects, American Enterprise Institute and Forum das Américas, Washington, D.C., September 10, 1982), p. 18. Econometric evidence supporting this argument is contained in William G. Tyler, "The Anti-Export Bias in Commercial Policies and Export Performance: Some Evidence from the Recent Brazilian Experience," *Weltwirtschaftliches Archiv*, 1983.

11. Anne O. Krueger, Hal B. Lary, Terry Monson, and Narongchai Akrasanee, *Trade and Employment in Developing Countries*, vol. 1 (Chicago: University of Chicago Press, 1981). The countries covered in the project were: Brazil, Chile, Colombia, Indonesia, the Ivory Coast, Pakistan, South Korea, Thailand, Tunisia, and Uruguay.

12. Lloyd G. Reynolds, "The Spread of Economic Growth to the Third World," *Journal of Economic Literature*, vol. 21 (September 1983), pp. 966–76.

13. Ibid., pp. 971–72. See also, Simon Kuznets, "Problems in Comparing Recent Growth Rates for Developed and Less Developed Countries," *Economic Development and Cultural Change*, vol. 20 (January 1972), pp. 185–209. Kuznets emphasizes the biases of GDP growth rates in developing nations—namely, an overweighting of the industrial sector in calculating the industrial-agricultural price ratios; and inflated estimates in the growth of service outputs arising from urbanization, industrialization, and militarization.

14. These problems include: poorly developed financial markets, the extensive public sector contribution to capital formation, foreign exchange constraints, unreliable data on capital stock, employment, wages and salaries, and debt equity financing rates.

15. Mario Blejer and Mohsin S. Kahn, "Government Policy and Private Investment in Developing Countries," Working paper (Washington, D.C.: International Monetary Fund, February 1984); Daniel Landau, "Government Expenditure and Economic Growth: A Cross-Country Study," *Southern Economic Journal* (January 1983); and Keith Marsden, "Links Between Taxes and Economic Growth," World Bank Staff Working Paper No. 605 (Washington, D.C.: World Bank, August 1983).

16. See also the following articles by Marsden: "Towards a Synthesis of Economic Growth and Social Justice," *International Labor Review* (November 1969); "Global Development Strategies and the Poor: Alternative Scenarios," *International Labor Review* (November–December 1978); and *Trade and Employment Policies for Indus-*

trial Development (Washington, D.C.: World Bank, 1982).

17. Keith Marsden, "Taxes and Growth," *Finance and Development* (September 1983), p. 41.

18. Internal Revenue Service, *Statistics of Income: SOI Bulletin*, (Winter 1983–84).

19. R. Joseph Monsen and Kenneth D. Walters, *Nationalized Companies* (New York: McGraw-Hill, 1983), and Leroy P. Jones, ed., *Public Enterprise in Less Developed Countries* (Cambridge: Cambridge University Press, 1982). Also see Ramgopal Agarwala, "Price Distortions and Growth in Developing Countries," World Bank Staff Working Paper No. 575 (Washington, D.C.: World Bank, July 1983).

20. L. H. Gann and Peter Duignan, "Nationalization as a Trade Culprit." *The Wall Street Journal*, May 24, 1984.

21. Keith Marsden, "Foreign Aid, the Private Sector, and Economic Growth," (unpublished paper, March 1984), p. 8.

22. Ibid., p. 11.

23. R. P. Short, "The Role of Public Enterprises: An International Statistical Comparison" (Washington, D.C.: IMF Working Paper, May 17, 1983).

24. Alejandro Junco, "Mexico's Private Sector Reels Under Government Control," *The Wall Street Journal*, June 29, 1984.

25. Dennis J. Maher, "Destatization in Brazil" (Paper delivered at the Conference on Trade, Investment, and Public Policy in Latin America: Trends and Prospects, American Enterprise Institute and Forum das Américas, Washington, D.C., September 10, 1982), pp. 16–17. See also, Thomas J. Trebat, *Brazil's State-Owned Enterprises: A Case Study of the State as Entrepreneur* (Cambridge: Cambridge University Press, 1983), and C. von Doellinger, "Estatizacão, Finanças Públicas e suas Implicaçoes," Câmara de Estudos e Debates Econômicos é Socials-CEDES, Relatório de Pesquisa 1, 1981.

26. Group of Thirty, *Foreign Direct Investment 1973–87* (New York: Group of Thirty, 1984), p. 7.

27. U.S. Department of Commerce data, 1984.

28. National Foreign Trade Council, *Charting a Realistic Trade Policy* (New York: National Foreign Trade Council, 1983), p. 18.

29. Group of Thirty, *Foreign Direct Investment 1973–87*, p. 1.

30. William Brock, *"Trade and Debt: The Vital Linkage,"* p. 1052.

31. Roberto Campos, *"A nôva demonologia,"* O Estado de São Paulo, May 22, 1984.

32. Council of the Americas, *The Impact of the Economic Crisis in Argentina, Brazil, Mexico, and Venezuela on United States Companies Operating There*, Technical report (New York: Council of the Americas, September 1983).

33. Keith S. Rosenn, "Regulation of Foreign Investment in Brazil: A Critical Analysis," *Lawyer of the Americas*, vol. 15 (Fall 1983), p. 351.

Discussion

COMMENT: Dr. Haar, I entirely agree with your point that private investment, either domestic or foreign, is the real engine for economic growth.

Unfortunately, private investment is fleeing most of Latin America. Earlier, it was said that $50 billion of Latin American private investment had left, an amount that seems small to me. My job is to mobilize capital for investment. I used to mobilize capital for investment in places like Latin America, but now I mobilize Latin American capital for investment in the United States and elsewhere. Therefore, both domestic private investment and foreign private investment are leaving Latin America.

What can we do about this situation? Can the political process be used to change this environment? We see no indication that people will take advantage of private investment opportunities in Latin America as they did twenty years ago. Whether because the influence of socialists in Latin America has expanded or because the politicians on the left are so effective, I foresee no improvement even in those countries that have suffered so badly. However well one may think of Mr. de la Madrid, he clearly does not believe in increased private investment. He says he will make exceptions to some of the investment rules but that he will not change those investment rules. The leaders of Venezuela have certainly not changed the philosophy there; instead, that country seems, with all its wealth, to be marching down the road of increased public investment and less private investment. The same political problems exist in the rest of Latin America, as far as I can see.

If, indeed, private investment is the engine for economic development and it is now discouraged, we ought to discuss what might be done or can be done to change the atmosphere. At the moment I share your pessimism that the political process is moving in the other direction, leaving no room for optimism.

DR. HAAR: I agree with you. I find it disheartening to see capital flight increasing. In my view the relatively high interest rates in the United States are undermining political stability in the region, as well. Consequently, U.S., Canadian, and Western European private investors are avoiding the region for *both* political and economic reasons.

As private capital, particularly local capital, withdraws, from Latin

America, what will that do to the tax base for governments in the region? On what will they draw for critical social services, for infrastructure, for exports? Unless another round of low real interest rates and hyperinflation occurs to lure back private capital, I do not know where the funding will come from. Take Brazil. I am not very optimistic in spite of the fact that it is a newly industrialized country. Brazil has, for example, a diversified internal economy, relatively speaking; a growing population; and an enormous market. If capital cannot be mobilized, however, it would be untenable for any national policy in Latin America to allow a system in which the government and the multinational corporations coexist well. There would be massive expropriations and nationalizations or, in a few instances, a complete retrogression to the 1920s, when some of the banana companies owned entire villages and told the president whom to appoint as minister of finance and minister of planning, and so forth.

I cited the Cartagena Consensus to illustrate how Latin American countries, especially the high debtors, define burden sharing. They want the IMF off their backs, they want lower bank spreads and lower administration fees, they want rollovers, and they want a spread out of the maturities. All that could be tied to export earnings.

The way to break the dependency cycle, however, is to assert independence. These countries need to assert independence, though, by getting their own economic house in order. Such measures do not mean decimating the poor; we are talking about macroeconomic adjustment and reversing the flight of capital. El Salvador, for example, has a marvelous opportunity to woo back some of that capital. The presence of a democratic government in power supported by the United States and others should inspire some confidence.

El Salvador must undo some of the exaggerated and foolish aspects of its nationalized banking and agricultural policies and pursue measures to bring money back from Miami into the country. It needs to revise some of its microeconomic policies within local corporations to create a healthy environment for private investment.

The Cartagena Consensus was a list of what the developed nations should do for Latin American debtor countries because of a local predicament. I say it must be a two-way street.

COMMENT: I think you are overly pessimistic. Mexico, for example, has made very great strides in improvement, going a long way toward restoring the stability of that country. Although Mexico was very slow to respond to the proposals of the IMF, once it got started, it made progress.

Venezuela's difficulties are not so great that it could not solve its problems overnight if it had the will.

Argentina is in a very grave situation, but as a very rich country with enormous natural resources, if it had the political will to correct the problems, it could turn itself around quickly. Solutions are there, and a rapid recovery is possible. Moreover, there has been more progress than some people recognize. As for the rest of the countries, they face very serious problems. But once the big four countries are accounted for, the amounts are not unmanageable for the banks.

COMMENT: Four years ago bankers were doing many very stupid things, and I may have been one of them—although I never made any fifteen-year loans to Venezuela at a 3/8 of 1 percent spread. Those types of loans were being made, however, and when a bank's objective is to make a 1 percent return on assets, it is a little difficult to lend money at 3/8 for fifteen years, pay taxes on that, support overhead, and make any money. Some really stupid lending was going on.

DR. HAAR: By the same token, though, everybody was cheering you.

COMMENT: That is right. Banks were being strongly encouraged to make these loans by the State Department and the Treasury to recycle the petro-dollars. The banks are not wholly to blame. I have been convinced by some of the comments here the past couple of days that there is a major problem that needs to be addressed. To try to find scapegoats is to misunderstand the problem.

COMMENT: Many banks in the United States appear willing to bear some of the burden of the solution. A number of us have been lobbying to encourage longer-term solutions to the debt problem, where we would bear some of that pain and some of the price.

Some of these recommended solutions, like those proposed at Cartagena—capping interest rates, capitalizing interest rates, deferring interest, and the like—have been proposed before by a large group of banks, not just foreign banks but regional U.S. banks and some of the money center banks.

COMMENT: I think the bomb of debt has gone off; I think it went off in every major country in Latin America, not only in Latin America but also in Turkey and a few other countries as well. There has been a default—what people are trying to find out is what to call it. The debt bomb has gone off, and it is with us.

What has been the response? Some very innovative ways have been found of getting around it. The Argentines have written dollar bonds. We have accepted some of them; all major banks that I know of have accepted dollar bonds. The U.S. government has not accepted them because it claims to be the only entity entitled to put out dollar bonds. That is a default, and we all have dollar bonds. When will the holders of those bonds be paid? Do I think that I will be paid when it says on that paper I will get paid? No, indeed. It will not happen. Some interest will accrue, of course. From a banker's standpoint, it is very important to have that piece of paper because if the banks do not receive a little interest every ninety days, the loan falls into the nonperforming category. Guatemala, Costa Rica, and Turkey all have pieces of paper like that—and they are all in default.

That sort of thing will just continue. We will find a way to call it something besides default. People will accept pieces of paper, but when it comes right down to it, there is no way those countries can possibly pay the interest, let alone the principal. It may take forty years to pay off; I don't know.

The U.S. government, though, is very innovative. In Mexico all the private debt that was insured by the Ex-Im Bank and FDIC was labeled a "political risk," which meant that people like us with a lot of insured debt could pass that on. "Commercial risk" is not so easy. In Bolivia, where the risk is patently political, it is labeled a commercial risk.

MR. MARKS: We should not panic. What can we do? First, we can see opportunities. My company, for example, is an agricultural concern. We had not been very active in Chile, but we learned that some of the native producers of citrus fruits, stone fruits, grapes, and the like were having difficulty in marketing their products and getting a reasonable return. We studied the problem, and, using our Dole label, we began to market those products during the off season in the United States. We have increased the return to the Chilean farmers by better than 50 percent. We did nothing dramatic, just what we could with our knowledge and expertise.

What else can we do? Perhaps we are in an unusual situation: in Honduras we are the largest single taxpayer in the country. We are exporters, and we are involved in a variety of domestic businesses. We have been in that country through a subsidiary for nearly ninety years, through governments and through revolutions. At one time the government called in the president of our company and said, "You have got to do this and this." He finally said to the president of Honduras, "Mr. President, here are the keys to the company, you tell me what to do."

We should not panic but look at the issues. We are discussing how to help a nation respond positively to the IMF and how to do it without mutilating our stockholders. We look at how much we export, what we earn, what export tax reduction would do for us, and what import tax increase would do for the domestic businesses in which we are operating. We cautiously give our views to the ministers, recognizing that we must do so very delicately because we could be accused of simply trying to influence the government for self-serving purposes. If we withhold our views, however, we are not being faithful to our shareholders, to the employees in that country, or to the government.

Not that we are always right, but we have been able to give some assistance on the domestic side. For example, we are the only beer producers in the country, producing beer there for about $4 a case. The production tax alone is over $4, so it is a heavily taxed product.

When the government wanted to increase the tax a few years ago, we consulted with them and asked how much we could increase the price. They told us to pass through the increase. We demonstrated to them, however, that if we did so, demand would drop so much that they would not get as much as if they permitted us a modest increase in the price of beer and increased the profit tax, which they did.

Again, I am cautiously optimistic. It is a very tough role to play because we have certain power. We have a lot less power than many people accuse us of having, though, and a tremendous responsibility. If a company is going to stay in a country for another ninety years, it has to consider what is good for that country and where its best interests meet the best interests of the employees and the stockholders.

DR. HAAR: That is very eloquent and convincing, and I think you are absolutely right.

MR. MARKS: Bananas, for example, are a tough business. Three years ago, not just in Honduras but in all our banana business, we wrote off over $50 million because of a worldwide banana problem. We were not the only ones. We had invested unwisely, trying to convert from flooded banana lands. After we concluded that we should not go back in bananas, we tried to help that community by converting to sugar. Sugar cane can stand a lot more water. Well, you know what has happened to the sugar market; we lost our shirts in sugar down there.

The reason we are in so many businesses in Honduras is that we have been there so long, and the available capital and the ability or willingness to take an entrepreneurial risk are very limited in that country. We are in a lot of small businesses, probably twenty or more, with many local proprietors. Indeed, one of the other things we are now looking at is a cooperative. It was started on its own, but we tried to help in its formulation. We are now trying to devise ways for the local small businesses to move toward greater ownership. Is there a way in which we can share profit and loss and get away from the ogre of transfer prices and share in marketing the product as well? Although the Hondurans have asked for this sort of arrangement, we are not sure they really understand what the risks are. In a small way we are trying to attack that problem and would welcome people's comments on how they might have tried that in other export businesses in Latin America or the Far East.

QUESTION: Are you the only beer manufacturer in Honduras? Has the government ever given any thought to using the tax money to create a local beer manufacturing concern or at least a joint venture for another kind of beer, for example?

MR. MARKS: First we do not own the subsidiary 100 percent; we own 53 percent of it. Except for the vice-president of marketing and the German brewmasters, it is all local management.

Carta Blanca opened a brewery and was not successful. I think the market is too small for somebody else to come in. A microbrewery might succeed but it would be difficult to enter on that basis.

COMMENT: We have dealt with so many numbers in our discussion of economic matters that I would like to change the topic to a theological aspect of what we have been doing.

For two days we have talked chiefly about the political and the economic problems. I take it as a matter of consensus that we are in favor of democracy in the political sphere. In the economic sphere, there is less consensus about capitalism and socialism. It is the third sphere, however, the sphere of pluralism that deserves a bit of attention. We must not be satisfied with the fact that one of us has one idea while someone else has another idea: Americans have one idea, Latin Americans have another; bankers have one idea, government officials have another, and so on. That would make communication absolutely impossible, and it leaves everything as a matter of force.

What we see in fact is that people do change their minds. Some of us more than others have experience of changing our minds. That is very important. How does that happen, and what brings it about? One of the reasons for entering into dialogue, discussion, and argument is to tempt that fate.

Second, it is also very important to recognize that the structure of a political economy, the differences in people's horizons, can be very creative. At the very moment when one man is deciding not to invest in Latin America, someone else is deciding to invest. Who can tell which one of them will pay the price or reap the rewards? The more centers of decision making there are, the more diverse the pluralism and the higher the probability that somebody in the mix will succeed. That in the end is good for us. That, by the way, is also how I came to my preference for capitalism.

There is a particular North American problem in dealing with this question of pluralism. I realize the United States is mainly a Protestant country, and there is no point in being American if you don't feel guilty. [Laughter.] We have a tendency not only in world forums but also in our own midst never to argue our own case. We understand the world to death. A friend of mine has said one of the greatest differences between Poland and the United States is here we have so many Marxists. It is absolutely astonishing the number of Americans who argue against America and, contrariwise, the number of Americans who never make the American case, granted it is a pluralistic case.

U.S. bishops have, until now, not presented to Rome their analysis of the U.S. economy. U.S. bishops and Latin American bishops have never argued about the U.S. economy and how it works. We get lectures all the time, however, from both Rome and Latin American bishops about economics. There is such a thing as too much humility in a pluralistic discussion. One of the most important reasons for an exercise such as this is to allow different people with very different points of view to make their own argument: if we all wait for somebody else to make theirs while we just listen, all sorts of things will be missing.

I want to conclude with one last comment. Two hundred years ago when Adam Smith looked at both North America and South America from a very great distance in Glasgow, he roughly predicted the results of these two very different experiments. His prescience has always suggested to me the importance of acknowledging fundamentally different views of the world and of what works. People can argue about them and make very different decisions about them, but time reveals degrees of success and failure.

The problem is that in the midst of living out the experiments, we cannot know how they will end—we are groping in the dark. From time to time our whole world view needs to be defined and examined. In the world some things work, and some things do not; alas, we cannot know until after it is all over which decisions were the right ones.

Dependency:
Ideology, Fad, and Fact

Michael J. Francis

Introduction

In the contemporary world a majority of the population lives in countries with governments that give public allegiance to an interpretation of world politics based on dependency theory or on some version of Lenin's theory of imperialism, or both.[1] These allegiances are reflected in speeches at the United Nations and in the domestic policies these countries formulate toward foreign investment and the Western powers.

The acceptance of dependency theory is so widespread and pervasive among third world leaders that international relations cannot be understood without taking it into account. All of the latest university-level introductory textbooks in international politics include sections on dependency theory, often as part of an explanation for what motivates the third world in North-South confrontations,[2] but sometimes as a theory of international relations lending itself to empirical testing.[3] Thus, even if dependency were wholly fantasy and had no intellectual links with reality, it would deserve examination because it provides the theoretical impetus for domestic and foreign policy in much of the world.

Although one can easily justify trying to understand the dependency perspective because it motivates policy, this paper is not intended as a description of dependency's main tenets. Rather, it is an attempt to demonstrate the strengths of certain parts of the theory for an audience of the unconvinced rather than of true believers. The argument is presented in two sets of proposi-

* Several individuals at Notre Dame gave me helpful suggestions on this paper, but my particular thanks go to my extremely diligent graduate assistant Thomas E. Gillespie who untiringly combed the library for materials and citations.

88

tions drawn from the writings on dependency. The first, the paper argues, are accurate. We can verify them by appropriate evidence. The propositions of the second set are more controversial, but a strong case can be made for each of them.

This paper does not attempt a balanced evaluation of the strengths and weaknesses of the theory. Its goal is to demonstrate to the skeptical that there is a basis for the dependency thinking even though there are many problems with the theoretical analysis. The other, unwritten, side of the paper would be an examination of the weaknesses of the theory. Many have already done that, and I feel no need to add to that body of literature (which makes many valid points).[4] So, this analysis is not an overview of the theory as a whole, but an explication of those parts of the dependency theory most useful for an understanding of contemporary international relations. This analysis ignores the political uses of dependency theory, which is another topic altogether.[5]

What Is Dependency Theory?

To avoid both a controversy over what constitutes dependency theory and a discussion of what issues divide its adherents, our description of dependency theory will be relatively broad. One place to start is with the oft-quoted passage from Theotonio Dos Santos:

> Dependency is a situation in which a certain group of countries have their economies conditioned by the development and expansion of another country's economy. The relationship of interdependency between two or more economies, and between these and world commerce, assumes a dependent nature when some countries (the dominant) can expand and be self-starting, while at the same time the others (the dependent ones) can only act as a reflection of this expansion, an expansion that can have positive or negative influence on the dependent countries' development. In whatever form, the basic situation of dependency produces a global situation in which the dependent countries are placed in a backward situation and under the exploitation of the dominant countries.
>
> The dominant countries thus impose a dominant technology, commerce, capital, and socio-political values on the dependent countries (to varying degrees in various historical moments) that permits them to impose conditions of exploitation and to extract part of the surplus produced by the dependent countries.
>
> Dependency, then, is founded on an international division of labor that permits the industrial development of some countries and limits this same process in others, submitting them to conditions and restraints imposed by the centers of world domination.[6]

The world Dos Santos sees is one divided between states at the periphery (the third world) and states at the core (the developed capitalist countries).

What happens at the periphery is shaped by, and dependent on, the policies of the core countries. This system works to the disadvantage of the less-developed states because it limits their options for development and because most profits go to the more advanced economies.

Another dependency assertion is that, whatever the history of development in the now-industrialized countries, the rules have changed, making development more difficult today. This is explained by Chilean economist Osvaldo Sunkel:

> In other words, the present international panorama of countries at different levels of development is not the aggregate of *individual historical* development performances. It is not a race which started somewhere before the Industrial Revolution, and in which, due to a number of factors, some countries reached advanced stages of development while others stagnated or moved slower, and therefore are now at more primitive or lower stages of development. The analysis of *dependencia* maintains that one of the essential elements of the development of capitalism has been, from its very beginning, the creation of an international economy which brought all economies of the world under the more or less intensive influence of a few European countries, plus the United States from the nineteenth century onward. Development and underdevelopment, in this view, are therefore simultaneous processes, the two faces of the historical evolution of the capitalist system, which are linked to each other in a functional way, inter-acting and conditioning themselves mutually.[7]

C. Richard Bath and Dilmus D. James, in an interesting survey of the dependency controversies and divisions, offer "four specific points on which *dependentistas* are in broad agreement."[8] The first is that the condition of underdevelopment in much of the world is intimately connected with the expansion of the Western, industrialized capitalist states. In other words, (1) the prosperity of the West is, at least at this stage, linked to the poverty of the third world. A related point of consensus is that (2) development and underdevelopment are two components of a single, unified system. They are linked, even dependent, on each other as part of a whole. Also, the dependency advocates do not see today's poverty in the less-developed countries (LDCs) as simply a temporary stage of precapitalist development. (3) Underdevelopment, in their eyes, is a persistent, natural condition. Finally, this school of analysis emphasizes that, (4) although the internal structures of the developing countries hinder economic growth, these structures continue to exist in part because they have strong linkages to, and support from, external forces.

This paper largely ignores the intellectual background and historical development of the dependency idea. It should be noted, however, that the concept stems from the experience of Latin America after World War II. In part, dependency theory was a reaction to a lack of emphasis in the scholarly literature on the external factors affecting economic and political development; but also, the acceptance of dependency analysis is linked to considerable frustration in Latin America and other less-developed countries over their failure to develop more rapidly.

Those with little knowledge of Latin America may find it strange that the Latin Americans feel such frustration, because since the late 1960s the area has experienced relatively good average annual growth rates in real gross domestic product. Although the growth is spread unevenly, from 1967 to 1980 the growth rates were between 5 and 7 percent.[9] As Bath and James observe, this "growth record is remarkable in light of the balance-of-payments difficulties, internal inflationary pressures, and growing debt-servicing burden that . . . afflicted the region" in the middle and late 1970s.[10]

But the discontent was caused by the failure of the improved economy to generate some of the expected by-products of growth. These by-products included "a reduction in income inequality, a diminution of the 'marginalization' of excluded social groups, the elimination of gross violations of human rights, broader public participation in the political process, and greater autonomy for Latin Americans in the control of their internal and external affairs."[11] Dependency provided an explanation for these failures and soon was translated into public policy by politicians who used a bastardized version of it to appeal to the masses.

One additional distinction needs to be made among the practitioners of dependency analysis. Although one can categorize the dependency writers in terms of a number of substantive issues, they are deeply divided methodologically. On the one hand, intellectuals such as Fernando Henrique Cardoso (often referred to as the father of dependency writing) do rather elegant historical analyses of concrete situations.[12] Their work is difficult to criticize because it involves assertions relating to specific points in time—generalizations regarding coalitions among groups and classes, links between particular groups in Brazil, for example, and the multinational corporations, and what effect the policies favored by that coalition had on the broader society. Cardoso has criticized rather testily those who draw sweeping theoretical propositions from his complex work or who want to quantify his thinking.[13]

On the other hand, the more empirically oriented social scientists believe that the assertions or tenets of dependency theory should be testable or, that at least some of the assertions should be subject to rigorous quantification. This division between dependency theorists mirrors the division among social scientists in general: on one side are those who prefer a descriptive or historical approach and are comfortable with value judgments, and on the other are those who believe that human and societal behavior lends itself to quantitative analysis and that a true science of social behavior is possible. Research done by those who work in the second category will be used in much of the analysis that follows, although one must keep in mind that a rather substantial line of dependency work, as represented by Cardoso, eschews what it sees as vulgar quantification. Speaking critically of the quantification approach, Lawrence Gould writes:

> In their efforts to subject dependency concepts and claims to rigorous, precise measurement and the standards of systematic critical inquiry, critical rationalists have forced the theoretical structure of dependency into a distorted form that ignores the richness and density of the "original copy." Meaningful inclusion of concepts and processes such as class alliances, culture, or the role of the state is ignored or handled incorrectly. [14]

The "Easily" Defensible Propositions. One can argue about the basic propositions of dependency theory, but for the purposes of this discussion we will start with two propositions in the dependency literature that have a good deal of evidence to support them. Of course, "proving" these assertions does not necessarily verify the entire theory, but it suggests that dependency needs to be taken seriously as an approach to understanding the Latin American situation and future.

Proposition 1: Because of their dependence on the developed "core" countries, the peripheral countries are experiencing a growing loss of national control over their economic, political, social, and cultural life. [15] This assertion is both background to, and linked with, the reasoning of economic dependency. The picture painted is of a new set of limitations on sovereignty that never existed before and that drastically limit the options of the third world states. Obviously, big states have kicked little states around since the birth of the nation-state system, but the argument is that prior to the growth of interdependence the "kicking" consisted of threats to invade, actual invasions, occupation, and perhaps a bribe or offer of protection in return for a favor, which usually consisted of joining an alliance. In the main, however, countries could do as they chose in terms of economic decisions. Now the international linkages intrude in the internal decision-making processes of the dependent states to such a degree that we are reaching a new stage in international politics. In the extreme, we could envision a world in which all important decisions are made in the core countries and the peripheral countries can only capitulate.

It seems valid to argue that the growing international interdependence has an aspect to it whereby the most dependent and weak lose some of the flexibility of decision making usually associated with sovereignty. The IMF-imposed austerity programs is a good illustration of this. It is possible to argue that austerity, balanced budgets, lower social welfare programs, and the like are necessary conditions for economic development in third world countries (or even in the United States). But the focus here is on the process: is not this a new phenomenon in international politics to have an international agency offering, indeed even imposing, very specific internal policies on such issues as taxation and government spending? Such a global organization would have been inconceivable prior to World War II. Even the *Wall Street Journal* points out that the reforms the IMF demands of the third world would be political suicide in the United States; yet Washington routinely supports such austerity for others.[16]

The argument in regard to development options in the third world is not that there is *no* choice, but simply that economic growth in LDCs is tied, to a great degree, to the prices of certain primary products, the availability of credit, and the availability of foreign investment. The free market experience of the Pinochet government in Chile, whatever its merits or problems, is an excellent example: the international recession was incredibly magnified, devastating an economic experiment that was being hailed as a model during its early days of seeming success.

Of course it can be argued that we live in a world in which the international commercial system affects the growth rates in all countries. Even in the United States some inflation has been fueled by the pressures of global inflation, by the OPEC price hikes, for example. But the dependency argument is that the difference in ability to resist outside influences is not just a minor quantitative difference between the developed core economies and the less developed peripheral economies, but an important and qualitatively distinct feature of economics in the third world.

The dependency argument suggests, however, that there are other new forms of interference or dominance in the postcolonial world. The foreign assistance programs of the great powers provide new instruments for the influence of the policies of third world countries. The question is not whether the aid programs are altruistic or avaricious, or whether the developed countries are primarily interested in the economic development of LDCs. The point is that the promise of economic aid is often used to influence the governmental decision-making processes of the developing nations.

Examples of this abound. In 1968 the United States withheld aid to Peru in an effort to get the Belaunde Terry government to make a settlement with the International Petroleum Corporation.[17] During the 1960s the aid program was used as a method of forcing Colombia to alter its currency evaluation processes and import procedures.[18] During recent years the relationship of the United States with the Dominican Republic has been dominated by the use of foreign aid to influence internal and foreign policy in that Caribbean state.[19] Brazil is another example: Washington slowed the flow of aid to the leftist administration of João Goulart and then flooded the military government that overthrew him with credits even before the new government could produce plans for utilizing the loans. Later, embarrassed by the dictatorial and torture-ridden nature of the new government, the United States lessened its financial support in an effort to get the government to "freshen" its international image. Although this writer takes the rather noncontroversial position of being against torture, if we are trying to understand the workings of the system, and if the torture of prisoners was a policy of the government (as apparently it was), then Washington was engaging in an attempt to influence the policies of that government. The arguments between the White House and the Congress regarding economic assistance to El Salvador during 1982 (caused in part by El Salvador's handling of the prosecution of the killers of the four women religious workers) has weakened the position that assistance to El Salvador is motivated only by the goal of economic development (although that goal certainly exists at some level of the bureaucracy).

Surely only the naive would not see that much of the impetus behind the U.S. foreign assistance program is the geopolitical influence that accompanies such a program. Despite the rhetoric concerning helping the poor of the world (rhetoric that is taken seriously within the foreign-assistance bureaucracy), a cursory glance at the pattern of who gets assistance and who does not reveals that it goes to prop up governments we favor. Empirical studies show a correlation between countries that have natural resources we desire and those receiving the most assistance.[20] Theorists of *realpolitik* have always considered foreign assistance to be an instrument of great power influence, an instrument great powers should and will utilize.[21]

That military assistance programs serve as channels of influence between Washington and the military establishments of Latin America, and thereby prop up the status quo, is also part of this dependency argument. The theorists see the influence of the U.S. military as further evidence that third world countries are losing control of their freedom to make internal decisions.

Since 1956 it has been argued before congressional committees that military assistance to Latin America is needed because the mixing of U.S. officers with Latin American military helps the Latin American officers to understand professionalism and the concept of civilian control of the military. Former Secretary of Defense Robert McNamara carried it further when, in the process of defending the military assistance program, he stated:

> In all probability the greatest return on any portion of our military assistance investment—dollar for dollar—comes from the training of selected officers in U.S. schools and installations. . . . They are the coming leaders of their nations. It is beyond price to the United States to make friends of such men.[22]

This training has taken the form of continuous programs in U.S.-sponsored schools in the United States and Panama over the past thirty years for Latin American officers. Given the largely conservative disposition of Latin American military men, and military officers generally,[23] this is a clear effort to help preserve the non-Communist status quo in Latin America. Obviously, defending a non-Communist status quo in Latin America is a goal that any believer in power politics would expect from a hemispheric power such as the

United States. Thus there is little surprise in finding that military assistance is used as a channel of influence. The point the dependency writers emphasize is the degree to which supporting the status quo limits Latin America's search for alternative paths of development and protects the interests of the multinational corporations (MNCs). There is more to the military assistance program than simply defending the status quo: The United States is seeking support for its foreign policy as well, and there is empirical evidence that military assistance has "a major impact" on recipient countries complying with U.S. foreign policy initiatives. (This is not seen in the case of economic assistance, however.)[24]

It is a bit more difficult to know what to make of the assertion that the third world countries are losing control over their cultures and social development.[25] It is obvious, walking down virtually any Latin American city street, that U.S. and European cultures are influencing Latin America (from Mc-Donald's hamburgers, to blue jeans, to rock-and-roll music). (In Eastern Europe the popularity of jeans and rock and roll is sometimes portrayed as a victory for our system—although some schools in the United States ban jeans and rock and roll.)

The influence of other cultures on Latin America is also difficult to evaluate because Latin American history is the story of various cultures sweeping across the continent: the Spanish, the British, the French, and now the United States. Presumably, though, the heart of the objection is that somehow the existing structures of Latin American (or LDC) societies may interact badly with the cultures of the core countries. It is clear to this observer that there is truth to the proposition that the patterns of life in Latin America and other third world areas are rapidly changing; the problem is to clarify specifically what harm and what benefits this change entails. The fact that Donald Duck comics convey an obvious ideology is not a convincing criticism, since we live in a world awash in ideologies of one type of another.

Proposition 2: The current economic growth in the less-developed countries is unevenly distributed among sectors of the society. Because income distribution is so badly skewed, the poorest half of most societies is left relatively untouched by economic growth. Statements relating to income distribution lend themselves to quantitative testing far more easily than speculation about the negative influences of other cultures. Moreover, the question of whether worsening income distribution is connected with recent economic growth has been subjected to a good deal of empirical study and testing. Increasingly sophisticated methodologies have been developed to control for changes over time, level of development, location on the periphery or near the core (or what is labeled "semiperiphery" for countries such as Brazil and Mexico).

More research needs to be done in the area, but the results of these quantitative research projects suggest that the much-heralded growth of the

95

modern sector and of GNP is not trickling down to the poorest levels, and it is at least arguable that in many of the most dependent countries, the poor are worse off than they were before the past twenty-five years of growth.

Some of the studies address the possibility that the MNC is a factor in this phenomenon. A 1979 study by Volker Bornschier and Thank-Huyan Ballmer-Cao confirms a hypothesis that greater MNC penetration leads to a greater degree of income inequality.[26] Another quantitative study, by Patrick Nolan, finds "a substantial relationship between income inequity and peripheral capitalism."[27] Steven Stack and Delore Zimmerman found that, independent of the level of development, being on the periphery of capitalist development has a "significant impact" on the degree of income inequality.[28] Peter Evans and Michael Timberlake conclude their quantitative work with the observation that "our results reinforce the idea that foreign investment exacerbates inequality not because it prevents capitalist accumulation in the third world but because the capitalist accumulation it fosters is so strongly exclusionary and inegalitarian."[29] Using rather different quantitative techniques, both Albert Szymanski[30] and Volker Bornschier generate findings in support of the idea that "private capitalist dependent development makes, in the long run, for less development in terms . . . of an equitable distribution of income."[31] The empirical research of David Snyder and Edward Kick leads them to conclude that for the period 1955 to 1970 dependency did increase income inequality.[32]

Other economists, who do not manipulate data but, rather, gather and evaluate statistics on income distribution over time, come to similar conclusions. In a study of that type, Keith Griffin and Azizur Rahman Khan wrote, in regard to Asia, that "in most countries we have studied, the incomes of the very poor have been falling absolutely or the proportion of the rural population living below a designated 'poverty line' has been increasing, or both."[33] Dealing simply with the income distribution figures for Latin America, David Felix recently concluded that "In sum, the Latin American income concentration is unusually high among LDCs, and higher GNP per capita levels scarcely reduce it."[34]

If it seems that there is great inequality of income produced by economic growth on the periphery, there are a number of possible explanations. Richard Rubinson's work suggests the following three factors: First, class formation in dependent countries has produced "a small elite whose economic interests are linked to investors in core countries. This externally-oriented elite impedes the development of an indigenous manufacturing class and ultimately controls an immense share of the wealth of the country." Second, because the production and export of food and raw materials are determined by this small elite in alliance with the dominant, industrialized countries, "there is no large-scale diversification of production. Under this type of production a small labor elite emerges which works in the export sector for wages substantially higher than for workers in the other sectors." Third, class relations in the developing countries are such as to worsen income inequality. This is because "the labor force as a whole has less bargaining power in relation to employers since they face a smaller more homogeneous set of employers." With weak governments in most dependent states, the workers are unable to obtain assistance from that quarter in their search for higher wages.[35]

It could simply be, contrary to the line of reasoning suggested by Rubinson, that rapid economic growth inherently exacerbates social inequality, as Mancur Olson claimed more than twenty years ago.[36] In any case, given the increased power of the multinationals in the most modern sectors of the economy, it is safe to presume that some mechanism is affecting the measurable growth of income inequality. Perhaps Rubinson's answer is too complicated. It may be that MNC investment is capital- rather than labor-intensive and will not immediately produce employment. This naturally brings up the "trickle down" idea, which will be discussed later in this paper.

The telling aspect of the findings on inequality is that the plight of the poor in Latin America, and even more so in Africa and Asia, is so desperate that praising a growth in GNP when the process is not helping the poorest certainly raises some questions regarding values.

The Controversial Propositions. This section of the paper reviews three dependency propositions that are less verifiable, either because of contradictory findings in various studies or because the nature of the proposition does not lend itself to verification.

Proposition 1: The condition of dependency makes economic growth more difficult for countries on the international periphery. The focus here is not income distribution but, rather, national income growth. It should be emphasized that dependency theorists do not usually argue that dependent countries cannot experience economic growth. Particularly since Brazil's dramatic growth of the late 1960s and early 1970s, to argue that countries of the international periphery cannot grow, even grow rapidly at times, is absurd. There is, however, a sometimes-stated and other times implicit theme in the dependency writing that over the long run dependent growth will be retarded because of the international system. This idea that dependency slows growth has been a target of such critics as Joseph Ramos who points, quite correctly, to the high growth rates Latin America as a whole experienced over the period of the 1960s and 1970s.[37]

There are two approaches to defending the proposition that dependency hinders economic growth. The first and most concrete is to examine the correlation between some measures of dependency and growth; the second is to compare the growth that has actually taken place with "what might have been" under the socialist economic structures favored by the adherents to dependency.

Early empirical studies of dependency came to often-contradictory findings in regard to growth, although it is probably fair to generalize that the first studies found that "the countries most integrated into the world economy have tended to grow more quickly over a longer period than those that are not."[38] To the contrary, though, other studies found that direct capital investment correlated negatively with development.[39] Others concluded that countries exporting manufactures grew more rapidly than those exporting raw materials,[40] a finding that countries lacking the ability to produce anything other than raw materials for export found discouraging. A later study concluded that nations with low per capita incomes are "substantially and significantly less able than richer nations to resist the retarding effects of investment dependence on economic growth"; it went on to conclude, on the basis of its regression analysis, "that the greater the level of investment dependence the less was the future of economic growth of the nation."[41] Another recent study observes that most quantitative tests of dependency theory show "that measures of dependency have very modest negative effects on measures of economic development."[42]

If the argument for proposition 1 is to be supported, its strongest case seems to be in the research of Volker Bornschier of the Sociological Institute of the University of Zurich. Although his findings on the relationship between foreign investment and growth have been the subject of a good deal of controversy,[43] the figures suggest that foreign investment initially has a positive effect on economic growth; over the long run, however, the countries with higher degrees of foreign investment grow more slowly than those with lower degrees of investment, after adjusting for countries' different rates of growth according to their level of development.[44] Another recent study, by John Rothgeb, also concludes that investment flows have short-term beneficial effects on growth but that foreign investment has a negative long-term effect on overall growth.[45] Research by Michael Dolan and Brian Tomlin concludes:

> In the first place, the findings of this study provide virtually no support for the postulates of conventional economic theories concerning the effects of linkages upon economic growth. On the contrary, the conclusions arrived at by Bornschier, et al. concerning the impact of direct foreign investment are corroborated here: direct foreign investment is *cumulatively* related to decreases in the relative rate of economic growth of countries. Perhaps equally important, however, is our finding that, in the short-term, investment is positively associated, at virtually the same magnitude, with increasing rates of economic growth.[46]

It seems plausible, therefore, to argue on the basis of the quantitative research of Bornschier and others that, in comparison to other alternatives, foreign investment and multinational corporations have a long-term negative effect on third world growth.

The other approach to supporting the proposition regarding slower growth rates and dependency is to cite the strong growth rates of the Eastern European countries and argue that socialism, with its ability to generate capital investment and to impose tight limitations on foreign investment, is the best approach for LDC growth. Thus the foreign investor and MNCs are positive factors in development if closely controlled but are detriments to development if allowed to operate too freely. This line of reasoning is difficult to refute because it assumes a comparability of the Eastern European economies and those of the LDCs—an exercise in imagination that may be too "iffy" for serious discussion.

Proposition 2: The "trickle down" process is not going to occur in the third world countries or will take such a long time to happen as to doom many future generations to poverty. A controversy exists over whether the relatively equitable distribution of income in the Western societies is a result of government policy or a natural evolution of capitalism. Regardless of which interpretation one favors, since a relatively equal income distribution does exist in the Western industrialized societies, it seems fair to ask the dependency supporters for reasons why economic conditions will not improve in dependent third world countries as well (as Rubinson suggests). The dependency theorists usually begin their explanation with some type of class analysis demonstrating why the wealth will not trickle down. They argue that it takes state intervention to open the doors to the trickle but that the undemocratic governmental structures and the highly stratified social systems prevent the equalizing of wealth. Albeit in sociological jargon, Bornschier argues the point as follows:

> More specifically, due to links with the world economy, . . . the political actor of a dependent country is less likely to be willing or able to act in favor of income equilibrium via the redistribution of incomes which is one of the ideal typical functions of the State in order to preserve the legitimacy of the society as a whole in situations that face centrifugal forces.
> The socio-political basis of such an inaptitude of the peripheral State is a specific class composition underlying the social formation process, namely a class coalition within the integrated sector segment against the marginalized majority of the population.[47]

Of course, most North American social scientists are uncomfortable with the use of social class as a tool of analysis. It is obvious, though, that the upper classes in the more capitalist LDCs have a great deal of political power and seem to be benefiting tremendously (and disproportionately) from dependent capitalist development. What are the implications of this? If one believes that economic growth eventually results in a more democratic political system and that democracy accomplishes equitable income redistribution, then presumably one can ignore class analysis and wait for the coming of democracy.[48] On the contrary, given the current hard evidence that wealth is not trickling down very far in third world societies and that income distribution is not improving, it seems fair to ask those who believe in a trickle down to provide evidence that this is happening in regard to the poorest half of the societies in question.

Proposition 3: The condition of being dependent is correlated with being undemocratic. The question whether government policies are a necessary component of a better income distribution becomes pivotal when considering the link between dependency and authoritarianism. The dependency literature portrays the dependent LDCs as poor, dependent countries governed by a small elite in cooperation with a repressive military that has strong links to the United States. In particular, it emphasizes that the repression of labor unions is needed to create the "favorable investment climate" so near and dear to the hearts of the stereotypical foreign investor. Probably the most blatant reference to this supposed link between repression and foreign investment came when Milton Friedman praised the Chilean model of development during the early days of the Pinochet regime for its ability to contain pressure for higher wages. Since the process of containment consisted of killing, torturing, and exiling labor leaders, the remark (which made sense in terms of the vocabulary of economics) stood as a kind of monument to the coldheartedness of the Chicago model. But does dependency relate to authoritarianism?

One initial problem in searching for that correlation is that there is a well-known positive link between economic development and democracy. Hence one must use a methodology to compensate for that relationship. At least two empirical studies take this into account and support the authoritarianism/dependency thesis. After making an adjustment for the development/democracy link, Kenneth Bollen finds a correlation between type of government and countries on the periphery or semi-periphery of the world economy. He finds countries on the periphery to be less democratic than those on the semi-periphery and both to be less democratic than core countries.[49] In another study Michael Timberlake and Kirk Williams find that the level of foreign investment within noncore countries tends to correlate with nondemocratic or exclusive political systems.[50]

If these two studies support the proposition, why not consider it verified? At this point, the question has not been researched empirically as much as it should (and will) be, and the relationships, while statistically significant, are relatively weak in both studies.

Conclusion

Obviously, dependency is controversial in part because it assaults a set of ideas claiming that free enterprise and foreign investment are essential for economic development in the third world. The goal of this paper has been to acquaint the uninitiated with some of the points of dependency theory and to suggest that it makes some valid points, even if one does not choose to accept the theory as a whole.

The most intellectually honest criticism of dependency theory would seem to be a kind of historical pessimism. Essentially, the argument would be that peripheral capitalism is no bed of roses and that some groups or individuals will benefit more than others. Further, the costs of totalitarian solutions are high and often unmeasurable, and at least capitalism has worked in some places. Finally, to make a leap into faith (or into the Kuznets curve),[51] the argument would urge the third world to wait patiently for the trickle down that probably will accompany its economic growth sooner or later.

There are, however, at least three very troublesome aspects to this defense of peripheral capitalism. First, whatever the merits of the argument, we must also recognize that what dependency theory criticizes, that is, the capitalist road to development, justifies the continued domination of a privileged few based on the belief that patience will eventually be rewarded when the trickle down comes. Unfortunately, many of those counseling patience are those who stand to benefit from the docility of the masses. In the same way that one must look a little askance at university professors when they extoll the benefits of higher salaries to professors, the uncritical acceptance of the costs of capitalism by those it benefits the most deserves a bit of skepticism. Second, at the risk of seeming excessively sentimental in this Hobbesian world, we must wonder if the suffering of the poor in Latin America and the rest of the developing world is really a price worth paying for capitalist development? More than half of the world's population live in countries with per capita incomes (in 1980 dollars) of less than $400, and, of course, many of those countries with $400 per capita incomes have extremely uneven income distributions. Thus, when we extoll the virtues of a system that produces a 3 or 5 percent per capita increase in GNP in the LDCs, it seems fair to ask if that is going to produce anything resembling a satisfactory life for the bottom half of the world's population in our lifetime or in the lifetime of our children. Third, are the circumstances of capitalist development that existed in the nineteenth century and that produced the prosperity so evident in Western Europe, North America, and Japan still present in the world economy today? It has been argued that there are many critical differences:[52] (1) Today new products or goods are produced outside the developing countries rather than internally. (2) Technology is also imported and embodies a capital/labor ratio that often is inappropriate to the factor endowments of the third world countries. (3) Contemporary production units are monopolistic or oligopolistic and are often owned and controlled by MNCs. (4) Rapid increases in population deepen the unemployment problem. (5) The industrialized countries were never colonies like the LDCs of today and hence got to keep the gains from increased production and international trade.

It is these differences in circumstances upon which the dependency argument is based. The answer the dependency advocates offer for third world development problems is usually a form of socialism with carefully controlled links to the world's economy. As a guide to policy, dependency suffers a number of problems, but as an antidote to those who believe in playing the intellectual fiddle of the status quo in a world of inequity and poverty, dependency theory suggest solutions with more immediate results.

Notes

1. This question of where Marxist/Leninist theories of imperialism end and dependency theorizing begins is controversial but not a topic for consideration in this paper. An excellent discussion of this is in Gabriel Palma, "Dependency: A Formal Theory of Underdevelopment or a Methodology for the Analysis of Concrete Situations of Underdevelopment," *World Development,* vol. 6 (July/August 1978), pp. 881–924. My general assumption is that there are some differences—and certainly there are many attempts in the Soviet press to enlighten those dependency theorists who stray too far from Lenin—in basic assumptions. See Liudmila Poskonina, "La concepción radical de izquierda brasileña de 'capitalismo dependiente': aspectos metodológicos," *URSS/AL,* vol. 6, no. 54 (1982), pp. 50–67. And one way we can place the various dependency theorists on an ideological spectrum is in terms of their acceptance of Marxist analysis. But for the purposes of this paper, the more centrist dependency writers such as Oswaldo Sunkel and Celso Furtado will be used to represent dependency thinking.

2. Steven Rosen and Walter Jones, *The Logic of International Relations,* 4th ed. (Cambridge, Mass.: Winthrop Publishers, 1982), chapter 5.

3. Bruce Russett and Harvey Starr, *World Politics: The Menu for Choice* (San Francisco: W. H. Freeman, 1981).

4. Tony Smith, "The Underdevelopment of Development Literature: The Case of Dependency Theory," *World Politics,* vol. 31 (January 1979), pp. 247–88; Joseph Ramos, "Dependency and Development: An Attempt to Clarify the Issues," in Michael Novak, ed., *Liberation South, Liberation North* (Washington, D.C.: American Enterprise Institute, 1981), pp. 61–67; and Robert A. Packenham, "The New Utopianism: Political Development Ideas in the Dependency Literature" (Woodrow Wilson Center, Smithsonian Institution, n.d.).

5. See, for example, Michael Novak, "A Theology of Development: Latin America," in *The Spirit of Democratic Capitalism* (New York: Touchstone Books, 1972), pp. 298–314.

6. "La crisis de la teoría del desarrollo y las relaciones de dependencia en América Latina," in Helio Jaguaribe, Aldo Ferrer, Miguel S. Wionczek, and Theotonio Dos Santos, *La dependencia político-económica de América Latina,* 3rd ed. (Mexico: Siglo Veintiuno, 1971), p. 180.

7. Osvaldo Sunkel, "The Crisis of the Nation-State in Latin America: Challenge and Response" (Paper presented at the Latin American Studies Association Meeting,

Austin, Texas, 1971). Reprinted in Yale H. Ferguson and Walter F. Weiker, eds., *Continuing Issues in International Politics* (Pacific Palisades, Calif.: Goodyear, 1973), p. 356.

8. C. Richard Bath and Dilmus D. James, "Dependency Analysis of Latin America: Some Criticisms, Some Suggestions," *Latin American Research Review,* vol. 9 (Fall 1976), pp. 3–54.

9. Because of the growth of population, when the figures are expressed in per capita terms, the rates are far less impressive.

10. C. Richard Bath and Dilmus D. James, "Institutionalism, Structuralism, and Dependency in Latin America," *Journal of Economic Issues*, vol. 16, no. 3 (September 1982), p. 675.

11. Ibid.

12. The most influential book is that of Fernando Henrique Cardoso and Enzo Faletto, *Dependency and Development in Latin America* (Berkeley: University of California Press, 1979). For an excellent recent example utilizing this historical approach, see Peter Evans, *Dependent Development: The Alliance of Multinationals, State and Local Capital in Brazil* (Princeton, N.J.: Princeton University Press, 1979).

13. Fernando Henrique Cardoso, "The Consumption of Dependency Theory in the United States," *Latin American Research Review,* vol. 9 (Fall 1977), pp. 7–24.

14. Lawrence Gould, "Against Trivialization: A Brief Commentary on Dependency and Epistemology," *Social Science Information,* vol. 22 (1983), p. 871.

15. Palma, "Dependency: A Formal Theory," p. 908.

16. "Just Imagine An IMF Plan for America: Lower Wages, Higher Taxes, Spending Cuts," *Wall Street Journal,* June 22, 1984.

17. Richard Goodwin, "Letter from Peru," *The New Yorker,* May 17, 1969, pp. 41–109.

18. U.S., Congress, Senate, Committee on Foreign Relations, "Colombia—A Case Study of the History of U.S. Aid," *Survey of the Alliance for Progress: Compilation of Studies and Hearings*, Senate Document 91-17, 91st Congress, 1st session, 1969, pp. 659–760. See also, Teresa Hayter, *Aid As Imperialism* (London: Penguin, 1971), pp. 107–19.

19. Abraham Loewenthal, "Foreign Aid as a Political Instrument: The Case of the Dominican Republic," *Public Policy*, vol. 14 (1965), pp. 141–60.

20. Richard Vengroff and Yng Mei Tsai, "Food, Hunger and Development: PL 480 Aid to the Third World," *Journal of Asian and African Studies,* vol. 17 (July/October 1982), pp. 250–65.

21. Hans Morgenthau, "A Political Theory of Foreign Aid," *American Political Science Review,* vol. 56 (June 1962), pp. 301–309.

22. U.S., Congress, House, Committee on Foreign Affairs, *Foreign Assistance Act of 1962, Hearings before a Subcommittee of the House Committee on Foreign Affairs*, 87th Congress, 1st session, 1965, p. 782.

23. Morris Janowitz, *The Professional Soldier* (New York: Free Press, 1960), pp. 233–56.

24. Adrienne Armstrong, "The Political Consequences of Economic Dependence," *Journal of Conflict Resolution,* vol. 25 (September 1981), p. 423.

25. David Sylvan, "Of Colonies and Coca Cola: The Concept and Measurement of Cultural Penetration" (Yale University, 1978).

26. Volker Bornschier and Thank-Huyan Ballmer-Cao, "Income Inequality: A Cross-National Study of the Relationship between MNC-Penetration, Dimensions of the Power Structure and Income Distribution," *American Sociological Review*, vol. 44 (June 1979), pp. 487–506.

27. Patrick Nolan, "Status in the World System, Income Inequality, and Economic Growth," *American Journal of Sociology*, vol. 89 (September 1983), pp. 410–19.

28. Steven Stack and Delore Zimmerman, "The Effect of World Economy on Income Inequality: A Reassessment," *The Sociological Quarterly*, vol. 23 (Summer 1982), pp. 345–58.

29. Peter B. Evans and Michael Timberlake, "Dependency, Inequality, and the Growth of the Tertiary: A Comparative Analysis of Less Developed Countries," *American Sociological Review*, vol. 45 (August 1980), pp. 546–47.

30. Albert Szymanski, "Comment on Bornschier," *Journal of Conflict Resolution*, vol. 28 (March 1984), pp. 149–56.

31. Volker Bornschier, "The Role of MNCs in Economic Growth: Reply to Szymanski," *Journal of Conflict Resolution*, vol. 28 (March 1984), p. 157.

32. David Snyder and Edward L. Kick, "Structural Position in the World System and Economic Growth 1955–1970: A Multiple-Network Analysis of Transnational Interactions," *American Journal of Sociology*, vol. 84 (March 1979), pp. 1096–126.

33. Keith Griffin and Azizur Rahman Khan, "Poverty in the Third World: Ugly Facts and Fancy Models," *World Development*, vol. 6 (March 1978), p. 295.

34. David Felix, "Income Distribution and the Quality of Life in Latin America: Patterns, Trends, and Policy Implications," *Latin American Research Review*, vol. 18, no. 2 (1983), p. 5.

35. Richard Rubinson, "The World Economy and the Distribution of Income within States: A Cross-National Analysis," *American Sociological Review*, vol. 41 (August 1976), pp. 646–47.

36. Mancur Olson, Jr., "Rapid Economy Growth as a Destabilizing Force," *Journal of Economic History*, vol. 23 (December 1963), pp. 529–52.

37. Ramos, "Dependency and Development."

38. Tony Smith, "The Underdevelopment of Development Literature," p. 250.

39. Christopher Chase-Dunn, "The Effects of International Economic Dependence on Development and Inequality: A Cross-National Study," *American Sociological Review*, vol. 40 (December 1975), pp. 720–38.

40. Richard Rubinson and Deborah Holtzman, "Comparative Development and Economic Development," *International Journal of Comparative Sociology*, vol. 22 (March/June 1981), pp. 86–101.

41. Jeanne G. Gobalet and Larry J. Diamond, "Effects of Investment Dependency on Economic Growth," *International Studies Quarterly*, vol. 23 (September 1979), pp. 435, 439.

42. Charles Ragin, "Theory and Method in the Study of Dependency and International Inequality," *International Journal of Comparative Sociology*, vol. 24 (January/April 1983), p. 124.

43. Szymanski, "Comment"; and Erich Weede and Horst Tiefenbach, "Some Recent Explanations of Income Inequality: An Evaluation and Critique," *International Studies Quarterly*, vol. 25 (June 1981), pp. 255–82.

44. See, for example, Bornschier's survey article "Dependent Industrialization in

the World Economy: Some Comments and Results Concerning a Recent Debate," *Journal of Conflict Resolution,* vol. 25 (September 1981), pp. 371–400.

45. John M. Rothgeb, Jr., "The Effects of Foreign Investment on Overall and Sectoral Growth in Third World States," *Journal of Peace Research,* vol. 21 (April 1984), pp. 5–15.

46. Michael B. Dolan and Brian W. Tomlin, "First World–Third World Linkages: External Relations and Economic Development," *International Organization,* vol. 34 (Winter 1980), p. 59.

47. Bornschier, "Dependent Industrialization," p. 384.

48. Of course it is controversial whether it is government policy or the natural workings of advanced capitalism that produces the better income distribution in the industrialized societies.

49. Kenneth Bollen, "World System Position, Dependency, and Democracy: The Cross-National Evidence," *American Sociological Review,* vol. 48 (August 1983), p. 477.

50. Michael Timberlake and Kirk R. Williams, "Dependence, Political Exclusion, and Government Repression: Some Cross-National Evidence," *American Sociological Review,* vol. 49 (February 1984), p. 144.

51. The argument here is that there is a natural concentration of income during the cycle of rapid growth followed by better income distribution (either because of political action or the natural evolution of mature capitalism) once development is achieved. The dependency argument would be that what Simon Kuznets has described will not come about in the case of today's LDCs because of the links the class structure within the LDCs has with international capitalism.

52. This list is drawn from Charles K. Wilber and James H. Weaver, "The Role of Income Distribution in the Process of Development," *Economic Analysis and Workers' Management,* vol. 9 (1975), p. 218.

Discussion

COMMENT: Dependency theory confuses capitalism with imperialism. Imperialism is the antithesis of capitalism because capitalism wants every producer and worker to become a consumer. If that is the case, it's a misnomer when dependency theorists denounce capitalism.

Moreover, if capitalism is exclusionist and inegalitarian, rather than looking at the size of multinational corporations, why not look at the size and power of the state, which looms so large in Latin America? What about the tax systems that these countries have to manipulate capital formation? And what are the welfare systems doing to the marginalized parts of the populations?

I also wanted to mention that when the Bornschier studies and the others discuss income distribution, besides not factoring in the population element, they fail to consider the pool of employable workers, which they ought to focus on. Nor do they figure the value of public housing, public health, subsidization, and a lot of the other noncurrency benefits given to the poor.

I would also point out that much of what the poor pay for in Latin American countries is bought from local companies that have been protected under government policies of high-cost import substitutions. Import substitutions do not allow U.S. firms to compete in Latin America, to produce a product affordable to the poor, or to make the local firms competitive.

What's more, you had the audacity to invoke Eastern Europe, with its slave labor, Soviet imperialism, and a permanent dependency relationship with countries within that bloc. To cite this region as a model is absurd. In the first place, the hard-working population in Eastern Europe would probably have done reasonably well under any circumstances, but would have thrived if it were capitalist. In the second place, consider the so-called "investments" from the other Eastern bloc nations, where much of the trade is by barter. The cruzeiro is far more attractive than the Polish zloty.

Finally, let me remind you that 15 percent of the land in Poland is owned by the private sector, yet it produces 85 percent of the country's hard currency from agricultural output. I find it reprehensible, then, to propose Poland or Cuba as a model.

MR. FRANCIS: Your comments stand on their own and, I think, are well taken. Without quarreling with you, let me point to some problems.

The Eastern European question arises because in fact the defenders of private enterprise in Latin America have been talking as if increasing gross national product were the be-all and end-all. I think that attitude is foolish both for the reasons I gave and for the reasons you gave. What capitalism wants is not necessarily what capitalism gets. What Eastern Europe would be like under capitalism seems to me beside the point.

Now, as for your point about the pool of employable workers, if the pool of employable workers is small, and the system can still operate, then maybe you need to start thinking about some other systems.

COMMENT: My comment concerns the issue of income distribution. If we concern ourselves strictly with statistics and compare the upper 10 percent with the lower 10 percent we come to the conclusion that in most of Latin America the income distribution has worsened. But is that the only measure we should look at? Many other measures of the quality of life have to do with access to safe drinking water, with child death rates, with life expectancy, with the educational system, and the like. There are different measures of the quality of life, and definitely some of these measures have improved. Now, the only way they could improve quantitatively is if they have reached the masses.

Up to the late 1970s the Latin American economies were still developing at a relatively fast pace, with the income of the upper 10 or 20 percent of the population increasing faster than the growth of GNP. Probably the income of a core of 30 or 40 percent of the rest of the population was growing at more or less the same rate as GNP, and the income of the lower 10 to 20 percent was growing at less than 10 percent.

The question we should ask, then, is, Are conditions worsening or improving for the lower-income groups in the population? Evidence is mixed on that point. Some evidence, in Brazil for instance, seems to indicate that conditions have worsened. We can make a case in many other countries, however—Colombia, Venezuela, Mexico, and several Central American countries—where the lot of the lower-income groups has improved over the past thirty years.

Part of this problem stems from economic policy in these countries. Most underlying theory of development advocates growth through import substitution, which has several stages. The first stage provides for growth. As the obvious consumer goods are substituted and produced internally, however, we go into the second stage where intermediate goods are produced. These require heavier capital investment and more sophisticated technology and have a higher capital-to-labor ratio.

At this point problems occur if the rate of growth is not fast enough, or if investment requirements are much higher than expected. In addition, the contribution of growth to employment becomes smaller and smaller as the import substitution scheme deepens. This is the case in most of the Latin

American countries, and of course the stages take different times depending upon the size of the internal market. The larger the market, the longer it will take to reach the stage where import substitution requires industries which are more and more difficult to cultivate.

It is also a good idea to compare what has happened with countries, such as Taiwan, that have opted for another strategy of development—the manufactured-export-led growth. There, the income distribution looks like that of a Northern European country—income is distributed very evenly among the population as a result of a very high rate of growth of gross domestic product in that country. This strategy for development promotes more employment and a more efficient use of capital than the import-substitution scheme.

MR. FRANCIS: Your point is well taken. Let me make a couple of observations, however. Taiwan carried out a very radical land reform and started out ahead in terms of income distribution; they solved a whole set of problems there. Even Guatemala, a stereotype of a backward country controlled by an oligarchy, has had a great increase in life expectancy and a decrease in the infant mortality rate.

A dependency theorist might argue that these occurred as a result of government policies and maybe even as a result of American foreign aid policy. These statistics reflect a track different from the developmental track; perhaps the two things are not linked. I would have to look at some figures, however, before I would want to defend that very hard.

QUESTION: In light of recent discussion, what is it that dependency theorists consider as a base line for comparing development? Do they agree on a definition of success?

MR. FRANCIS: There is a lack of consensus, to some extent because people are trying to defend a theory. Sometimes, although the theory starts crumbling around the edges, people continue to defend it.

On one side, people cite increases in gross national product. On the other side, people point to all the poor people; they say that the same number of poor people seem to be around now as twenty years ago. They say don't talk to me about an economic miracle when there are income distribution problems, high unemployment rates, and the failure to develop democracy.

Perhaps we can begin to find some middle ground for the determination of standards. Twenty years ago the dependency theorists argued that growth cannot occur if a nation is dependent. Now, suddenly, these countries have growth, and the dependency theorists have backed off from that stance and now have brought up a different set of measurements.

QUESTION: Has anyone focused on the percentages that must be achieved for success under any system? Have people agreed on employment levels, on growth in GNP, or on any other indexes that, if achieved, would mean success?

MR. FRANCIS: As I understand the free enterprise argument, the unemployment question would not be addressed for some time, and high rates of unemployment would be tolerated. We would just have to be patient through the hardships. In other words, we should not worry about Chile's 24 percent unemployment now, only if Chile has 24 percent unemployment in twenty-five years following this same model.

In short, the sides will not agree to accept the same set of measurements; They won't declare that this is the winner and this is the loser in the ball game.

COMMENT: The longer life expectancies and lower infant mortality rates in developing countries are interesting not only in the current figures but also in the rate of improvement. The rate of improvement in these figures in Latin America has generally been faster than it was for either Europe or the United States at comparable stages of development. And that's been true starting in the early decades of the 1900s.

I see a greater problem, though, in what happens when state solutions are attempted in Latin America and adversely affect the middle class. The recent experience in Colombia of Betancourt as a result of political pressure from the guerrillas as well as from attempts to improve the lot of the general population has led to higher taxes and fewer benefits for the middle class, yet this is the very class that is the basis of the creation of democratic institutions for Latin America. If this class sees no hope for the future, we have serious problems in making long-term progress.

The question of whether income disparity is necessarily an evil thing has to be considered in light of the problems of trying to reduce those inequalities. In some ways, greater income disparity is not necessarily a bad thing because we cannot simply hold down two classes in order to try to improve the third one.

COMMENT: The dependency theory often gives rise to a conflation of two different statements: one, that there is an economic maldistribution occurring in countries that are profiting overall from a growth in their national product; and two, that the poor in those countries do not benefit. That is, not only is that income gap growing, but in absolute terms the poor are not benefiting. Here empirical evidence might be beneficial. About five years ago I followed those arguments very closely as they related to Brazil. I could not find any conclusive evidence that the poor were worse off absolutely as that country increased its gross national product.

Moreover, at least some evidence suggested that even as the gap grew, the poor benefited. We must be aware of what we are arguing about when we say that the increase in the gap is bad.

It may be, as the speaker just said, that it is not necessarily bad if, as the gap increases, the poor benefit. Mr. Francis's paper on dependency theory, however, assumes that the gap increases to the detriment of the poor in every case. In his paper, he argues exactly that point. He claims that benefits, for instance, are "not trickling down" and claims that findings support him. The findings then listed do not support these claims at all. They do show an increased gap, but they do not show, as he states, that there is no trickle down.

That represents the kind of confusion I see in much of dependency theory, and it has an ideological basis: inequality is bad, and we should try to wipe it out or reduce it. This conviction drives us in the direction of socialism.

Although the last statement in the paper suggests possible solutions, I do not view them as such. The strength of the paper lies in its critique of what exists.

The paper contains alternatives, one of which is socialism. If we include such countries as China, the Soviet Union, and Eastern Europe, one could make a case that the gap between those at the top who run the country and those lower in society is bigger in the Socialist countries than in the Catholic countries. Obviously, they have no more money to control, but they do have more resources under their control. Government officials in Socialist countries are often thrown out of office charged with corruption: that is, they have used their power to benefit themselves.

We saw this pattern in China and in a number of Eastern European countries. If we want to talk about the benefits of socialism as it exists, not theoretically, we cannot do it on the basis that the gap between the rich and poor does not exist under socialism. I argue that it exists and that it is even more severe than it is in Catholic countries.

MR. FRANCIS: You raise an interesting but virtually undoable research problem. Many have tried to analyze this gap in Eastern European countries, but the research that I see suggests that the gap is far smaller in Eastern European countries than in Western countries. We can always fall back on the argument that the officials have a lot of personal wealth accumulated through graft stashed away, but it is impossible to prove. Moreover, it's not just in Eastern European countries that people are thrown out of government office for corruption.

COMMENT: There is considerable empirical evidence on the Soviet Union for what I have said.

MR. FRANCIS: What does the empirical evidence consist of? Of course, it is obvious that some people conceal their personal property, but the degree of importance of this practice to the economic activity of the country cannot be easily measured. I don't say you're wrong, necessarily, only that I don't know how to quantify it.

I think one of your observations is very much on the mark. I also find dependency theorizing more important as a critique of what's going on than as a source of solutions for the future.

As for the gap between rich and poor, that argument, of course, is still going on among economists. A new article on Brazil in one of the economic journals reports that the bottom 50 percent, in fact, are getting worse in absolute terms. At least from a common sense point of view something is wrong with a development program that increases the incomes of those at the top at the rate of 10 percent and the incomes of those at the bottom only 1 percent.

Of course, the argument could be made that in the long run it all works out.

QUESTION: I would like to challenge your common sense on that issue. According to John Rawls's theory of justice, if the only way to achieve a 1 percent gain for the least-advantaged group were to increase the gain for the most-advantaged group from 10 percent to 20 percent, and thereby increase the gap even further, then, according to Rawls, we would have to do that. If we cut in half the gain to the most-advantaged group from 10 to 5 percent and in the process reduce the least-advantaged group's increase from 1 percent to ¾ of a percent, according to my understanding of Rawls, we would not be morally justified.

I would also like to hear more debate on the work by Bornschier. What I understood the speaker to say is that, in looking at the absolute poverty and at the improvement or deterioration of the situation of the least-advantaged group, Bornschier is not fully accounting for the benefits that poor people in some Latin American countries are receiving.

How do you account for the sum total of benefits received by poor people, at least in urban areas, in Latin America? How do you figure the differences in the way welfare benefits are distributed, the protected economies, the underground economies, and so forth? Is this really an undoable research project?

MR. FRANCIS: This issue raises some very complicated questions. If we try to figure the welfare benefits in, of course, the Eastern European case may be strengthened more than the other cases because the number of welfare backups in the Eastern European or communist countries is fairly high.

If you're going to talk about helping poor people, consider that in Cuba, the poor people are really being helped a great deal—and I'm certainly no fan of Cuba. If a peasant is asked which he prefers, Cuba or Brazil, he might choose to live in Brazil. If you tell him he is going to be a peasant, however, he might be better off living in Cuba. In Brazil there is opportunity that does not exist in Cuba. But if a person is to be at the bottom, it might be better to be at the bottom in Cuba rather than in Brazil.

COMMENT: When they let the barriers down and allow the people in Cuba to make a decision on where they would like to live, they leave. Don't forget that all the Marxist countries have barriers to keep people from leaving. Eastern Europeans cannot leave either. If peasants in Cuba with a chance to go to the United States or Mexico or Brazil were allowed to leave, they would leave.

QUESTION: Would you care to speculate on how the situation in Cuba might have been if the Cuban refugees who came to the United States and succeeded so well had been in charge of a truly democratic Cuban government, as opposed to the Soviet–subsidized reign of Fidel Castro? Without the money that the Soviet Union pours into Cuba daily, certainly Fidel Castro would have gone down as a classic failure.

As we talk about improving the condition of the Cuban people, we should consider some of the points raised earlier, such as the quality of life, the foremost consideration of which should be religious and other freedoms. How could the people in Cuba possibly be characterized as better off today than the people in any country where they enjoy freedom and suffer poverty? In your view, would Cuba be better off as a democratic country run by people who came to this country?

MR. FRANCIS: I haven't the slightest question that Cuba would be better off. My point is, however, that the peasants have enjoyed many benefits from the Cuban revolution and the peasants have not fared very well in Brazil.

QUESTION: Mr. Francis, I am interested in your views on the impact of multinational corporations in Latin America. Dependency theory seems to start with a condition and then attempt to place blame for that condition. I am concerned that some of the blame in your paper is quite specifically directed toward multinational corporations. I've worked for only one multinational corporation in my career, but I find no similarities between my experience with that multinational in Latin America and what your paper identifies as the influence of the multinationals. It's been quite the opposite. A statement in your paper, for example, says that workers are not able to gain an adequate wage because their governments do not have the muscle to deal with the multinationals. That is simply not true in Latin America today. Within the past six months workers in Chile, Peru, Venezuela, and Mexico have had either increases directed specifically by the government or increases directed by the government for federal employees, which industry inevitably matches. The idea of multinational muscle exerted against the governments of these countries seems to me to come out of some very bad historical examples, which I find difficult to replicate today in the industrial experience in these countries.

ITT in Chile perhaps was a bad example. I know very little about its actual involvement, other than what I've read. If there is another ITT in Chile today, it is certainly not well known. As a matter of fact, the muscle exerted in the Chilean economy today is exerted by Chilean corporations, not by multinationals, at least in our business.

Our opportunity to provide employment in countries like Mexico and Peru is limited by policies adopted by those governments. I find no link between those governmental policies and multinational corporations or the influence of the multinational corporations on those governments. Quite to the contrary, dependency theory seems to be clearly linked to the policies that these governments are adopting. These policies in turn limit the employment opportunities for the people who live and work in those countries. In a number of places in your paper, however, you refer to empirical evidence, and I am interested in what empirical evidence supports your statements.

MR. FRANCIS: We social scientists prefer to look at this situation over the long run; if something has improved in Chile in the past six months, it will probably get worse again. Ted Moran has written a good article that appeared in *World Politics* in which he makes the point that this bargaining balance shifts under certain kinds of circumstances. Historically, multinationals have had the ability to kick governments around but now suddenly find themselves kicked around by governments. The position of the corporations vis-à-vis the governments varies with the kind of industry, the kind of investment, and the length of time in the country, however.

We social scientists look at one set of evidence; as for the multinational managers, they know that their hearts are pure, and they know that they are there trying to do their best and can see how employment is created by their immediate investments. My argument would be that they are too close to the situation for a true perspective. Whether you find my argument useful is another matter.

QUESTION: Isn't it at least as arguable that dependency theorists adopt an abstract set of categories for viewing empirical reality that leads them to make certain choices, to see some things and not to see others, to focus on the gap in incomes over the absolute incomes and the like?

MR. FRANCIS: Some of these empirical studies were not done by people who were necessarily prodependency, however. They gathered the evidence systematically to see if it confirmed the theory.

113

QUESTION: I think one of the strongest things that came through in your paper was that at least in some cases in some countries the investment from the outside harmed the creation and existence of indigenous business. That finding would support dependency theory, if the gross national product is increasing because of the outside and not because of the inside.

Could you develop that point a little? Is that the case generally throughout all these countries or just in some? Does multinational investment from the outside harm the development of indigenous business because the wealthy elite would rather deal with business from the outside, where they can make more money, than deal with local business?

In the Philippines, for instance, a bishop implied to me in conversation that, after Aquino was killed, even the business people demonstrated in the streets, because they knew that Marcos would be tying in much more strongly with the outside, hindering their own efforts for internal development.

MR. FRANCIS: Certainly you identify a lot of the arguments of dependency theorists. In another sense, we could argue that businessmen are almost stateless, that they are in fact pursuing profits, and that a businessman who happens to reside in Buenos Aires will not behave any differently from a businessman who happens to reside in Arlington, Virginia. Latin American concern with losing control of the economy reflects a rather old-fashioned belief in nationalism.

One set of studies, however, discusses the difference between the behavior of local entrepreneurs and the behavior of multinational entrepreneurs. My understanding is that various of these studies have found different approaches to the creation of employment, for example. Some studies argue and produce convincing evidence, at least to me, that multinationals tend to bring in more capital-intensive investment and therefore do not employ the same number of people with the same amount of investment. Perhaps they may not even bring in the investment; they may mobilize local investment without using labor-intensive techniques.

QUESTION: A dependency economist from Mississippi could argue that his state has historically been on the periphery and that the core in the Northeast has really controlled the economic development of this country. Furthermore, he could argue that although there certainly were economic elites in Mississippi, they had ties to the northeastern establishment and that when things got rough, they shipped the wealth back to New York. If you were the governor of Mississippi, would you go for a quick-fix, Socialist solution, or would you do what most of the governors are doing and encourage investment, that is, enterprise zones and the like?

MR. FRANCIS: A quite valid point. One of the problems of dependency that I have not dealt with is why capitalism practiced across a national border differs from capitalism practiced within a country. In an earlier paper on dependency, I used a long quotation from a detective novel set in Colorado, in which the characters complain about letting businessmen come in from New York City, take the land, leave the pit, and not clean up the mess after them. The quotation sounded exactly like the kind of thing that occurs in dependency literature, in which the Mexicans or the Chilenos complain that "they've taken the copper and left us the hole."

The dependency theorists have not been able to explain why crossing a national border causes capitalism to be somewhat different from capitalism within this country. Is Colorado's relationship with New York any different from Bogota's relationship with New York? While some differences exist, there are some basic similarities, too.

COMMENT: Down in South Carolina we hear a lot of talk about Yankee imperialism. [Laughter] Mr. Francis, your paper combines many very idealistic approaches, observations, and problems. Idealism is certainly worthwhile, but if it is not tied together with pragmatism and sound alternative approaches, I find idealism to be a broken reed.

A developing country is in many ways like an adolescent. In five or six years my sixteen-year-old daughter will want to claim her sovereignty and move out on her own. Just like my daughter, a country newly sovereign has several options for maintaining itself.

My daughter could decide to go back into the company firm and have the protection of the family operation, but she sacrifices some of her sovereignty. Some former French colonies in Africa, for example, followed this approach.

A second approach is to declare true sovereignty, to set up an independent business, or to go into independent farming. Although this is maintenance of sovereignty, the risk is high. It is very painful and likely to lead to very slow development. A few countries, like Burma, have tried this approach at various periods.

The third approach is to get a job with somebody else. Now, if she does that, she will sacrifice some of her sovereignty, at least until she develops her savings, learns skills, and makes contacts. Every individual and every country must make a decision on how much sovereignty to compromise.

The peripheral countries you mentioned earlier include not only the Dominican Republic, Brazil, and Nigeria, but also Canada, Australia, Belgium, the Netherlands, Switzerland, and Austria—all peripheral countries. The core countries are six or seven: the United States, Japan, Germany, France, Britain, and maybe Italy and the Soviet Union. All others are peripheral countries.

MR. FRANCIS: That, of course, depends on how we define peripherals. This is

115

a good point on which to close because it brings me back to one of the most important points of dependency theory: your view that your daughter's growing up and moving out are analogous to options for national development is ridiculous.

The Dominican Republic has, after all, been around for a long time; it is not sixteen years old. It may look like a sixteen year old because the United States or the Western developed countries keep it looking like a sixteen year old by maintaining Trujillo in power and thwarting what might be seen as natural economic growth. Whether we agree or not, that is an absolutely key point to dependency. Dependency theory does not see development as just a game where countries start maturing at different times.

According to dependency theory, the underdevelopment in the Dominican Republic is linked to the development in the Western world. Whereas the Dominican Republic may think it will grow up and move out, in fact it will not grow up or only at a very slow, skewed rate.

The Role of the Catholic Church in Latin American Development

Archbishop Marcos McGrath, C.S.C.

The contribution of the church in the whole area of economic development is, as Stalin once said, not a matter of troops, which we don't have. Nor is it a matter of economic power or wealth, which we don't have, particularly the churches of Latin America.

The contribution of the church to development is a vision we share and a vision we try to incarnate into the realities that affect us all. A passage from the Book of Proverbs provides a good introduction to this idea:

> Doth not wisdom cry? and understanding put forth her voice? She standeth in the top of high places, by the way in the places of the paths. She crieth at the gates, at the entry of the city, at the coming in at the doors. Unto you, O men, I call; and my voice is to the sons of man. O ye simple, understand wisdom: and, ye fools, be ye of an understanding heart. Hear; for I will speak of excellent things; and the opening of my lips shall be right things. For my mouth shall speak truth; and wickedness is an abomination to my lips. All the words of my mouth are in righteousness; there is nothing froward or perverse in them. They are all plain to him that understandeth, and right to them that find knowledge. Receive my instruction, and not silver; and knowledge rather than choice gold. For wisdom is better than rubies; and all the things that may be desired are not to be compared to it. I wisdom dwell with prudence, and find out knowledge of witty inventions. The fear of the Lord is to hate evil: pride, and arrogancy, and the evil way, and the froward mouth, do I hate. Counsel is mine, and sound wisdom: I am understanding; I have strength. By me kings reign, and princes decree justice. By me princes rule, and nobles, even all the judges of the earth. I love them that love me; and those that seek me early shall find me. Riches and honour are with me; yea, durable riches and righteousness (Proverbs 8:1–18).

It is this wisdom that we bishops of Latin America feel that we must try to bring to the very complicated present situation affecting our peoples and

117

affecting inter-American and international order.

I congratulate the organizers of this dialogue. We often say that war is too important to leave in the hands of the generals, because it affects peace and happiness in the world for all men. By the same token, business is too important to leave in the hands of businessmen, and religion is too important to leave in the hands of bishops, ministers, and priests only. In other words, these are all human affairs in which each of us has a particular role, but in which we must get together to share our different visions because we are working for the whole man and for a whole planet. When we do not, then we pull apart, as any academic has witnessed in a university without interdisciplinary dialogue.

Religion and the Temporal Order

What does the church have to say about social problems, economic problems, and political problems?

I speak of the church in relation to the temporal order as we see it in the Catholic church. This is a general Christian approach, however, with some exceptions noted later.

In "moral theology" we used to say that all of man's actions come under the aegis of religion under the aspect of their moral consideration of good or evil. This is quite obvious. If there is good or evil in the action, then it has a moral connotation and therefore is of interest to any religious body.

In the present context, however, we would say that in a different manner. We would say that the church is interested in the whole temporal order because of its vision of man. There is a different, more meaningful way of saying it. In 1965 when Pope Paul VI made the first trip by a pope to the United Nations, he said: "I come to you as an expert not in politics nor economics or sociology, but as an expert in humanity, the vision of man."

This vision has been the particular emphasis of the present pope, John Paul II. Shortly after he was installed as pope in 1978, he had a very felicitous expression. "Whenever," he said, "we pronounce that word 'man' or 'mankind' we should do so with profound reverence."

During his episcopacy and papacy, all his documents have centered upon this concept. All the roads of the church, he said, lead us to man, to man and woman and their dignity and to their rights and the preservation and promotion of those rights, both personal and social.

In many ways, then, the role of the church beyond its immediate religious sphere, the role of the church in the social temporal order, is its insistence upon the dignity of every human being and what this means in terms of human rights and duties, both personal and social.

The social teaching of the church, as we call it, or the social doctrine of the church, as some call it, is really an area of "moral theology," a reflection in faith upon human relations. We will describe how this theology has evolved in our times and has become much more existential without ceasing to be very traditional.

This social teaching of the church is an integral part of evangelization but has not always been quite so clearly stated by the Christian churches. We know of the social Gospel movement here in Protestant churches of the United States, and we know of the social reform movements in the Catholic church, beginning in Europe in the past century and taking shape in this century.

The clear affirmation that the insistence upon social justice is an integral part of the preaching of the Gospel, however, is something new for us. It was stated with clarity in the Second Vatican Council and very specifically in the World Synod of Catholic Bishops in 1971 in Rome. This affirmation has been worked out more and more emphatically in all of our key documents, so that whether it is in preaching from the pulpit, or in catechism to children, or in the university, or in forums such as this, social justice is not a question of carrying out a religious teaching and then separately speaking about social justice. Justice is a integral part of the Gospel itself—social justice, the insistence upon personal human rights, and the consequences of social rights and organization.

Social justice is to be taught by the pastors of the church in the Catholic vision of things and in most of the other Christian churches. The priests ordained in apostolic succession are charged with preaching the Gospel. "Go therefore and teach all nations," says the Lord, "all that I have taught you, and I will be with you until the end of time" (Matt 28:19–20).

Social justice is an integral part of the preaching of the Gospel; it cannot be ignored. We cannot *not* condemn injustice; we cannot *not* praise the good, both personal and social. It is part of the Gospel to do so.

This social moral teaching by the church must be carried out in constant dialogue with people enmeshed in the social problems they touch on—not only for reasons of winning their confidence and having them better disposed to accept the teaching, but also because: (1) they are equally members of the church and participate equally in the mystery of salvation, in the body of Christ; and (2) they are specifically competent in their areas. The Second Vatican Council insists a great deal that because the lay person lives in the daily texture of civil and secular life, he must incarnate Gospel values in that structure. It is the role of the pastor to announce these principles and seek, with the laity, their real and concrete significance.

The Puebla document expresses this beautifully when it says that this Christian anthropology, this whole vision of man that the church gives us, must be worked out in our countries "in historical models for the future," in every area. Therefore, the dialogue must be continuous: our social teaching is a growing thing, not denying the past but growing as new challenges occur.

When Pope Leo XIII put out his great encyclical in 1891, *Rerum Nov-*

119

arum, the social problem at that time was the typically nineteenth century European conflict of capital and labor. When, many years later, Pope John XXIII put out his encyclicals, *Mater et Magistra* (1962), and *Pacem in Terris* (1963), the key problem of social justice had become the contrast between the rich and the poor nations of the world—a problem that Leo XIII did not touch on directly, simply because it was not clearly defined in his time.

As new problems arise, then, we have to bring our Christian view to bear on them: through dialogue we discover what our guiding lines of action should be. This means, very obviously, that church social teaching is a dynamic, ongoing, growing body of doctrine that is not infallibly stated as are our doctrines on the Triune God or Christ, our Savior. Social teaching is not in that order of infallibility. It is a practical, prudent application of the Gospel to the world, which the pastors have to carry out in dialogue with the laity. Although authoritative statements in church social teaching should be respected, they can be questioned. They should be questioned with the respect that they deserve, however, and a sincere desire to find the most faithful sense of the Gospel in the social problems we touch on.

This understanding of our social teaching is very important, and it has taken specific shape in our times. What we call social teaching of the church in the decades of the 1930s, 1940s, and 1950s, just before the Council, was put out in manuals under that title. It contained various chapters on the family, corporations, labor unions, and the like. Although it was very useful, it had two major drawbacks, which were criticized by many of us in the Council in 1962–1965.

First, it was based immediately on the natural law rather than on the Gospel itself. Second, it tended to be very dogmatic and stiff, not flexible, according to new circumstances and conditions that alter the social problem and its moral dimension.

The Council stressed a return to the sources of our faith, meaning that our social positions should spring from the Gospel, from our vision of man in the whole biblical sense. The natural law developed by so many philosophers of various origins is very useful for interpretation of the philosophical basis of discussion, and it is necessary. But it is the Gospel that is specifically Christian.

Moreover, we should not pretend to have facile formulas to solve all social problems. We should be able to reflect upon them, pointing out the good and the evil aspects, to give some guidelines, and to condemn some things that are obviously condemnable and recommend others that are obviously recommendable. The church, however, does not pretend nor should it ever pretend as church to propose political models, economic models, or social models for the solution of society's problems. This is not the church's role as "magisterium," the teaching authority. It is the role of Christians and all other people living and working in society.

The role of the church is to help us as a conscience to seek what is good and evil and to give guidelines. That is the nature of the social teaching of the church.

This concept is useful for what I have to say later on; it also indicates the value of dialogues such as we are holding here. A few theologians discussing multinationals among themselves would have some interesting things to say, the heads of multinationals would have some interesting things to say, and people in government would have some interesting things to say about multinationals. Brought together, however, their ideas become much more enriching and meaningful. This is the way we should carry out dialogue for life today.

An example of the value of such dialogue in Panama has been very helpful to us. About five years ago we put together a group of economists, some business men, several bishops, several theologians, and a few social workers. What bound us together was that we were all believing, practicing Catholics and that we were all deeply interested in the problem of poverty in Panama. We have been meeting on and off for the past five years. In a few months we are finally putting out a book on poverty in Panama, its causes and possible solutions. The announcement of it has awakened a great interest in many sectors of the country. We hope it will lead to many and broad discussions on the topic in the search for solutions.

The Latin America Context of Faith and Culture

We must bear in mind the variety in Latin America, from the Rio Grande down to Patagonia, as a caution against our tendency to speak in generalities. Many people today, for example, still refer to Latin America as South America, leaving out Central America and Mexico altogether. The very term Latin America is ambiguous because some parts of that area are not Latin. They are English speaking or Dutch speaking, particularly in the Caribbean area. As a term, though, Latin America applies to the whole area.

Quite obviously, there are close similarities—historical, cultural, religious, and linguistic—among the countries and peoples of Latin America, far more, for example, than within the continent of Africa or Asia.

The contrast now at issue is that between North America and Latin America, which also lends itself to oversimplifications. These two branches have grown from the European tree but are separate and different, with different histories and different developments. For centuries they remained separate—separate and, perhaps, opposed. I find it a gross exaggeration for people to talk about Latin America as an area of special friendship or special treatment on the part of the United States. It has never really been so except for passing moments. We are most aware of this in Latin America.

The influence of the United States in Latin America began to grow in the middle of the nineteenth century with the expansion of U.S. trade, particularly in Central America. The hegemony over our lands, which once belonged to Spain and some briefly to Great Britain, passed largely to the United States. This, however, does not mean there has been any real affinity between the peoples of North America and South America. Clearly there has not been much rapport because of the tremendous difference in approaches to so many realities. The only meeting of people taking place right now of any size is the migration of Latin Americans to North America out of economic necessity, political refuge, or fear for their lives. These people tend to be absorbed into the United States, when they can stay, and cease to feel their roots in Latin America. Therefore, they do not really become a bridge, as one might hope they would be, between the two continents. The students that go to the United States from Latin America are mostly paying students, usually from the upper-class families.

For some years I was the bishop chaplain of university students through all Latin America and traveled to centers in Europe and North America. The bulk of our students who study abroad go to other Latin American countries, because they can do so on the money they have or on the small scholarships they obtain. The second level of economic opportunity is that of Europe, because with smaller scholarship sums they can get into a university in Spain or even in other Western European nations. The Russian bloc as well is now offering many scholarships to Latin America, often covering all costs.

In the United States, there are very few scholarships available for Latin American students. Increasing opportunity for Latin American students is now receiving more support, as part of the Kissinger Report, for example. Until now, though, to go to the United States a student has had to compete at a very high academic level to get into the outstanding universities, although the decline in students is making it a bit easier now. A student has to pay his way in the United States, which means that of the 50,000 students from Latin America who study here, 90 to 95 percent are from the upper classes. This concentration of upper-class students really precludes a meeting of peoples. It is a meeting with only a part of our people.

Many of our higher economic groups in Panama have talked to me about the problem that occurs when their children, who finish in a private high school in our country and then go to the United States for four or five years of university, come back. They are twenty-three or twenty-four years old and do not really know their own country; they are not really identified with the social problems of their own country or their own people. The poor students, on the contrary, who go through the public schools and the universities, which are full of political problems, waste a lot of time in politics. They get bent this way and the other, but they certainly are exposed to the problems of the country. This situation concerns us and bears on the question of the United States and Latin America. In short, we want our better-qualified students to have the opportunity of specializing in the United States—but students from all social classes, aware of their country, and educated with an interest to serve it.

U.S. citizens coming to Latin America also tend to associate with a higher economic, social, and cultural level of society. They constitute what I once called the "embassy crowd." They may live in Santiago, in Buenos Aires, or in Lima. They attend all the major receptions at the U.S. embassies, they go to the golf clubs, they go to the country clubs, and they deal with the upper level of our society. When they come back to the United States, they give lectures on the country they have been living in. Of course, they have not really been living in that country; they have been living in what could also be called the "Hilton circle," a certain well-cushioned area of society with very little exposure to the real problems of most of our people. This is another caveat we should have in mind when we talk about Latin America.

In business contacts with firms in Latin America, American businessmen mingle with the upper level of society and are likely to be insulated from knowledge of the realities faced by the majority of the people in the countries where these corporations work. Unless individuals find some way to break out of that insulation and unless companies have correspondents in these countries who are themselves making that effort to be in contact with those harsh realities, those individuals and companies will be part of the problem of the ever-widening gap between the rich and the poor.

One other question is also very interesting: the religious, cultural, and ideological differences between North America and Latin America. These are sometimes characterized around the notions of Protestantism and Catholicism or at least British Protestantism and Hispanic, Lusitanian, or Iberian Catholicism. A lot can be said for this contrast, but it is also an area in which grave oversimplifications sometimes tend to falsify the problems.

In the wake of Weber a great deal has been written about the relationship between Protestantism and the rise of capitalism. We are all aware of this line of thought and grant it some validity. A great deal has also been written about the effects of Spanish Catholicism in preserving traditional social patterns of organization. Some might jump from this notion to the very broad conclusion that the Protestant ethic, which is also lived by Catholics in the North, is the source of progress and of the production of wealth and that the Catholic ethic is somewhat medieval in its pure "social" interest, emphasizing sharing but not producing.

I believe that this question must be handled with care, because many factors come in. The Protestant Reformation took place in the sixteenth century, and the Industrial Revolution did not come about until several centuries later. Other factors are clearly involved.

In addition, at the time of independence of both North America and Latin America, 1776 to 1821, probably Latin America was much more culturally advanced than the United States. The nineteenth century, however, was a disastrous period for Latin America. It was a period of infighting between clericals and anticlericals and liberals and conservatives, and of growing economic and political dependence on the North, which destroyed many values and many strengths of our people and set us back considerably. To ignore that century and to blame the present problems of Latin America entirely on the previous Hispanic colonial period is to ignore much of our history.

This omission can be illustrated by one aspect of the Kissinger Report. The report makes many excellent points, especially in its economic recommendations. It also states, as many others including the pope have done, that the basic problem in Central America is poverty and social injustice. Logically, then, this has to be our first and fundamental concern. Then, however, the report rather superficially attributes this problem to the aftereffects of the long Spanish period of colonialism and feudal organization and ignores the fact that certainly since the latter part of the nineteenth century Central America has been mostly under the aegis and domination of the U.S. economy. Most of the problem comes from this period, not from the previous historical period under Spain. The distribution of land, the concentration of wealth in the hands of a few, the subservience to mono cultures and mono products—these are fruits of nineteenth and twentieth century economic developments.

As for the church itself, I would briefly categorize its history in Latin America in four periods. This arrangement can help define the present period.

The First Period: Conquest and Colony, 1492 to 1821 (the Year of Generalized Independence). The early period of conquest was like that of the conquerors themselves, the conquistadores: remarkable and outstanding, an exploit that evokes tremendous human admiration but also that reflects many of the narrow traits that came out of the crusade mentality of the Spanish (they had just expelled the Moors and the Jews) at the close of the fifteenth century. Throughout the sixteenth century the missionaries had a continuous fight with the conquerors. The missionaries tried to hold back the conquerors from excessive use of the sword and to bring about a more benign, humane consideration for the Indian populations and later for the black slaves that were brought into the colonies.

Some outstanding figures arose at this time, and a concept of social justice in international rights originated during this period that is only now being rediscovered and reevaluated. The energies of Spain and Portugal declined in the latter part of the seventeenth and in the eighteenth centuries, a decline manifested in the colonies.

The Second Period: Conflict and Disintegration, 1821–1900. Even so, in 1821, the key date for the independence of most of these countries, the local churches were rather well organized. They had, for example, large numbers of local clergy—priests, monks, and nuns—and well-organized catechetical works.

By 1900, the church was, however, characteristically bereft of clergy, with hardly any native clergy in many of these countries, and much disorganized. During this period in the nineteenth century there occurred bitter infighting for political control, in which the clericals wanted the church to continue to have direct influence in state affairs and the anticlericals wanted to push the church out of state affairs and to control it in some ways.

In 1899 Pope Leo XIII, in view of the chaos in politics and the weakness of the church in Latin America, called all the bishops of Latin America to Rome for the first Latin American Synod. He insisted upon a renovation of the church, a restrengthening of the participation of the laity, the better preparation of candidates for the priesthood, and other measures.

The Third Period: Rebirth of the Church in Latin America, 1900–1945.
From 1900 to 1945, the third period, a rebirth of the church occurred in Latin America, brought about largely under the guidance of the Holy See and the various church movements, mostly of European origin, which culminated in the Second Vatican Council: the biblical movement that had such difficulty getting under way in the modern Catholic church and that grew and took shape in our countries as well; the liturgical movement and the more active participation of the laity in the rites of the church; the catechetical movement; the movement of social doctrine and social awareness; the ecumenical movement that increased contact with Christians of other faiths. By the time of World War II some very strong, outspoken expressions of renovated Catholicism were evident in several countries in Latin America, particularly in Chile, Argentina, and Cuba.

After World War II and the immediate prosperity that this brought to Latin America through sales to the Allies, a great recession came and a new kind of poverty in which the belt of misery tightened around our cities. People came in from the land and had no place to work, no schools, no health facilities, and no homes. The movement of the church began to concentrate much more on these social aspects. Between 1945 and 1960 occurred the birth of the Christian Democratic parties, the Christian Democratic labor unions, and all kinds of Christian-inspired university groups, farmer groups, and business groups looking for a Christian answer to this new social crisis.

The demographic explosion as well as the swelling of the cities and the recession following World War II suddenly produced this highly critical situation.

Just at this time came the Council. With it the church stepped into a new era. The Second Vatican Council (1962 to 1965) was certainly the most significant religious event of this century. I think we can say that universally, for all religious bodies, and particularly for the Catholic church and the other Christian churches. In general the Council exerted a powerful effect on the religious view of things in all religions of the world.

Three aspects of the Council are particularly significant: a *return to our sources of belief, a going out with this belief to the world, and a reflection on the Gospel and the world.*

First, this return to the sources of belief signified a tremendous new input of the Word of God, going back to the Bible itself, and emphasizing the Gospel in everything we do and say and believe and act upon. In this we very frankly recognize our tremendous debt to our Protestant brothers who continually promoted the reading of the Scriptures when in the Catholic church we relied rather upon the preaching of our priests without each going directly to the Word of God.

Now, we approach more directly the Word of God in the life of the church and in the teaching of the church. It is really tremendous what this return to the Scriptures has meant to the church, particularly in Latin America. In any country now, in the hills the peasants use their Gospel, the New Testament or Bibles, in study groups or reading circles, where they talk about the meaning of the Gospel for their daily lives. This sweeping change is, in large measure, the result of the Council. Returning to the sources also means living that Word of God in our Christian community in our sacramental lives, as was done in the early church, that of the Apostles.

Second, the going out to the world as church has much to do with today: evangelizing that world with the Gospel in our hands, stressing the dignity of man. The Council presents a beautiful vision, which is so important for us to grasp and to live ourselves if we are believing Christians: man is created in the image of God; man is called to be the son of God; man is called to build this world, dominating all that is in the world and placing all at the service of man, but of all men and of all women, not as an exclusive or preferential service of some over others.

This vision is important because it helps to restore to us as Christians a historical dynamic that we had largely lost. The historical dynamics of the early church were very strong. During the Middle Ages religious life became static. The Renaissance ushered in a new vision of things but largely the Roman and Greek as opposed to the biblical vision. The Protestant Reformation did not possess a historical dynamic of its own. This began to spring up from other areas such as the Hegelian historical dynamic that has dominated most thinkers since the nineteenth century. Now we are returning to a strong biblical, historical dynamic, which is so necessary for our sense of our individual lives, our social purpose, and the importance of what we are doing in the world.

Third is the reflection on the Gospel and the world, as expressed in the famous Pastoral Constitution "The church in the World Today," which every Catholic should know and read and reflect upon a great deal.

Here I would point out four things: first, the relationship of temporal society with the kingdom of God. The kingdom of God in our Christian biblical Gospel has begun and is within each of us and among us insofar as we already live the life of God, which is love, our redeeming love. At the same time, however, it is being developed in the temporal structures and society that we construct. We are called as human beings to build a better world, a world that is not accidentally related to the world to come, but a world that in some ways prepares the world to come for eternity. It is not simply that it is a nice thing not to kill your neighbor; it is not simply a nice thing to help the sick to become healthy or the poor to have a better station in life. These are good in themselves, but they also prepare the kind of society, a civilization of love as Pope Paul VI calls it, that is the kingdom here in preparation for the kingdom to come. An intrinsic relationship comes about that does not *identify* the kingdom of God with temporal structures but does relate them intrinsically.

Second, this theological reflection of ours has a new bent to it. We have been used to theological reflection that starts with statements of faith and deduces from them our conclusions. For example, God is one in three persons. From this revealed truth we deduce in our reflection much about person, about nature, about the relationship between the persons in God, about the relationship between the son of God in his divine nature and in his human nature, and so forth, in what we call speculative theology.

There has always been, however, a role for "inductive theology," but it has come strongly into its own in our own period. What is it? Basically, it is a religious reflection that derives from a consideration of the reality we live in and looks at that reality through the eyes of faith. We try to see the human social problems in that reality. Then we reflect upon them with the light of the Gospel and project outward what we believe we should do about this situation.

Those who as young men or women worked in some specialized religious or Catholic action groups will remember the famous inquiry method, the "see, judge, and act." Inductive theology is see-judge-act. We look through the eyes of faith at the problems; we judge these problems and then project out to the world. This is the method the church had been using broadly for the previous thirty to forty years, but which was consecrated by the Council to become the method to complement the deductive. We do not discard a deductive procedure, because God has spoken and from His Word we deduce. We also have the inductive approach, however, which expands the area of religious consideration to take in our modern situations and problems and illuminates them through the light of faith, so that we can walk more clearly in such circumstances.

Third is the growing sense of the *local church*. When I was in the seminary, it was a bit dangerous to talk about the *American* church or the

African church or the *Latin American* church. Such terminology was considered divisive and somewhat schismatic. Now we use it commonly, the "church of Panama," the "church of Buenos Aires," and so on. We have returned to an old sense of the local church, which comes from apostolic times. All the churches, as apostolic foundations, grew up as "communities of saints" in their place. The Book of Revelation, the last book of the Bible, for example, is addressed to the faithful in each of the seven cities of Asia Minor to which John wrote.

The sense of the local church that we find in the first Christian groups of Jerusalem described in the Acts of the Apostles (chapters 2, 3, and 4; cf 2:42), is that of a community of faith, around the Eucharist, with a strong sharing or "communication" of material goods. This sense of community becomes fundamental in the strongly renewed sense of our church today as communion—a communion that is active communication, on all levels, between people who make up the community: communication in love, communication in service, and communication in goods in sharing what we have. This communication in sharing becomes, in a certain sense, the very basis of the Catholic approach to social justice. This sharing must go beyond our immediate communities: it must reach out to other communities, and it must reach out to the world community. Unless we have this sense of sharing, something is lacking in our Christian view of things.

The local church has another aspect also: as it takes on the qualities of the local people, it should express these qualities in liturgy, in song, and in prayer and should address itself to the problems of the local community. At the same time, if it is an authentically Catholic community, it will be in strong contact with all the world communities of the church and particularly with that of Rome, whose vicar is, for us, the visible head of the church, the successor of Peter.

The Council years, 1962–1965, coincided with the growing shift of Christianity from North to South. Father Walter Buhlman, a German Capuchin missionary, a few years ago published "The Coming of The Third Church," which traces this shift.

The first church was built in and grew up around the Middle East, the Holy Land, and North Africa. For centuries it was a population center of the church.

The second church, from the early Middle Ages until the twentieth century, was centered in Europe and North America. In the beginning of the twentieth century about 70 percent of the Christians in the world were found in Europe and North America. By the end of the twentieth century, however, about 22 percent of the Christians will be in Europe and North America, while the bulk of the Christian population will be in the South. About 60 percent of the Roman Catholics in the world will be in Latin America. This is the coming of the *third church*.

This factor is extremely important because a prevailing habit identifies Christianity, culturally and historically, with the West and particularly with its European origins. This is historically true for the second church. It is daily less so with the coming of the third church.

In a certain sense the Second Vatican Council was the first truly ecumenical council, not in its doctrinal value, of course, because every council is ecumenical in its teachings for the entire world. It comprised, however, bishops from the entire world, and it presented the problems of the entire world.

Application of the Council in Latin America

For the application of the Council in Latin America, the two general conferences of Latin American bishops are of special moment.

The Council ended December 8, 1965. Even before that, though, we held some meetings of experts in the diverse areas of the Council's considerations to apply the Council to Latin America. I was charged with the organization of the first meeting, which took place in a town called Via Mao on the outskirts of Porto Alegre in southern Brazil. Although we went about it timidly, the meeting was such a success that CELAM (the Council of Latin American Bishops) decided to hold more meetings. This contributed to a growing consciousness of the church of Latin America and the church as a factor of unity in the development and integration of our continent. When CELAM, in 1967, proposed to Pope Paul VI a meeting of all the bishops of Latin America to apply the Council, he was delighted. We took as the title of the meeting "The Church and the Present Transformation of Latin America in the Light of the Council." The meeting took place in August 1968 in Medellín, Colombia. It came out with a striking set of sixteen brief documents on key areas: peace and justice, human promotion, and the church structures. What had a particularly powerful effect, because of the problems of our peoples, were the statements on peace and justice. Because Medellín suffered from one of the difficulties of the Council, the results were rather unequal. Although the Council had marvelous vision and marvelous presentation of doctrine and moral orientation in general, we were not aware of how much pedagogy was required to implement so much reform. Radical and even moderate changes would not come about quickly without very serious adjustments and much suffering. The pedagogy required after the Council we learned by hard experience. The same happened after Medellín. The years immediately after the Council, 1965 to 1975, saw the first working out in the church and the world of the new thrusts of the Council. For many, this brought on a state of flux and incertitude, a lack of clear identity as church, as priests, as religious, even as lay persons—a loss of old moorings and horizons. This went hand in hand with a period of protest against all authority—we remember 1968—which in church circles was described with the French term—"contestation." Council renovation was not easy. It took a decade or more to combine tradition and renewal into a dynamic whole.

In 1977 a group of bishops from Latin America were called together by CELAM, and it was proposed that we hold another conference ten years after Medellín, in 1978, to discern and guide the process of church renewal in Latin America. Rome approved, and the preparations got under way. It was actually held in 1979, after the deaths of Paul VI and John Paul I. After John Paul II was elected, one of his first major acts as pope was to come to Mexico to inaugurate the Third General Conference of Latin American Bishops at Puebla.

The preparation for this general conference was remarkable. Throughout 1977 an inquiry went out to the Bishops Conference of Latin America. Delegates of these conferences met twice, in five separate regional meetings. Five bishops, one from each of the five regions of Latin America, acted as a central committee. With the assistance of specialists they drew up a working document on the basis of the reports from the twenty-three bishops' conference and the five regional reports. This first working document was rather defensive, wary of some church situations in Latin America.

In 1978 we had another round of consultations. The steering committee sent this same document out. The bishops' conference sent it on to every parish, to thousands and thousands of church communities, the base groups and the many apostolic, social, and prayer groups of the church. A few months later the reports started coming in, from all these groups, through the bishops. They gave a stronger, more sure point of view. The people expressed great confidence in their church. There was evident growth in the Scriptures, in the life of communities, in sacramental life, in local vocations—lay, religious, and priestly—in social awareness and commitment, as Christians. We went into the General Conference of Bishops, at Puebla, confident that we were speaking for our church, thanks to the broad-based consultation we had carried out, perhaps the largest ever held in Latin America. As a result, Puebla is a faithful presentation of the renovated church of the Council as it is being lived in Latin America.

First, its theme is, "A liberating evangelization for communion and participation in the church and in the world." It is a jargon we must translate. *Liberating evangelization* means not only evangelizing, not only preaching the Gospel, but a Gospel that liberates, intends to bring people into communion and participation in the church and as citizens of the world in their communities. This should be the projection of the Gospel: spiritual and social.

This liberalization is basically a liberating or freeing from the sin that is in all of us. It places first emphasis upon personal conversion. Even though the books of sociology and certain ideological schools may tell us that changing structures changes people, we hold the opposite: it is people who make structures. Without new men, there will be no new structures. Without new

130

men and women, the structures of the continent cannot be renovated.

I talk to Cubans, in Cuba, and they tell me that the new man, the new Marxist man, that was supposed to come about as a result of Socialist structures in Cuba, has yet to be found. There are as much corruption, lying, and vice as before. Unless the man is changed, we cannot expect him to work for better and more just human relations and structures.

The thrust of Puebla is the work of "evangelizing," that is, announcing the Gospel, and living it, in the church, and in the world. This means growing lay participation in the life of the church, particularly on the popular levels, and a freer church, separate from and independent of the traditional power centers—political, economic, and military. It stresses more active participation of laity in the church, especially through the formation of small church communities. As individuals and as communities in the world, we share fully the task of promoting human development and the formation of social awareness and conscience for this task. Puebla stresses anew the necessity for living the basic Gospel option for the poor in our Latin American situation. This is not something we have invented; this is Christ. One of the most quoted texts in Puebla is that of the Gospel of St. Matthew, chapter 25, verse 40: "And the King will answer them, 'Truly, I say to you, as you did it to one of the least of these my brethren, you did it to me."

It is simply the Gospel: finding Christ in our suffering brethren. This commitment must be projected beyond the individual poor, whom we must assist, to a consideration of the structures that bring about, prolong, and intensify poverty. This brings us to our responsibilities and an insistence upon sin, personal sin and social sin, and the structures that prolong and intensify the injustices that our sins bring about.

I think all of us who are interested in reflecting upon the living of our faith in the world today will want to have those instruments for that reflection.[1]

Puebla Document: See, Judge, Act

The Puebla document develops itself in three parts, the "see, judge, and act" or the pastoral vision, reflection, and action. We do not look at things as though we were looking at them for the first time; we look at them with the eyes of faith. As we look at Latin America, we find that the crucial human problem in Latin America today is poverty. Our role as pastors or as religious leaders is to preach the Gospel and to live the Gospel; but the living of the Gospel is seriously impeded by the frequency and intensity of poverty among our people—particularly, as the text points out, because that poverty could be overcome and is not being overcome.

In 1979, this was the concerted opinion of the many economists that we consulted along with other experts.

There was lacking a clear political (and moral) will to fight to overcome poverty. Worse, the gap between the rich and the poor already scandalously great as compared, for example, with the United States, widens yearly. Careful studies by the United Nations Economic Commission for Latin America renovation was not easy. It took a decade or more to combine tradition and renewal into a dynamic whole.

We have had great social progress, great economic progress in the decades of the 1950s, 1960s, and 1970s. The present debt problem is holding everything in suspense, as we know. Withal, the development of Latin America in the past generation has been astounding, but it has been a one-sided development: it has not been an integrated development embracing all our people.

A report of the United Nations Economic Commission for Latin America calculates how much of the national budget in each of our countries would have to be invested every year, so that in a ten-year period the gap could be closed. Of course, it is not so simple, as many of us who have worked in social areas know. Economic progress cannot be bought. Somehow, however, the UN analysts tried to calculate what investment would be required; the sum is well within the capacity of our countries, particularly with more international understanding.

The Puebla document passes on to a doctrinal reflection and judgment of this situation. We have the tripod, the truth about Jesus Christ, about the church, and about man. Then the discussion of what we mean by evangelization and how it should be carried out. This brings up the whole question of evangelization and culture; evangelization, religious feelings, and popular expressions of the people; and evangelization and human promotion—how to understand the intimate connection between the Gospel and social questions in the temporal order. There, Puebla restates the meaning of the social teaching of the church. I think it is admirably done. The statement is a real contribution of the church in Latin America to the thinking of the universal church. It is the best statement we have yet. It takes advantage of many other statements of the universal church, particularly the 1971 Vatican Synod in that intervening period.

Finally, the document addresses the relationship of ideology and politics. Ideology as presented in the Puebla document is the particular explanation of social realities from the point of view of a specific, interested group. Normally, political parties have their ideologies. Normally, any professional group has a certain ideology, and this is good. It is a kind of platform in which groups express their values, their views, and their recommendations for action.

The problems with ideologies begin when they become absolute and when a particular ideology excludes all other ideologies or interpretations or pretends to cover the whole area of explanation. This cannot be. It would mean only one political party, only one economic model, only one social model. Puebla calls these false absolutes "idols." Only God is absolute. There are "false gods" that would justify themselves alone and above all else. The ideology of national security becomes "a false god" in Latin America, when governments say that to preserve themselves in power they can justify recourse to arbitrary imprisonment, torture, or murder. This would turn the government into God. Also, Puebla reminds us, the state is not the government alone. The state is the government and the people and their territory. Security must be ensured for the people and the national boundaries as well, not simply for the government.

Marxism and some forms of capitalism, Puebla points out, become absolute ideologies, which pretend to be above human rights or the criticism of other points of view.

In Puebla, the church insists a great deal upon the fact that in its evangelizing labors, when it stresses human rights and human and social values, it does not identify itself with any ideology nor with any socioeconomic or political party or program. Its role has to be above them and therefore ideologues cannot claim to be the expression of the church, nor can they preempt or attempt to sway the expression of her religious faith.

The third part of Puebla is the numerous pastoral projections. Then follow the priority areas for these projections: *the poor, the young, the constructors of the pluralist society,* and then finally *the international order.* Puebla concludes with an insistence upon a plan, pedagogy, and method for working out in each country this plan of integral evangelization. Fourteen years after the Council in 1979, we were aware that pedagogy requires pastoral planning and coordination. In fact, things in the church of Latin America are settling down. There is now overall a pattern of development in a renovated church. This has come slowly. On October 11, 1984, we will celebrate twenty-two years since the beginning of the Second Vatican Council.

Puebla and Liberation

One point of great interest to us is the church's position regarding the theology of liberation. The doctrine of Puebla is a "liberation document." The term "liberation" came into wide general use throughout Latin America when the former term "development" appeared to many inadequate. Pope Paul VI coined the expression, "Development is the modern word for peace."

In Latin America, however, development (or *disarrollo*), as used by the international organizations, came to signify merely technological development, with very little insistence on the human and social condition, the better distribution of the fruits of development and the growth of national product, or the incorporation of the marginal elements of society. This narrow application created a rejection of the term by some socially interested groups that looked for a new term, a broader term that could involve simultaneously the religious

133

and the social dimensions. "Liberation" thus came into use.

Liberation is frequently used in the text of Puebla. Nowhere, however, does Puebla mention the "theology of liberation," because there is no one theology of liberation: there are many theologies. Some of them we would absolutely reject; others we feel are a valid expression of the Puebla document and of scriptural and church doctrine.

The basis of liberation theology is its method—a religious reflection developed from the reality we live in, seen with the eyes of faith. We look upon this reality, we see the problems and values involved, and we project our reflection into our pastoral action. The basis of liberation theology is a strong awareness of poverty in our area, the fruit of social injustice that must be overcome. Social injustice is a state of social sin that we must overcome, as stated in the Puebla document. This is part of the church's attitude toward the problems of Latin America.

Some "liberationists" would pretend to include in their pastoral vision an interpretation that is ideological. Facts, of course, can be interpreted in many different ways, and we are all free to discuss interpretations of causes and solutions. When a person interprets a fact ideologically and tries to make that absolute and final, then we find it very hard to discuss matters any further.

Dependency theory is a good example. There is the *fact* of dependency that no one can deny. Various *interpretations* of dependency, however, may be questioned and discussed. Some ideological interpretations may convince one person but not another. In the same way, we talk about poverty in Latin America: it is a fact. Social injustices are also facts.

The problem with one school of liberation theology is that it has accepted the Marxist analysis as scientific. Adherents of this theology accept Marxist social analysis because, they claim, it has been proven to be "scientific." They do reject Marxist metaphysics, however, because it is atheistic.

There is no such thing as economic science, we answer, and particularly no *a priori science,* which pretends to be part of the very reality under discussion. It would be begging the question. In a recent volume of essays edited by Michael Novak, there is a very sensitive and sympathetic criticism of Gustavo Gutierrez, considered the first principal liberation theologian, which points out some of these ambiguities.[2]

As I see it, however, the problem is methodological. It amounts to including in a supposedly "objective" view of reality a given ideological interpretation, even before introducing the Gospel, and the light of faith. What happens, then, is that elements of faith are criticized on the basis of the accepted ideology and cut to its size. Ideology judges faith, which is the reverse of good and valid theological method, in which faith must judge ideology.[3]

This brings about another consequence. The theology of liberation schools that employ Marxist analysis speak of one sole history, secular and salvational. In this view they tend to identify the kingdom of God with the temporal order. Never is that identification made in the Scriptures; never is that stated as the Catholic position. The kingdom of God is coming; it is here; but it is to come in its fullness only at the end of time. No single political, socioeconomic structure can ever equate itself with the kingdom of God because human institutions are so full of human imperfection.

The Church's View of Social and International Reality

The church's view of social and international reality is a rather uniform view of things. Some people set Cardinal Obando y Bravo, of Managua, against Cardinal Raúl Silva of Chile. They hold exactly the same doctrinal and social positions, but they are in very different situations. Therefore, what they say sounds different. Cardinal Obando, who is vigorously protesting the repression of human social rights under the Sandinista regime, is pictured to a rather ingenuous audience in Western Europe and North America as a conservative defender of vested rights of the oligarchy, which is not at all true. He was one of the first to take strong positions against Somoza, to give strong moral authority to the movement to overthrow his regime. Now he is simply trying to continue his defense of human rights under a new regime, that of the Sandinistas.

It is what Cardinal Silva has had to do in Chile. He is no radical. I know him very well. He is a wonderful man, who is basically a conservative. He was forced, however, to set up a commission on human rights, which he called "Vicariate of Solidarity," to defend the people who were being "disappeared," as they say—who were jailed, tortured, killed, and secretly buried. He set up a very elaborate scheme for the whole of Chile to carry out a constant investigation of all those who disappeared and to support their families through soup kitchens all around the country. Although this became the great thorn in the side of the Pinochet regime, it had to be done simply in respect of basic human rights. We cannot allow people to be snatched off the streets, tortured and killed and allowed just to disappear, without saying something about it.

Here are two cases. The two Archbishops have very different personalities, but they hold the same principles. Cardinal Silva is a Chilean of Spanish descent. Archbishop Obando is a Nicaraguan of Spanish and Indian descent. They differ in that sense and in the color of their skins, but they hold to a renovated Conciliar and Puebla position, based on the Gospel, for human rights. Certainly it is a liberation position—a liberation that is personal and then social, a liberation that is striving to make the presence of the church felt in the building of a better world. This liberation asserts that the great construction of the world that God has placed in our hands is not skyscrapers or technological advances, all of which we must bring about and put to the service of mankind, rather it is the building of human community. This human community is the preparation for the world to come: the living of love, which is the great commandment of the Scriptures; the great commandment of our Lord, to be built and developed personally and socially. This is the meaning of the church's presence in society.

For us this means an option for the poor, not exclusive but *preferential.* We have to work with all members of society, and this option is to be shared by all of us. If there is injustice, then by opting for the poor, we also save those who perpetuate that injustice, because we are bringing about a betterment of their own situation and they themselves are saved. And they themselves are living the kingdom which we should live.

The building of community involves sharing. I think this idea of sharing in solidarity, the sharing that occurred in the early Christian communities, is a very simple notion, but one that extends to all levels of society and to all kinds of problems.

Many, perhaps, have heard Barbara Ward speak. It was always a thrilling experience to hear her. As she spoke about the poor in the world, she stressed the necessity of going beyond our frontiers to be genuinely humane people, universally human and catholic in our love for all people. We had overcome our problems of inequities within our individual frontiers, she would say, because of movements for justice, because of taxation, and because of social controls. Something similar, she says, has to be developed worldwide. Christians should think and feel along these lines.

Nonetheless, we have to be shocked by the fact that it is specifically the Western, more Christian areas of the world—so exaggeratedly ahead of the rest in the possession and use of material goods—that show little interest in effective approaches to softening the gap.

There is not only a gap here, but also a real dependency of the poorer upon the richer nations in most of their economic decisions. Added to these questions of international scope are our many internal problems: polarization, violence, corruption, inefficiency, military intervention, and lack of integral democratic process. These problems make us weaker, too, in facing the international dilemmas. Moreover, to this is added the lack of unity between our countries vis-à-vis our relations with North America, Europe, and Japan. In fact, much energy and precious funds are spent on costly rivalries: between Ecuador and Peru, or Chile and Argentina, or, most sadly, in the Central American conflicts.

The bishops of Latin America have spoken out frequently and strongly on internal issues of justice and human rights but have said very little about international rights or the structural causes of what we might call international injustice. Most of what we have said in this area, even in Medellín and Puebla, is taken from papal documents, including the great social encyclicals of recent popes. We have an awareness, a sense that the international structures weigh upon us and impede the full development of our people. We have not, however, given the matter full attention. This is a very serious void, which must be attended to.

On the whole, the bishops in Latin America do not support any economic model as such. Within their countries, they are certainly more inclined to reform capitalism. Very few are inclined, properly speaking, to socialism and certainly not to Marxism.

The church in Latin America should be more involved on the international level. Occasionally, I am called to these gatherings because I speak English, because I have contacts in the United States, or because I am from Notre Dame. We need more contacts of this kind. When the bishops in the United States develop a document on the economic order, particularly in what touches on the international sphere, they should have some input from the Latin American churches and from the European churches. If we can set up a broader dialogue, we can help ourselves a great deal and think creatively together, as Christians.

Finally, my impression is that although the church has criticisms of multinationals, most of the criticisms are really questions. We have the impression that the multinationals are creating or furthering an international economy within our countries, which offers a higher wage scale but does not integrate fully into the local economy, therefore tending to increase the contrast between the rich and the poor.

Some believe that the multinationals do not look beyond their own operations, toward the integral development of the third world countries, a logical but unsatisfactory viewpoint.

These matters, however, are discussed in greater detail by other contributors.

Notes

1. The Medellín documents (1968) and the Puebla document (1979) may be obtained in English from the National Conference of Catholic Bishops, 1312 Massachusetts Ave., N.W., Washington, D.C. 20005.

2. Joseph Ramos, "Reflections on Gustavo Gutiérrez's Theology of Liberation," in Michael Novak, ed., *Liberation South, Liberation North* (Washington, D.C.: American Enterprise Institute, 1981), pp. 50–60.

3. The Instruction of the Sacred Congregation of Doctrine of the Faith, in the Vatican, on "Liberation Theology," made public on September 3, 1984, asserts the church's views in this vein and at length.

Discussion

QUESTION: Although you mentioned many issues in your presentation, the question of population was noticeably absent. How can economic development take place with population growth like Latin America's? It seems impossible for almost any economic system to meet that need. Isn't there something that the church as well as concerned laymen should be doing toward assuming responsibility for population? I think it was only recently that my ancestors found out that you could get to heaven by having only one or two children instead of twelve. And I wonder if it is not something that we ought to be focusing on there.

Second is the question of individual industry. With so much emphasis on sharing, it was only recently that some of us learned that we could undertake and pursue a life of personal industry, leading to expanded employment, and still get through the eye of a needle. We only recently learned that building a business, employing people, and trying to conduct our business fairly were acceptable in the eyes of the church and in the eyes of God. Before, these activities may not have been thought worthy because the concept of sharing led away from husbanding resources and employing those resources for a business.

Your comment about reforming capitalism makes me suspicious that the American bishops will speak to the American population and the American business community not to praise the virtues of capitalism, but to raise our consciousness. Their cautions could then be taken out of the historical context in which they were delivered.

Could you address those issues further?

ARCHBISHOP MCGRATH: The question of population growth is obviously difficult, given the church's position on artificial means of birth control and, more particularly, on sterilization and abortion.

We have a problem in Latin America because many times the aid given to our countries by the U.S. government through the Agency for International Development also supplies the means of artificial birth control and sterilizations. For example, one of our pastors recently received food through AID, which also mistakenly sent him a whole carton of artificial birth control instruments. He sent it back with a little note. In those areas of Latin America where artificial means of birth control have been pushed, they have been strongly rejected as a cultural imposition and as an imposition upon the rights of the people.

The population growth in many of our countries has nevertheless declined considerably. In Panama the annual natural increase in the population has declined from 2.9 percent to about 1.9 percent, which reflects a considerable slowdown in the birth rate.

Recently, some of our Holy Cross fathers met in Panama for our thirty-fifth anniversary of priesthood. One of them has worked for many years in Bangladesh, which is just slightly larger than the area of Panama but with less inhabitable land because about one-third is under water. Panama, however, has 2 million people, while Bangladesh has 101 million people. As he looked out the window of the airplane, he said, "Where are the people? I see no houses; nobody is here. You've got plenty of room for expansion."

We are not overpopulated yet. I have seen the situation in Bangladesh. The church is stressing responsible parenthood, introducing family planning and clinics for natural family planning.

The church in Latin America is also increasing its understanding of these problems. As a matter of fact, our major problem in Central America and other culturally underdeveloped countries is the number of children born out of wedlock. If we solve that problem and have not only family planning, but families, we will overcome the major problem of birth increase. We will have solved the problem of children who are not cared for, who start with a strike against them, who do not have the support of economic, cultural, or spiritual formation.

To address your question of the individual in industry, I would say that in our evangelization we stress personal responsibility in the social order and the person before the structures, man before economy. The man must be honest before an administration can be honest.

If this concept is extended through a broad process of evangelization, through the formation of community groups among the *campesinos* and the workers and in the middle-class areas, it will have a strong effect. The idea of personal responsibility brings about a different approach to the social question, evoking particularly a willingness to solve one's own problems.

General Omar Torrijos, who ran our country for a good while until he died in an airplane crash, created a certain sense of dignity for the poor, but he was also a give-away person. He created paternalistic expectations, which are very difficult to overcome. We have to strive for people to do the best they can themselves in communities. Sometimes people tell us, for example, that they do not have any school in their community. They have the land; the government will give them the materials. We say, why don't you build it yourselves?

Put in your weekends working on it. Put up some schoolrooms.

This can be done. The approach that emphasizes the rewards of personal industry is very much a part of the kind of personal change that evangelization could bring about.

COMMENT: I was very heartened by the emphasis you placed on democratic institutions and also by that which you placed—more sotto voce—on reformed capitalist institutions.

I notice in your remarks and typically in church documents, however, a hesitancy to move in this direction. It seems to me, though, that there is an embarrassment about it, an embarrassment that comes from certain lacunae in Catholic social thought over the last 150 years. Some issues are not addressed, and some experiments have not been accounted for within it.

First, I think poverty is not so good a focus as the creation of wealth for the poor. Creation seems the theological category that best matches the cultures that have created wealth, which have led to that exaggerated distance between rich and poor countries. If we think in terms of creation, we will see the importance of institutions. Certain institutions bring about development for poor people. The challenge for Catholic thought is to learn how to identify and promote such institutions.

Second, the metaphor of liberation is actually the wrong metaphor because it has built within it assumptions of oppression. Because "liberation" carries the germ of oppression, those who adopt liberation as the true metaphor are thereby implicated in its opposite. The metaphor suggests that people are poor because they are oppressed, rather than because poverty is the natural state of humankind.

On my second point, one reason we are embarrassed to say that we are in favor of reformed Catholic institutions has to do with the misreading that Catholic church documents have given to the liberal tradition. Pope John Paul II in *Laborem Exercens* attributes to early capitalism some beliefs that he would probably be hard pressed to identify in any single liberal writing. There really has not been a full-dress treatment of that liberal tradition. These thinkers were not materialists. They were not guilty of economism in the sense attributed to them.

In addition, attention to the building of institutions that do work to liberate human beings both economically and politically is missing in the church documents. The institutions of religious liberty were overlooked, as I mentioned, but also the importance of patent laws, encouragement of invention, and so forth, have been ignored.

In 1800, according to Oscar Handlin, there were only about 5 million people in the United States, yet there were already more business corporations than in all of Europe. It is possible to create an environment that supports a multiplicity of small enterprises, which hire the vast majority of people.

Even in the United States the major corporations employ only 16 million out of a work force of 107 million; the vast number of Americans work in small enterprises. Catholic teaching contains very little encouragement of the vocation of building businesses. When I talk in Latin America, I am always reminded of just how guilty businessmen feel about being businessmen. They get no cultural support.

I think it would be extraordinarily helpful for the Catholic church to support a set of institutional arrangements that stimulate small business. It is crucial for Latin America.

GUILLERMO CHAPMAN: My comments concern liberation and oppression. First, oppression in Latin America is not a problem of the multinationals' oppressing the people, but the overall setup in many of these countries is very oppressive. Some countries have rigged cost-of-living statistics to allow wage adjustments below the increase in the cost of living, so that real wages could decrease and make it easier for business to function. Moreover, in the banking structures of many Latin American countries there is an incredible concentration of economic power. In those institutions, then, there is oppression, with good cause to call for liberation.

Defining liberation is problematic. Some people interpret "liberation" as aimed strictly against the multinationals. I use neither "oppression" nor "liberation" that way, but rely on the overall context.

Another problem arises with oppression. Probably the people at the bottom of the social scale are those who are not oppressed by anybody but are poor because they do not participate in the market economy. They are not employed by anybody. Nobody pays them even misery wages. Because they do not participate, they have a very low income and exist in extreme poverty. The problem, then, is not oppression or liberation: it is a lack of participation, of not being integrated into the modern economy. This problem of liberation has many nuances that we have to take into account.

On another point, I agree that Catholic social teaching does not encourage the formation of business, which is a key economic function. We have to perform this function. That point is well taken, and I would like for us to expand it.

QUESTION: A few years ago when Cardinal Arns of São Paulo was interviewed, he questioned the whole concept of Western-style development, because the results were urbanization and materialism. He seemed to support a return to a more rural, agricultural society, the small-is-beautiful approach.

How widespread is that feeling among Latin American bishops, and how does it affect the development process?

ARCHBISHOP MCGRATH: As Archbishop of São Paulo, a city that increases every year by 400,000 new inhabitants, he might very well speak that way. The conditions are really impossible, almost as bad as those in Mexico City. The growth of these cities, the flood of people away from the land, and the lack of facilities in the countryside and on the outskirts of cities have created a monstrous problem.

I cannot interpret his remarks because I was unaware of them. Although I know him well, I do not know his thinking on that particular point. As for me, I do not see a general move in that direction.

As for the question of participation in the economic process, it is reflected in various ways in our documents. Michael Novak is correct to say that the church does not have an adequate terminology to discuss this issue. Even the pope is a little embarrassed when he talks about these questions. He does not talk about "communism," for instance; he talks about "social collectivism" by which he means communism. When he talks about "liberal capitalism," he uses different terms. He uses "capitalism" or "pure capitalism." In Latin America "capitalism" is not often used because it is used there rather demagogically, in political contexts. To use it in religious texts, then, can be misleading. In Latin America "liberal" means something quite different from what it does in the United States. When we talk about social development in the Medellín document, for instance, we use the expressions "underdevelopment" and "development" and we use "marginal" and sometimes "the facts of dependency." But I see no single developed position of the church in Latin America. Instead, I see different tendencies and different positions, but no official church position.

COMMENT: Please comment on the concept of entrepreneurial development which seems to have gained fairly widespread acceptance.

ARCHBISHOP MCGRATH: In our part of the world I foresee a great interest in promoting small agro-industrial concerns. Recently, Guillermo Chapman and I have been instrumental in setting up a foundation in Panama with Swiss money. A very fine Protestant family with $1.5 million to lend wanted to operate in some part of Central America; they contacted me and arranged with the Catholic church in Panama to lend to small producers, farmers, shopkeepers, and the like who cannot get bank loans because the amounts they need are so small. That sort of program is very attractive.

QUESTION: In the context of liberation theology, I was surprised that you would specifically name Gustavo Gutierrez as one who exemplifies what is really objectionable in liberation theology. Can we draw you out a bit more about the debate on liberation theology?

Second, could you comment on the process of the formation of the consensus at Puebla?

ARCHBISHOP MCGRATH: About your first question, regarding Gustavo Gutierrez, I know him very well and have for many years. He is without doubt a very good, spiritual priest, very dedicated, very loyal to the church.

In his famous book published in 1973, *A Theology of Liberation*, he makes the statement that liberation theology is not a question of a new theology, but a new way of doing theology. This is the heart of the problem: theological reflection should begin by examining reality with the light of faith. He, however, already includes in his view of reality elements of Marxist analysis. He tends to include a political option and implies that without a political option there is no mediation of the faith. He does not say so explicitly, but the implication is there. Many of his followers, like Raúl Vidales, the Mexican, have expanded his ideas into an option for Marxist class conflict and the use of violence.

Another example is the great theologian Jon Sobrino, writing in El Salvador, who is most orthodox in his personal life and in his own faith. His theological writings throw out hypotheses that others have picked up and applied. He is probably responsible for what we call *la iglesia popular* (the popular church), and many Christians have followed that line of reasoning as far as it will go.

It is somewhat like putting medicine on the market before it has been tried: that is one of the problems with theology today. Theologians used to debate these things among themselves; now they present their ideas on the front page of the newspapers, and people without a grasp of the whole theological context will apply them in ways that can be dangerous to faith and to the church.

Your next question concerned the method of writing the Puebla document. The method for the Puebla document was quite different from the process the U.S. bishops use in writing their major pastoral letters. The U.S. bishops invite in experts on a subject, listen to them, and then work their opinions into the document. The draft document is circulated publicly, and criticism invited.

What was done for Puebla was done in two phases. In January 1977 we met in five areas of Latin America; not all were bishops, but each country sent representatives. We listed what we thought would be the important points for meeting ten years after Medellín. Out of that list came a working document, which was then sent back to the local churches. The bishops made copies and sent them to all the parishes and all the movements, and then they went to the grass-roots groups and base communities.

This document was the basis of discussion for 1978. All the groups gave their opinions or their reports. It was publicly handled. These ideas went into the bishops' conferences. Then each conference of bishops made up its full report, all of which were voluminous. All of these reports went into a final working document, which was sent back to all of us and to the base groups before we went to the meeting in January 1979.

When we got to the meeting in Puebla, we did not use any of these documents. That is where the difference lies. These were all preparatory documents. We then set up commissions. Cardinal Lorscheider proposed the pattern of the one document we would publish, based upon the previous text. Then a steering committee of five was elected, on which I was selected for membership.

We worked all through the night to receive and incorporate into the outline suggestions made by the bishops. We presented an outline of the working document the next morning. We divided ourselves into commissions and went to work on it. In two weeks we edited this document. What each of us had was about fifteen volumes of reports and suggestions from all the base groups, parishes, and bishops' conferences from around Latin America. That is the difference in method. I find a certain value in each of the two different methods.

The text relevant to your question regarding social teaching is this, section 472 in the Puebla document:

> The contribution of the Church to liberation and human promotion has gradually been taking shape in a series of doctrinal guidelines and criteria for action that we are now accustomed to call "the social teaching of the Church." These teachings have their source in Sacred Scripture, in the teachings of the Fathers and major theologians of the Church, and in the magisterium (particularly that of the most recent popes). As is evident from their origin, they contain permanently valid elements . . .

This is where the distinction comes in:

> . . . [elements] that are grounded in an anthropology that derives from the message of Christ and in the perennial values of Christian ethics. But they also contain changing elements that correspond to the particular conditions of each country and each epoch.

Then the document describes how we put this together:

> Following Paul VI, we can formulate the matter this way: attentive to the signs of time, which are interpreted in the light of the Gospel and the Church's magisterium, the whole Christian community is called upon to assume responsibility for concrete options and their effective implementation in order to respond to the summons presented by changing circumstances. Thus these social teachings possess a dynamic character. In their elaboration and application lay people are not to be passive executors but rather active collaborators with their pastors, contributing their experience as Christians and their professional, scientific competence.

Clearly, then, it is the whole Christian community, in communion with its legitimate pastors and guided by them, that is the responsible subject of evangelization, liberation, and human promotion.

This passage is the best succinct formulation on the social teaching of the church that I know.

QUESTION: Do you have any advice for us in North America so that we can tackle what I consider to be the gravest problem facing us: the scarcity of priests?

ARCHBISHOP MCGRATH: One obvious positive response is what we call pastoral vocational work: promoting the image of the priest, along with all of the spiritual motivation and the prayer.

Our Lord says if there are not enough laborers for the harvest, pray to the Father that He send them. We feel the vocation comes from God, but we have to let it be known, of course. Over the past seven years, almost since Puebla, we have experienced a great increase in vocations to the seminary in Latin America. A few weeks ago I was in a seminary that had never had more than sixty seminarians; it now has 130 seminarians. In Panama it has been the same; in fact, we had to put up a new building. That phenomenon is occurring all over Latin America and in some parts of the United States.

While we are increasing our seminarians, we also have to see that the church becomes more and more corporate in its attitude toward participation of the laity; this encouragement of lay participation is here to stay and will intensify.

I see the distance between laity and clergy shrinking. Much that priests had to do before the laity can do just as well. For the first time, the administrator of an archdiocese can be a lay person. Before, he had to be a priest. Why? The chancellor can be a lay person, man or woman; it always had to be a priest before. These changes are opening up new areas, and I think this is very healthy. In Latin America we are promoting lay ministers and married deacons a great deal. Moreover, a large sector of the church in Latin America would like to see married priests—not that they would like to see priests who are entering the seminary marry. But they would allow older people who are married and have families to be ordained to the priesthood, which is quite a different concept.

If we took a poll of the bishops—certainly in Brazil—a majority would like to permit married priests but would not want to abandon the celibacy of the clergy as the normal standard.

QUESTION: In the United States small is not necessarily beautiful, but small is very effective. Small companies today are creating more new jobs than the big companies are. More than half the major inventions that resulted in new industries in the past twenty years have come from either individuals or small companies. I have written a book about this phenomenon and can talk about it at great length.

Is anything being done in Latin America to create the atmosphere in which people can become creative in small companies? What kind of atmosphere makes people comfortable, encourages them to create, and assures them that if they do create, something will come of it?

A new idea is one of the most unusual things that ever happens. It's also one of the most creative, most important, and most valuable. New ideas cause revolutions, not just social revolutions but industrial revolutions. Our own country provides many examples. It does not take much to stimulate individuals to invent. What is being done in the underdeveloped countries to make it possible for people to create?

MR. CHAPMAN: I do not have an overall view of what is being done in Latin America. In general, to be effective these things have to come from the bottom up. It is very difficult to detect them until after they have been successful. Maybe many of these initiatives are in progress at this moment. I hope there are many we are not aware of. I do know of a few.

An institute in Colombia, for example, works very closely with the University of the Andes. For many years now scientists and professors have been working to develop simple technology for harnassing small creeks to generate electricity. That power would then be used for simple machinery for very light industry in the rural areas. This research is beginning to have an impact in Colombia and beyond. The whole concept is similar to the foundation, mentioned by the archbishop, which was established in Panama with money from a Swiss family.

It resembles somewhat Russell Marks's description of what Accion International is doing, but with some differences. If I understood what he said, Accion is subsidizing interest rates. We have taken the position that just allowing the very small entrepreneur access to the formal trade market is a subsidy in itself. If he can pay 17 percent, which is the normal commercial rate of interest in Panama now, he is much better off than paying 180 percent, which is the equivalent rate of interest through informal credit mechanisms which exist in my country and all over Latin America. It is not necessary to subsidize the rate of interest, only to allow the small entrepreneur access to 17 percent credit. The foundation guarantees part of the loan to a commercial bank. The bank has to share the risk. There are probably many initiatives like that; I know of some in the Dominican Republic, as well as in parts of Central America.

ARCHBISHOP MCGRATH: One step forward is the increase in vocational schools, shopwork, and the like, so that the mid-level technologist is becoming much more available. In the past many people could be hired to carry the bricks, but nobody to lay the mortar. Now it's beginning to work out better.

QUESTION: Latin America now has many excellent scientists and technologists. When a professor of physiology gets a Nobel Prize for discovering the mechanism of action of insulin in a pancreatic cell, however, his $150,000 does not feed very many people, except his own family, of course. Over the years I have not sensed an atmosphere that encourages creative individuals to want to become entrepreneurs.

ARCHBISHOP MCGRATH: In Panama, probably typical of the rest of Latin America, the national economy employs 85 percent of our population, creating a job for every $10,000 or $12,000 invested. The international economy, which includes banking, creates a job for every half million dollars invested. Therefore, it is the smaller enterprise that employs our people, stimulates production, provides income, and makes possible development.

QUESTION: Archbishop, I was struck by your emphasis on the Scripture as a new factor in the renovated life of the church in Latin America.

You seem to juxtapose Scripture and reading of Scripture to what you called the natural law, which we might call critical reason or prudential judgment. I am uncomfortable with the implication that an unmediated reading of Scripture can occur, that one can come to it without a set of intellectual filters in place. If there has been one clear teaching from the great and welcome renaissance of Catholic biblical scholarship in the past forty years, it is that no such thing is possible and that the attempt to do it is at least one contributing factor to the disingenuous view of some social realities that you describe.

We have seen this somewhat in American Catholicism over the past three years. In the process leading up to bishops' pastoral letter on war and peace, one often found oneself in conversation with very well-intended, highly motivated people who really believed that one can draw a direct-line conclusion from the Sermon on the Mount to U.S. foreign policy. I'm not exaggerating. I have heard that idea put in precisely those terms at all levels of the church, from archbishops on down.

Given the importance of the base communities in the renovation of the church in Latin America and given no one's wish to go back to a purely propositional Catholicism but to bring the richness of the Scripture into the full life of the church, the evangelization in all its aspects—how do you reconnect Scripture to critical reason? How do you educate these base communities so that the possible distortions of an unmediated approach to Scripture can be handled, so that the ideologization problem is resolved, and so that the Scripture becomes a meeting point for people of good will to think about a

147

religious response to social reality, rather than a partisan instrument used to bless preconceived political agendas?

ARCHBISHOP MCGRATH: First, we must understand that Scripture, while an inspired revelation, comes to us through human office. The literary genius of each of the scriptural texts has to be part of our formation. As we educate our pastoral agents, our delegates of the Word, they receive quite a bit of this formation, so that they do not have a superstitious approach to Scripture, believing that every word is somehow magical. The revelation of God comes through these inspired books, but inspiration comes through human messengers. Scriptures have to be understood in their human context. The book of Genesis, for instance, is not giving us a scientific explanation of the creation of the world. This is part of the basic approach.

Second, formation should grow out of Scripture, so that in our liturgy—whether the Mass or the liturgy of the Word with no priest present—the person who comments on scriptural readings should know them in the context of the Bible. Ideologues use Scripture as a hook to promote whatever they want to promote on a particular occasion. In preparing sermons, then, a priest must avoid this error.

There are two ways of approaching Christian base groups in peripheral communities of a city or in a rural area. We can bring in a problem off the streets: what can we do, for example, about the lack of transportation? There are no buses. A person has to get up at 3 or 4 a.m. to get a bus. We have to protest. We can bring this protest in and then find a scriptural text to back it up, which is a backwards approach. Using Scripture in this way puts it in a very relative and manipulated role, not that this sort of problem is outside scriptural concerns.

Approaching the Scripture responsibly, does not mean that one simply cannot find scriptural formulas for all social problems, least of all international political problems. We will find, however, the basic attitudes toward man and toward life there.

As for a natural law, I certainly believe in a natural law and in the utility of the natural law for explaining things in a moral context. For us, though, revelation is much more than the natural law. The Gospel, the Beatitudes, and the sermon of our Lord at the Last Supper contain truths far more profound than what we can establish by reasoning from natural law. Therefore, our social teaching goes beyond the natural law. It certainly includes natural law. The doctrine of love, which is the heart of Christ's message, however, is much more than natural law.

QUESTION: Would you say more about what should be done regarding questions of international justice and injustice?

American businesses are concerned not only with their own interests but also with operating justly in host countries. Yet many Latin Americans claim that paying higher wages widens the gap between rich and poor, and therefore they argue against the higher wages. The companies are caught in a bind: they are not allowed to operate in the most efficient way because it differs from how some of the local corporations operate. What guidance can the church give on this issue?

ARCHBISHOP MCGRATH: Stating that sometimes multinationals contribute to a double wage scale, paying higher wages than the local economy for the same kind of work, does not necessarily lead me to conclude that they should pay less. It is simply a statement of fact. The consequences of a double wage scale should at least be considered.

We bishops in Latin America have concentrated very much on our pastoral jobs in our own dioceses, in our own countries. Through our observations, discussions, and participation, we have developed a real awareness of the problems of our people. The church is very close to the people in Latin America; the pastors, the bishops, and the priests have a special affinity with the poor because they need the most assistance and the most presence. Therefore, the problems on a local level are much better understood.

Some excellent documents are coming out from bishops all through Latin America that are helping to create a Christian awareness and participation. For a time some of the richer people and professionals, the business managers and so forth, felt that the church was neglecting them. I got that criticism from many of my friends, and I think it was partly true. What we have been trying to do, however, is to incorporate them with us into the overall pattern. They are not being neglected religiously because all kinds of spiritual movements are open to them. But perhaps we have neglected to address their professional obligations in a Christian context.

In the past several years an awareness of this need has grown, and we have seen a reaching out to create centers of dialogue and promotion on all levels so that we can incorporate the professionals and the managers into the process of consideration of Christian presence in the social order.

We are still far from reaching much adequate reflection on the international order, as you point out. As a member of the organizing committee at Puebla, I was very much aware of its absence. Its absence was so glaring that we had to create a special commission to do something about it because the document would have been deficient without at least one section on the international problem.

That section, however, does not represent a sufficient awareness on the part of the church of Latin America as a whole, a defect we must correct. We are turning in upon ourselves, and we must look more toward Latin American integration into the international scene. When we talk about international problems, we tend to quote other conferences of bishops in Europe and North

149

America. We are aware of the problem, however, and awareness is the beginning of the solution.

We are beginning this process in the Central American area. For instance, we will issue a document next month that we've been working on for the past five months: *The Church in Central America: Its Consideration of the Central American Problem*. It should be very helpful. Everyone but the church has offered an interpretation of Central America. Now we are offering ours, which we hope will help other people.

A central benefit from an encounter like this AEI seminar is meeting so many interesting people and exchanging points of view. I see this dialogue as the heart of a new awareness of the social role of the church, encouraging us to put our beliefs into practice and to live them. Thank you for this great opportunity.

The Role
of Multinational Corporations
in Latin American Development

Guillermo O. Chapman, Jr.

I wish to present a Latin American view of the global interdependency between Latin America and the United States. In general, I will address the role of U.S. multinational corporations (MNCs) in Latin America, and more specifically, their role in Central America and in my own country, Panama. I will also discuss some U.S. government positions on development issues. In both cases, I hope to refer to the perspectives and concerns of the Roman Catholic church in Latin America. In this way, I intend my remarks to supplement those of Archbishop McGrath.

Evaluating Multinational Corporations

It is important to define a few standards against which to evaluate the performance of MNCs in the area.

First, I recognize that the corporation's primary duty is to its shareholders and that to meet that duty it must make profits. Corporations will not engage in activities in Latin America or anywhere in the world that, at least in the medium-range term, are not profitable.

With this caveat, what can Latin American countries ask of the MNCs that operate in their midst? In general, they should expect a contribution to the improvement of the quality of life of the general population and especially of the poorest of the population. Today the distribution of income in Latin America is quite skewed. By being there, by being active and trying to achieve their basic goal, the multinationals should also help achieve a fairer distribution of income in these countries. The use of resources to generate a job should be reasonable, in comparison with the cost of generating a job in the overall economy (maybe multinational corporations are spending too much money to create each new job).

Second, over the life of the company it should steadily improve the real wages paid to its employees.

Third, these companies should have a positive effect on the balance of payments in the country in which they operate, and this effect should be better than what is achieved by traditional exports. From a Latin American point of view, if a country is generating a positive balance of payments from traditional exports and an MNC is not contributing to that positive balance, why should the country allow the multinational corporation to operate?

Fourth, part of a contribution to improved income distribution should come through financing social programs in the public sector: health, education, water supply, and the like. The way this comes about is through taxes paid to the local government.

Fifth, the company should contribute to economic growth: that is, it should be profitable enough to do all of the above and at the same time be able to reinvest in the country in which it operates.

After defining these very general standards for gauging the performance of corporations, we should now look at the activities of the MNCs and the contributions they make in light of these criteria.

Activities of the Multinationals

Some factors that influence the activities in which multinationals engage are the size of the local market (that is, the resource endowments of the country in which they want to operate), the business climate, and geographical location. The largest countries in Latin America attract corporations engaged in industries that require relatively large markets to operate efficiently. They are active in consumer goods, intermediate goods (that is, industrial goods and consumer durables), and, to a much lesser degree, heavy industries.

Most of the multinationals involved in industry in the larger Latin American countries are primarily seeking a share of the local market. Most are engaged in import substitution, producing in the host country goods that were previously imported from abroad.

In the medium- and smaller-sized countries, the activities that attract multinationals are determined mostly by the resources available. The exploration and exploitation of oil and minerals is a case in point. Many of these activities have been bought out or nationalized.

In tropical agriculture the activities center on bananas and sugar. Export processing is especially important in those countries with available manpower and a good geographic location in relation to the U.S. market. Mexico, some of the Central American countries, and some of the Caribbean islands have thus become export processing areas oriented toward the U.S. market.

Finally, the services sector makes its decision to operate based mainly on location and climate. International banking services fall into this category.

I will now share my impression of the degree to which these different types of activities meet the standards already defined. The industries that are directed mostly toward the local Latin American markets have been inefficient generators of employment. They have tended to use large amounts of capital per job created. This has happened partly because most companies import into Latin America technology developed for advanced industrial nations, technology ill attuned to Latin America's relative resource endowment: that is, to the relationship of labor, capital, and land in Latin America.

The very nature of the process of import substitution eventually leads to these inefficiencies in the generation of employment. Although at the onset industries with a high labor content can be developed, heavier capital is required for increased employment in production of more sophisticated goods or intermediate industrial goods. In addition, more sophisticated and advanced technologies are required. All of this tends to make employment generation much more inefficient.

Reinvestment in these activities is a function of local market growth. If the market expands and additional capacity is required, additional investment takes place. Many companies, however, especially those producing durable goods, do not look for other markets. That is, these companies do not seek to export or to market new products within the Latin American countries. These activities provide relatively modest reinvestment in the countries.

In the case of oil and minerals, the governments have very strong negotiating positions. In general, companies engaged in these activities have made very good contributions, though reinvestment outside their own industry has been low. I think a sizable collection of taxes has come from oil and minerals.

As for tropical agriculture, we find several practices detrimental to development. First is the transfer price both for imports and for final products. By definition, then, these companies pay as little in taxes as they can get away with. Second, most of them have very antagonistic labor relations, a source of constant conflict. In general, they are looked upon with strong suspicion, even by the local business community. Part of this suspicion, of course, is grounded in historical precedents because of the history of the involvement of these companies in local politics, of corrupting public officials, of buying off legislators, and like practices.

Another type of activity, export processing, satisfies most of my criteria, although it too has some weaknesses. One is that it tends to be very volatile: it's here today, gone tomorrow. By its very nature, given the competitiveness of the business internationally, these companies pay very little in taxes. They are, however, very good at employment and foreign exchange generation.

The banking services that have recently developed in some of the Caribbean islands and Panama have very few links to the domestic economy. When they grow, they grow because of the international need for the services there, but they generate very little for the local economy, employ only very highly trained members of the labor force, and pay very little in taxes.

Although the country does not lose any economic resources by their presence, the psychological costs are important. Building a bank building causes a construction boom and attracts deposits that can greatly increase gross national product figures, giving the impression of growth and of improved economic conditions. Actually, however, very little happens beyond the official statistics and outside the main cities.

In the case of Panama the banking industry has created, for instance, a second dual economy. The original dual economy, mentioned in all the literature on Latin America and on developing countries in general, embodies a contrast between the contributions and links of the modern and the traditional sector. We have another duality in the modern sector between the export service activities and the domestic sector activities.

Those activities oriented toward the export sector pay very little in taxes, generate very little employment, have few links to the domestic economy, and are under foreign ownership. Business activities in the traditional modern sector, by contrast, pay their way in taxes, generate comparatively more employment, have many links with the rest of the economy, and are generally under local ownership.

Of course, there is no such thing as the perfect multinational. Each type of multinational makes a given type of contribution. Most of these contributions, with a few exceptions I have mentioned, are positive. One of my first conclusions, then, is that if a country is to rely on multinationals as one of the elements of its development strategy, it has to attract conscientiously a mix of multinationals. It has to set up a system of signals by which it tells the world what types of multinationals it would welcome.

Those that are attracted should be attracted to generate contributions to balance of payments, employment, or whatever, so the mix achieves an overall desirable result. No single multinational and no single activity would make all the contributions one would need to generate development. In general, we ask the multinational to be a good corporate citizen, to abide by the rules of the game within the government, and to pay its taxes as it should.

It has been said that multinationals tend to retard economic growth in the countries where they are present. This is very hard to believe.

As one in the field and naturally aware of what multinationals can do, I find it difficult to accept that multinationals actually retard economic growth. One has to recognize, though, that they do little for the very poor directly. Because most of the very poor either do not participate in the market economy or are on the fringes of the market economy, any direct connection between a multinational and the improvement of the lot of the very poor in a country is very limited. Because multinationals have to compete in the world market and therefore need labor with a certain level of training, it is very difficult for them to have a direct influence on the very poor.

The problem of the very poor, then, must be solved by other components of development—the local government or small business. There is really no single, easy formula for development.

The Socialist Alternative

Socialism, as I see it, offers no real alternative. Some have pointed toward the improvement of social indicators in Cuba: indeed, it is really a very impressive record, especially in terms of public health and education.

Over the same period Costa Rica and Panama, however, have achieved the same degree of improvement in health and life expectancy that Cuba has. We do not have to go to a Socialist system to achieve those goals. They are achievable under a quasi-capitalistic and quasi-democratic system as we have in the rest of Latin America.

Moreover, comparison of the performance of Latin America with that of the Eastern European countries is unfair. East Germany, Czechoslovakia, and Poland were already industrialized countries before World War II and had a large, highly trained work force and even some physical infrastructure at the beginning of the recovery after the war.

Finally, I have not been able to find a good example of a third world country that has become a developed country under the Marxist scheme. Neither is this problem of development a question of the village economy versus the multinationals. We also have to recognize that the formal market economy is incapable of solving the problem of unemployment.

Solving Unemployment

In Latin America over the past twenty years we have had relatively high rates of economic growth; yet we have maintained relatively high rates of unemployment. The contribution that this economic growth makes to employment is not enough to guarantee that over the next ten or fifteen years unemployment will come down to a frictional level of 5 or 6 percent, the level acceptable by the social conditions of the country.

We must recognize that economic development will require a good mix of multinationals and a strong local private sector, with heavy emphasis on small business plus the so-called village economy or appropriate technology activities. Small businesses and appropriate technology are really the means to filling the employment gap that the formal economic structures of these countries are not able to fill.

Maybe those of us directly or indirectly in the business community are at fault here in relation to the clergy and the hierarchy of the church. We have to recognize that even though the clergy are not experts at business, they have to address themselves to these very sensitive social questions. When the business

155

community looks at social issues from the outside without really contributing ideas, help, or programs, many times we find that the church has fallen into the hands of the leftists and of groups that propose measures offering no real solutions to the problem of development.

Conclusions

In conclusion, I will offer some observations about the problems in Latin America with as much honesty and humility as I can marshal.

Many of the causes for the problems in Latin America can be attributed to erroneous policy decisions that our governments have made, to bad structures in place for many years, as well as to positions of the U.S. government.

We must consider the question of U.S. intervention: even if the U.S. government does nothing with respect to Latin America, that is a form of intervention.

Because the United States is bound to intervene in Latin America, we should ask what type of intervention is appropriate. I have three main suggestions. First, U.S. intervention should be nonpaternalistic; second, it should support Christian values; and third, some economic policy mistakes of the United States vis-à-vis Latin America should be corrected in the short term.

In the past many programs offered to Latin America by the U.S. government were manufactured in the United States. They were written by U.S. experts, by an industry of experts who specialize in development programs and present them to these countries on a take-it-or-leave-it basis. Even the Kissinger report reflected that paternalism, when in places it reads "our program."

The alternative that I suggest is that the United States stand ready to support programs developed indigenously by the Latin American countries themselves and that foster certain values the U.S. agrees to support.

Many of the programs we have had in the past, including the Alliance for Progress, were not even government programs. Local governments in Latin America put together programs in which they really were not interested so as to obtain financing for certain projects they did want. A reversal of this historical attitude is required for programs to work.

The programs have to be supportive of values that give priority to the very poor, respect human and political rights, and foster democracy as a system of government. We must ensure that these programs are managed with honesty and that there is accountability in the use of public funds in Latin America. I strongly urge the United States to avoid supporting military regimes because it is evident from the history of Latin America that military regimes do not support economic development and because in the medium or long term such support really works against U.S. interests. That has been the case for the support of Trujillo in the Dominican Republic and Somoza in Nicaragua.

Finally, some current policy mistakes in the U.S. position on Latin America must be corrected. Now, in addition to all the difficulties that Latin American countries have paying their debts, there is the added difficulty of quantitative restrictions in the U.S. market on steel, shoes, and textiles, with talk of putting quotas on the import of copper into the United States.

This situation reminds me of what happened with the German reparations payments after World War I. Germany was asked to repay its debt, but it was denied access not only to the U.S. market but also to the rest of the European market. Without access to the U.S. market, Latin America has no way to pay its debt because it has to earn dollars to pay this debt. Part of the problem lies in the fact that the U.S. tax system is set up to encourage multinationals to minimize the taxes they pay in Latin America to get a reasonable tax break in the United States.

In sum, the Latin American situation calls for very urgent reform in economic policy, elimination of regulation and control, reduction of state participation in the manufacturing and agricultural sectors, a revamping of taxes, a restructuring of public finance, and a redefinition of development strategies in general.

As for the U.S. government and U.S. multinationals, realistically one should expect that their own interests will be the main motivation behind their decisions. This is an understandable, valid position. Let us be sure that it is enlightened self-interest, however, inspired by Christian values.

Discussion

QUESTION: Why is there such a negative perception of multinational corporations in the U.S. population and in Latin America? Is it justified?

MR. CHAPMAN: Historically, some of these companies have not been the best corporate citizens and they have sometimes engaged in very bad practices. Some of these companies have been the source of very gruesome reports. In addition to the worst practices, there has always been the tendency of price transferring and of tax avoidance, along with instances of companies being in countries where their presence was not justified.

Mostly, the problem is that the governments have not set up a clear system of signals indicating which types of activities are desirable in the country and which are not. They should be discriminating, because not all multinationals are good.

Some of the critiques of the multinationals originate in countries like Brazil from the same writers who gave us the dependency theory. This view reflects a different vision of what development should be. These theorists are very critical, for instance, of multinationals for manufacturing consumer goods, because this tends to foster consumerism and a set of values that are not Brazilian. This might be a valid criticism, but the Brazilians must decide what type of development they want. If a given company fits particular development criteria and is willing to behave according to the laws, then we welcome it. If it is not, it has no place.

COMMENT: Mr. Chapman has taken a very good position on multinationals for now and for the future. We should not forget, as he has pointed out, however, that some of the practices in the recent past were very undesirable. This is especially true in some countries more than others.

Americans unacquainted with our history have difficulty understanding how the Central Americans can hold simultaneously a great admiration for the United States and a very deep resentment toward U.S. public policy in Central America over the past several generations. It has been in support of these companies and their practices, however, that the military has intervened. This has not left good will. We must recognize the past while looking toward the future.

QUESTION: Mr. Chapman, if each country in Latin America followed your prescriptions for the multinationals as a condition for hosting those multinationals, each country would be asking its multinational businesses to make a commitment to export and not only to export, but to export nontraditional exports: that is, to add to the export picture.

You also recommended that the United States should eliminate trade restrictions and recognize that Latin America will not be able to repay its existing debt unless it has free and open access to world markets for its exports.

Don't these recommendations present us with a very difficult trade-off? If exports are indeed important to rebuild the Latin American economies and those exports go to the United States, these invariably replace domestically produced goods in the United States.

Therefore, free access to the U.S. market will diminish employment in the United States. People in the United States are being asked to support the economic recovery of the people in Latin America. This arrangement represents a request for a trade-off, and it's the concept of trade-off that I wanted you to address.

MR. CHAPMAN: I don't agree with the position that if the quantitative restrictions on goods exported to the United States from Latin America are eliminated, it will result in a loss of jobs. It would result in a certain degree of restructuring of the U.S. economy. This restructuring would derive from a recognition that some industries in the United States are no longer competitive and that resources committed to those industries will have to be released and put into other industries where the United States has a competitive edge.

Moreover, Latin America as a whole has become the most important U.S. export market. A healthy Latin America means potentially more jobs for the U.S. worker, more jobs than could be artificially saved by protecting industries that are no longer competitive. If the United States asks the Latin Americans to be realistic and to restructure their economies, the United States should practice what it preaches and do the same.

As for my prescriptions for multinationals, I have to insist that the Latin American countries cannot go deeper into the export of commodities, because historically that guarantees a deterioration in the terms of trade: every year it takes more bananas to buy the same tractor. If we keep on producing more bananas or sugar, we will be worse off. The income gap will widen. Therefore, having recognized the causes of the widening income gap and worsening terms of trade, we should stay away from commodities.

Because no country will be good at everything, there has to be room for specialization. The smaller countries will have to find their niches where they can get one half of 1 percent of the U.S. market, which could prove to be a tremendous boon for that specific country.

QUESTION: Archbishop McGrath, How do we resolve that seeming conflict between what is good for Latin America and what is good for the United States?

In their document on the economy, will the U.S. bishops address the effects of overseas imports and recommend some sort of protection for those jobs because we have our own poor and unemployed, or will they accept the data that we have discussed and recommend export opportunities because of their potential for job creation?

ARCHBISHOP MCGRATH: This is not really a theological question. As Mr. Chapman was saying, it is really a question of a trade-off in specialization. The eternal task of government is to try to work out the trade-offs involved. It is quite obvious that if the Latin American countries that are trying to pay off their debts cannot export, they have nothing with which to pay their debt.

QUESTION: I am in the apparel industry. In the past ten years approximately 400,000 jobs have been lost because of imports into this country from nations with a lower labor rate.

I think we should be extremely cautious in how we go about increasing the exports from the Latin American countries. If we lower the barriers in a dramatic or sudden way, job losses will occur.

To go back to the issue of taxation, Mr. Chapman, how do you reconcile the need for taxes to finance social programs for the poor with the provision of tax incentives to attract new companies?

MR. CHAPMAN: Having to promise a tax holiday to attract companies is a fact of life. Many countries are competing to attract the same types of industries— apparel, assembly, electronics, gadgets, and the like. The way to attract them is to offer a tax holiday. That in itself is an initial cost that the countries have to incur to attract a company. At the same time, these are labor-intensive industries. They employ a large number of people, who then collect wages and pay taxes. Immediately, therefore, these companies contribute to fiscal revenues of the country. In the medium term, once the tax holiday is over, they pay taxes. If the country were in the seller's position instead of in the buyer's, then the company would have to pay taxes from the first. It all depends on the market conditions for each specific activity, whether the country has to give away taxes.

As for the question of trade, I do not recommend eliminating the barriers or import duties. I do recommend eliminating quantitative restrictions, or import quotas, which have been set up in this country in the past five years. Some recent analyses indicate that more jobs have been lost in this country in the past three or four years as a result of reduction of Latin American imports than were saved in industries protected by the import quotas.

QUESTION: Mr. Chapman, how should the IMF and the banking industry handle intervention?

MR. CHAPMAN: In principle the IMF tells these countries that if they want the financial help of the IMF, they can have it, subject to putting their own house in order. Couched in those terms, it is a sensible and valid approach because we face a short-term problem in which the governments have large budgetary deficits and the countries have very tight merchandise accounts, surpluses that do not allow them to service the foreign debt.

The object is to generate some savings, reduce the size of the deficit in the public sector budget, and increase the size of the merchandise account surplus in the foreign account so that the debt can be serviced. To allow these things to happen, the IMF will give short-term financing at a reasonable term. For example, it will allow short-term financing to be repaid over the next ten years at a below-market cost of 7 or 8 percent interest.

The problem, however, is that the financing provided to the countries is very limited. It is not enough to pull the countries out of the slump. In addition, the major countries that are financing these loans are having problems themselves and do not want to provide financially shakey countries with larger funds. This is one side of the question.

The other side of the question is that Latin America has undergone three successive years of economic contraction, and some countries that have already suffered major privations because of economic recession or contraction are politically very explosive.

The reasoning behind the IMF approach is clear, but we must recognize that the IMF does not have enough financial resources to back the approach. In addition, the situation of the governments in these countries is such that if they do adopt these measures, they might write themselves out of a job because a revolution or other political explosion might ensue. We must reschedule the Latin American debt and provide additional funds to the IMF, the World Bank, or other international lenders.

QUESTION: Do you accept in principle the right or obligation of these lending institutions to intervene?

MR. CHAPMAN: It is a system with a quid pro quo. No country is forced to enter into an IMF program. It is strictly voluntary. Countries enter into the program if they want IMF resources. Venezuela, for instance, has refused to talk to the IMF. It has said it will adjust its programs without discussion with the IMF. Venezuela will not subscribe to a stand-by agreement and will not abide by its rules. Venezuela, of course, can afford to do that. Maybe Mexico in a few years will also declare its independence.

So far Argentina has also taken a very tough stand vis-à-vis the IMF, mainly because of internal political reasons. It would be politically very costly, given the internal situation, to accept the IMF conditions.

QUESTION: Do multinationals have a right or obligation to intervene?

MR. CHAPMAN: I was using the term intervention to characterize official action by the U.S. government. I was not thinking in terms of the multinationals per se.

COMMENT: Maybe the word intervention is misleading. Perhaps a multinational has an obligation to use its influence to foster what it believes to be the best interests of the country in which it is operating.

MR. CHAPMAN: I don't agree. I believe a multinational should be a good corporate citizen, do what it knows how to do, do it well, and abide by the law. It should avoid participation in local political problems.

Multinational Companies
in the Third World

Rolando Duarte

A great society is one in which its businessmen abide strictly by their consciences in matters of business as well as in matters of private morality. I would like to discuss a moral vision for multinational businessmen who play such a crucial role in the development of the third world.

Third world countries generally share certain characteristics: they have low per capita income, high birth rates, high mortality rates, low educational standards, population growth greater than the growth of their gross national product, and high unemployment. In addition, they are exporters of raw materials and importers of foreign capital and manufactured goods. Other common characteristics pertaining to social, anthropological, and political disciplines could certainly be mentioned. Although incomplete, this summary provides an introductory sketch of third world countries.

In contrast, the rich industrial countries—the so-called center or core countries—are importers of raw materials, exporters of manufactured goods, and suppliers of loans and other direct investments. Their educational levels are advanced, per capita incomes are high, and low birth rates combine with low mortality rates to produce a low overall rate of population growth.

Today, multinational corporations (MNCs) supply a bridge between the third world and the developed world. Most of these MNCs have their headquarters in the developed countries, and about 60 percent or more are U.S. owned. It is said that the production generated by the MNCs and by their subsidiaries worldwide is higher than all other exports from the Western economies. According to some researchers, by the end of the century, MNC operations will double world trade and will favorably affect the balance of trade throughout the third world, provided that conditions of internal stability and cooperation prevail and improve. The broad investment strategy of MNC managers is, therefore, of obvious and crucial significance to the third world.

Historically, the MNCs have already played a large role in the development of Latin America. Like the third world in general, Latin America has been the recipient of substantial capital investment emanating from MNCs

163

operating in public services, petroleum, mining, manufacturing, trade, banking, farming, and agro-industries. In the 1960s—encouraged by the availability of large internal markets, the possibility of expansion in other areas, and the need to help host governments implement import substitution policies—a number of MNCs established a fairly large manufacturing base in many Latin American countries, especially those countries with large populations such as Argentina, Brazil, and Mexico. In Chile, Bolivia, Venezuela, Peru, and Colombia, the MNCs traditionally invested in profitable mineral extraction such as petroleum, copper, iron, and tin. In Central America, by contrast, the major share of MNC investment was concentrated primarily in trade, public utilities, petroleum, banking, hotel management, and some manufacturing.

To mention one well-known example, in the early part of this century, the United Fruit Company operated in all parts of Honduras and on the Pacific coasts of Guatemala and in Costa Rica. That company changed and developed new towns, transforming what were rain forests and jungles into bustling ports, railroads, and processing centers that brought prosperity and new employment to the area. In the 1970s, however, the investment environment changed. Political pressure from elected parties and labor organizations brought with them land seizures and strikes, causing many MNCs to wind down operations.

Recently, I read an account by Lee Tavis of the operation of the Dolefil Company in the Philippine Islands, one that reminded me of the investment of the United Fruit Company in Central America.[1] Like the United Fruit Company, the Dolefil Company has established well-planted fields, special houses and schools for its management, and a cluster of lodgings for the rest of the workers. Nearby villages have been transformed into full-fledged towns with local government, town halls, public markets, stores, and craftsmen attending to the needs of the people. I sincerely hope, however, that the political and social unrest that we see emerging in the Philippines today will not result in the same degree of turmoil I have witnessed in Central America. It is not inevitable that MNCs produce such unrest.

On the contrary, it is desirable and necessary that the third world—the countries at the periphery of development—welcome demand from the core countries for the raw materials and goods of the third world, provided, of course, that the terms of trade remain profitable to the third world countries. Study and research show that the third world economies have improved and developed substantially since the Korean War. Import substitution and manufacturing begun in the 1960s increased the gross national product of many third world countries, stimulated their employment, and improved the balance of trade.

A 6 percent annual rate of domestic growth was the goal of developing countries. This compares with a 2.3 percent average population growth rate in Latin America (in some countries the rate is close to 4 percent). Indeed, much improvement and modernization were achieved throughout the region, in the cities, in education, in health, in production, in the balance of foreign trade, and in bettering the general standard of living and working.

More recently, however, the increase in petroleum prices for non-petroleum-producing countries, the spectacular rise in interest rates, and the worsening terms of trade for raw materials vis-à-vis manufactured goods reduced many progressive yet poor countries to the border of collapse. The comparatively mild recession that occurred in the Western developed economies resulted in even greater burdens for the countries on the periphery. Latin America in particular has been hit hard by balance of payment deficits, acceleration of unemployment, social unrest, and political instability. Some countries have experienced violence, terrorism, revolution, internal warfare, and guerrilla actions.

Right now the situation is grim. It is impossible to expect that the developing countries will eliminate the current accounts deficit overnight, nor can they miraculously reduce the number of unemployed, increase production, or change the terms of trade relating to their own resources. The economic problems are especially acute in those nations without internal stability. As we have seen in El Salvador, general social unrest hinders determined governmental efforts to increase employment and production or to broaden income distribution. Nevertheless, some countries are taking important steps on their own. Mexico, Venezuela, Brazil, and Argentina have already begun to help by adopting policies of austerity in government expenditures, moving public employees to the developing private sector, and assisting international corporations in new ways. It is too early to predict results, and much more remains to be done.

Despite these efforts, there is an urgent need for new capital inflow, now and for the years to come. I have seen, for example, a recent publication from a Swiss bank that discusses in detail the external financing requirements for a group of twenty-four developing nations. These nations had a bank debt of over $200 billion in 1982, of which $42 billion was newly borrowed. The external debt of all third world countries was estimated at about $350 billion. Predictably, the writers of the Swiss report do not expect an instantaneous change in the export proceeds of the less-developed countries. If we are to avoid a financial debacle for both the third world and the lending nations, it is essential that the third world obtain renewed aid from official government and multilateral financial institutions. Loans with long-term maturities and the lowest possible interest rates are in order.

Yet our appeal is also directed to the private sector of the industrialized nations. Private corporations will have to cooperate and participate in the funding of the third world debt. New borrowing and direct investment will be needed to carry these nations out of the slump and to enable them to adjust their economies to a point of financial equilibrium.

Any successful action depends upon international cooperation, mutual understanding, and dialogue between East and West, North and South. We must all learn—and this is the most important point—to coexist in friendship on our small planet.

The need for international cooperation has been recognized at different levels, but notably at a new conference on trade and development held under the auspices of the United Nations. Many other persons have examined the difficulties facing the international economic order in an age of global interdependence. The adequacy of market forces has been questioned by some; others weigh price systems, competitive advantages in international trade, and the international division of labor against the needs of a new international economic order. Much sane advice is being offered to the IMF, the World Bank, and other multinational financial institutions to improve and enlarge their lending assistance. The Law of the Sea Treaty, for example, provides for a greater sharing of the benefits from the exploitation of seabeds. We must try to correct the so-called international inequalities and provide for a global interdependence among the different nations from our beloved world.

This approach has been accepted and approved fully by the third world and with some reservations by the industrial countries, especially the United States. President Reagan's Caribbean Basin Initiative and the recent Jackson Plan are positive moves in that direction. Our friends from the North have shown a definite concern for improving the living conditions and general economic health of the Central American and Caribbean nations. The actions of the United States will complement efforts in the area to develop free, pluralistic, peaceful societies with justice and freedom for all.

To reinforce what I said, I would like to relate the following story. Many years ago a friend, a Salvadoran businessman with a very prosperous enterprise, envisioned for the future an economically vital Central America. He envisaged freight cars of goods coming through Mexico from Canada and the United States, destined for the countries in Central America. He envisaged a "dry canal" in the lower part of the Central American isthmus. There would be an oil pipe from Mexico on the Atlantic Coast to supply petroleum for the Central American refineries. He saw the establishment of many institutions of higher learning, postgraduate schools of business and technical disciplines, and development centers to foster trade and industry. He imagined a chain of tourist resorts to attract thousands of travelers to the Yucatan, just as the Mayas had done ages before.

The completion of any one of these projects envisaged by my friend would be enough to change the economic structure of countries such as ours. The virtue of my friend was to think and act big and not to be satisfied with tiny actions that just patch the many holes and limitations of our economies.

Having lived for so many years with military rulers and dictators who violated our civil soul and deprived us of democratic, civilized government, today we are striving to bring self-government and prosperity to Latin America. I believe that those grand projects and large investments that my friend and others imagine will require the resources of the multinationals. We know the limitations imposed by the size of our markets and the degree of peace, as well as the stability of trade with our countries. Yet we know that a great deal can be done by these private corporations to alleviate our general economic condition. We need their help to fulfill the dreams of our people.

We call upon the businessmen and concerned individuals who have been blessed with democracy to support our great and painful efforts to achieve a democratic society that will truly provide the best and the most lasting safeguards for human rights. That cooperation will bring peace and justice to our people, and it will help us to write with golden letters a heroic and significant page in our modern history.

Note

1. See Lee A. Tavis, ed., *Multinational Managers and Poverty in the Third World* (South Bend, Ind.: University of Notre Dame Press, 1982), pp. 187–252.

Discussion

QUESTION: Mr. Duarte, your vision of the role of the multinationals seems to differ substantially from Mr. Chapman's. Would you comment on those differences?

MR. DUARTE: It is a question of priorities. We now have a balance of payments deficit. That deficit is causing a reduction in our standard of living; incomes are declining. The terms of trade will not change. The price of petroleum will not go down, and the price of raw materials will not go up, whatever we produce, for years to come.

We need time to prepare ourselves politically and socially for the democratic process. For our economies to develop and for our incomes to increase, we need the help of direct investment and loans from the multinational banks to move the position of our countries forward a little bit, allowing us time to organize in a better way.

MR. CHAPMAN: I really don't see any major differences between what Mr. Duarte has stated and what I think. El Salvador is passing through some very special circumstances now. If I were a Salvadorean, my first priority would be to attract as many multinationals as I could in the shortest possible time without asking very many questions.

QUESTION: How many multinational corporations are represented in each of your countries right now?

MR. DUARTE: I would say about twenty.

MR. CHAPMAN: I would say about 200 in Panama. At least a hundred international banks are registered in Panama.

COMMENT: The contrast between Panama and El Salvador is worth exploring, particularly as it relates to the attitude toward business and in particular toward multinationals. This attitude bears upon some of the issues addressed in this session. Clearly, the environment for multinational business or indeed for any business in Panama today is quite different from the environment for business

168

in El Salvador today. In El Salvador it is very difficult to do business for many reasons, some relating to the civil unrest, but many more relating to the economic condition.

MR. CHAPMAN: There are very important differences between Panama and El Salvador. In Panama we have a very open system in certain segments of the economy, making it very easy to do business. Very obvious examples are the banking system and the re-export trade. The general rule is, if a firm will be based in Panama to conduct international business, we will open up the country for it. A corporation can be organized in two weeks, which is as fast as it can be done anywhere in the world. We set very limited regulations and provide a very attractive tax setup.

If the operation is oriented toward the local markets, however, then the rules of the game are completely different. Consumer goods are most likely to be subjected to price controls. Corporate income tax rates are very stiff, higher than those in the United States.

A firm interested in retail merchandising would find no legal way of doing business because foreigners are not allowed to own retail businesses in Panama. On top of that very stiff labor laws regulate relations with employees.

COMMENT: Despite those restrictions, if one goes into the supermarket in Panama, he will find virtually every consumer product for sale that he would find in a supermarket in the United States.

MR. CHAPMAN: Yes. Generally, we have a very open tariff system. The average import duties are comparatively low, especially in comparison with the rest of Latin America.

What I described as the rules for the internally oriented economic activity in Panama apply to all activities in a country such as El Salvador. No distinction is made between an export-oriented activity and a domestic-market-oriented activity. The same rules apply, along with very high taxes, very stiff labor regulations, and price controls.

MR. DUARTE: We have some manufacturing in El Salvador. One-fourth of our gross national product comes from the manufacturing sector, which is a very large proportion. Maybe that is not the case in Panama, where most of the goods are imported. In a supermarket in El Salvador, about ninety percent of the goods are produced in the country or imported from the rest of Central America because we have regional integration in Central America, free trade between the Central American countries.

I have made a list of the enterprises now run by some multinational companies. Even though we have violence, terrorism, and unrest in El Salvador, we are still working hard, and we are still manufacturing. We have two

169

Japanese textile factories, Texas Instruments, IBM, ITT, and Phillips, for example. Our situation is completely different from Panama, which provides services. We are a producing country; we manufacture.

QUESTION: Let me phrase my question another way to Mr. Chapman. If you were in El Salvador, why would you be doing your utmost to attract multinationals into that country?

MR. CHAPMAN: I draw a distinction between a general case for Latin America and the specific case for El Salvador. For Latin America generally I would recommend a mix of multinationals that would bring about different contributions to development, which none of them could make unilaterally.

Looking at the very broad picture, we would need to be selective to achieve that mix. In the very special circumstances of a country such as El Salvador, however, we could not afford to be choosy. In the short run, it is not a problem of selecting the best mix, but of attracting whoever cares to come into the country.

QUESTION: I am interested in the historical events that Archbishop McGrath raised in his remarks on the pattern of past U.S. intervention in Central America. I want to know how that pattern might condition possibilities for cooperation today.

I address my question to Mr. Chapman, Mr. Duarte, and Archbishop McGrath. To what degree in Panama and in El Salvador does the past history of the United States vis-à-vis Central America influence the possibility of political and economic cooperation today? What standards guide a cooperative political-economic engagement? How do we, after acknowledging our history, transcend it? Can we avoid choosing between two impossible historical choices, given the multitude of pressures operating on us?

ARCHBISHOP MCGRATH: As Guillermo Chapman remarked earlier, it's not a question of the United States intervening or not intervening, but of how it intervenes. It's already there. A presence is an intervention, and the United States is strongly present in many ways—economically, politically, socially, culturally.

First, we should consider feelings. Is there a feeling of rejection because of the past? Does this limit the possibility of a positive presence? Obviously, some hurt carries over from the past, from what some companies have done and from what the military interventions have signified in support of U.S. business and U.S. public policy. This is quite obvious.

The result is, however, that everything is viewed with a certain amount of suspicion. About the Kissinger report, for example, Latin America wonders how serious U.S. intentions are. Will it really entail economic assistance, or is it some kind of camouflage for more military and political control of the area? I sense a Doubting Thomas attitude that comes from past experience. This is understandable and quite rational.

Of course, it is quite obvious that not only is there no opposition to a presence (as business people or anyone engaged in economics would say), but there are various demands put on that presence.

MR. CHAPMAN: A very prominent Costa Rican said to me recently that Costa Rica could work out good arrangements with the United States because the United States had never intervened militarily in Costa Rica. Doubtless there is a drawback to a history of intervention. Costa Ricans have no axe to grind, which is obviously not the case with Central America in general and more specifically with Nicaragua and Panama, where the Marines have gone in, or with the Dominican Republic and Haiti where the Marines have even taken over the government. That historical fact probably does not weigh on the American conscience because it was quite unimportant from a U.S. point of view, but it was very important for that little country in which the U.S. military intervened.

. Of course, some Latin Americans have no ideological anti-U.S. position; they understand that these are different times and different circumstances and that most of the U.S. population, the present government leadership, and the present religious and business leadership do not feel tied to those historical patterns. Among certain groups in Latin America there is also a reserve of good will, an acknowledgment of the good intentions of the United States toward Latin America.

Yes, the historical background is important, but it is not the only element. The really important element today is communication. With good will, with interest, and with frank and open discussion, the historical fact can be accepted. We Latin Americans have to accept our own historical mistakes as well.

MR. DUARTE: We don't like that word intervention—it does not seem to be the right word just now. We like *cooperation* or *collaboration*. If a guerrilla in the western part of El Salvador is asked about the U.S. presence there, we know what he would answer, of course.

Domestically, we do not want the Nicaraguans or the Cubans intervening in our country. What we have requested, the United States has done, and we are thankful for that. They have given military and economic aid. We haven't asked for troops to help us in our internal war.

QUESTION: What is the climate for nonprofit organizations in Latin America, and what role do they play? Nonprofit organizations would seem to provide an opportunity for some of the more wealthy in these countries to distribute their

171

money to the poor without its leaving the country. These organizations also provide an opportunity for idle people to work in a nominal way.

ARCHBISHOP MCGRATH: The largest nonprofit organization in Latin America is the church. It also has the largest number of people working voluntarily in many ways. Generally speaking, however, there is much less tradition for creating foundations or legacies for nonprofit endeavors. These things are just beginning in many of our countries.

Some years back a very prominent, wealthy member of the Jewish community died in Panama. I later received a visit from the rabbi, a good friend of mine, who said that when the man died, he had left no money for the synagogue or for any social endeavor.

I had to tell the rabbi that the Catholics were just the same. There is very little sense of legacy; people are not given to making donations in life or after death, or to setting up patrimonies and foundations. It indicates a lack of responsibility, a lack of social sense, a lack of constructive contribution to the development of the economy. This attitude is beginning to change, however.

Probably many of the social groups patterned after the U.S. style of Rotarians, Kiwanis, and the like, which do operate fund-raising activities and do contribute to setting up nonprofit institutions, generally are not run by private individuals. They turn them over either to the church or to some private institution or, more commonly, to the government, which maintains them. Not many of them are run by the individuals that created them. The school systems in most of our countries are not considered nonprofit enterprises. They are governed as though they were'intended to earn a profit, which they obviously cannot. This creates a real difficulty. This policy comes in the aftermath of a nineteenth century liberal tendency to control the whole educational system, particularly the Catholic school system. Government controls make it difficult for private schools.

A residue of that tendency affects a good part of our countries, particularly in Central America. Central America suffered a great deal during the nineteenth century, especially Guatemala, Nicaragua, and Honduras, from the battle between the clerics and the anticlerics, That conflict has left in its wake restrictions that impede many nonprofit ventures because of jealousy on the part of the state.

Although there are some nonprofit organizations, the church is certainly the one with the largest number of hospitals, the asylums for the aged, orphanages, and soup kitchens. The church also sponsors many operations for feeding preschool children. That is the largest enterprise, and it is nonprofit and tax free, and it does a great deal of social promotion in this regard.

COMMENT: I am interested in the actual military situation in El Salvador. Suppose the United States today gives $1 million of economic aid, but tomorrow night the guerrillas blow up a bridge or burn a field. Our economic aid burns away as fast as it's given. What is the prospect of defeating the guerrillas or in some way stopping the guerrilla war? What degree of popular support do you think the guerrillas have? When I asked this question of Archbishop Rivera y Damas, he said the guerrillas have very little support.

MR. DUARTE: I completely agree: right now the guerrillas seem to have no public support for their operation. The two elections we had in 1982 and 1984 prove that: 1,700,000 people voted. The people chose the democratic process.

We are at the beginning of the democratic process. We have come back into the democratic community, something everyone in El Salvador had hoped for. Even the people on the right have chosen the democratic process. They supported a political party in the elections, they voted, and in a very hard-fought campaign they came in second. Only the left did not participate in the democratic process.

In general, we are in the process of becoming a democratic society. We are in the process of learning to be a pluralistic society. Before the elections and during the campaign, the party of the right and the party of the left practically insulted each other on television and radio. Now, however, it is completely different. Everyone has started working for the benefit of the country, working to foster improvement in trade and production.

With respect to the guerrillas, your observation is true; every day a bomb goes off or they attack a different town. It's easy. Anyone can do it. Three or four people can do it. This activity will have to be controlled, of course, and to some extent it is. According to some information, if the line of munitions and food from Nicaragua were stopped, the guerrillas would have a very difficult situation. They would have to leave their arms at the border of Honduras and go back to Nicaragua.

QUESTION: Mr. Chapman, how would you explain to the United States why it is so urgent to provide economic assistance to Latin America?

MR. CHAPMAN: What the United States decides to do vis-à-vis the Central American situation, specifically the Salvadoran situation, has to do with whether Central America is judged to have any strategic value for the United States. If it has no value whatsoever, then it can just go down the drain. Yet I happen to think that it *is* important for the United States. I also think it is important for the United States that Central America not align itself with the Communist side. If we agree on that, then we need to find the most effective way to prevent Central America from going to the Soviets. From the U.S. point of view, the most effective way is to help the present Salvadoran government or eventually U.S. troops must be sent to Central America. The choice comes down to that, provided the United States wants to keep Central America from falling into Communist hands. To me it is a very simple proposition.

173

Economic Revival:
The Role of the Private Sector

Russell E. Marks, Jr.

My involvement with business in Latin America probably began in the most primitive circumstances. The first country I lived in was Bolivia in the 1950s, not very long after the revolution in 1952. At that time the country was in extreme disorder. Bolivia was also the first country in which the United States attempted a stabilization program, a phrase that has been subsequently used in a number of other countries. The pattern of stabilization programs was created in Bolivia. In retrospect, we would probably have to admit that while it was well conceived, it did not work. Although it seemed to be working for a time, cultural conditions in Bolivia made its failure almost inevitable. Frequently, economic considerations that seem to us perfectly rational do not work in Latin America because cultural circumstances work against much of the kind of development that we have come to think important.

In my view, it is not possible to talk about national sovereignty as we once talked of it. No country in the world, including the United States, enjoys anything beyond nominal sovereignty today. We must accept the proposition that interdependency is a fact of life and will become an even stronger consideration in our planning and in our actions over the long run.

The private sector in Latin America has always been closely involved in the concept of dependency. It has been said that the multinational corporations increased dependency. The criticism seems more political than economic, however, and consequently much more difficult to combat in rational terms. Today, however, the private sector is suddenly being called upon to do a great many things in the hemisphere.

After a period during which the private sector was excoriated by both domestic and foreign critics, suddenly even Latin American governments are calling for more private activity. Unfortunately, the call for more private activity in the hemisphere comes at a time when the private sector is perhaps weakest. Over the period of development in the late 1950s the private sector grew in Latin America. Since then it has become a less important element in almost every national economy: its percentage of gross domestic product has declined in most countries, particularly during the recent economic crisis.

174

During this period the strength of the private sector was eroded considerably faster and deeper than has the strength of the public sector.

Several factors are relevant to this decline of the private sector. In the United States at the beginning of this development epoch in Latin America, we thought that economic growth would eventually lead to better distribution of wealth and, following that, to political stability and more participatory government. We had an objective in promoting that economic growth. The United States worked very hard to promote growth in Latin America. Evidence has shown, however, that economic growth does not necessarily lead to better distribution of wealth and political stability, though I still think that the sequence could eventually occur. In fact, I am still convinced that our aims may still very well be achieved, though over a somewhat longer time than we thought in the early 1960s.

At the time this development process in Latin America was most promising, we assumed that the rate of growth would be constant. That, of course, was also a false proposition. As I look back after this period of economic destruction in our hemisphere, however, and judge what has happened by the standards we applied at that time, I believe that it looks as if we did the proper thing.

Even the borrowing seems justified, given the recirculation of petrodollars at the very low interest rates. In fact, state economic planners would have looked foolish then if they had not borrowed very large sums of money. The main concern then centered on infrastructure development, industrial manufacturing development, agricultural development, and eventually consumer development.

Of course, money was borrowed in large sums at low interest rates on the assumption that the rate of growth that was already very high would continue. Furthermore, it seemed that if the rate of growth continued, those countries would be able to service that level of debt over a long time.

What happened, of course, was that external conditions caused that premise to fail. Not all problems in Latin America were internally generated. The oil price increase originally unbalanced the economies to a certain extent but then allowed them more money to grow. In addition, the increase also provided the import-substitution theorists and implementers in Latin America a large fund to finance the development of public corporations, allowing them to make the public sector the engine of development all over Latin America.

As state corporations were formed throughout the region, state bureaucracies sprang up to supervise the activities of those state corporations. Over time, then, a great deal of money was invested in both of those efforts. When the collapse occurred, the countries that first experienced financial crisis had to borrow money to cover operating deficits. They no longer borrowed for investment but to cover operating deficits in the state corporations and in the administration of government. When that happened, it was obviously impossible to continue to service the debt, and the crisis became obvious to all.

As the crisis deepened, the private sector, excluded from sources of credit, eroded. As the state corporations grew and were obliged to continue to grow to maintain this principle of economic development, they absorbed all the available domestic credit.

First, foreign corporations in Latin America were obliged to borrow outside the country. Shortly thereafter, local investors had to borrow outside the country, because they were frozen out of local sources. Finally, the state corporations began to borrow outside the countries. During the period of private sector borrowing while state corporations still had access to domestic sources, however, the foreign-owned and domestically owned private corporations had to restrict operations because they realized that they would not be able to service their debt. The problem was clear to them earlier than it was either to state corporations or to the administration of the state.

During this period agriculture dropped in importance around Latin America, so that by 1982 approximately 71 percent of imports in many countries in Latin America were agricultural products. At that time agriculture was largely a private sector activity. An erosion of private sector activity in agriculture, manufacturing, and commerce occurred during that time. Confidence rapidly diminished. Both resources and people fled the country.

As we look at the situation in Latin America today, we face the argument that the sorts of austerity programs imposed by the IMF are too restrictive, limit the prospect of growth too much, and cause a rent in the polity of these countries. Yet, some contend that unless inefficiencies that have developed over the years in the economies of these countries are squeezed out, no additional funding would be sufficiently productive. Our task now is to balance the contentions. At this time the private sector in Latin America has a great deal to contribute. During the period of deterioration some things have happened that are not necessarily bad and must be considered as we look toward the future. What good things have really happened?

All over Latin America I sense a new awareness of the value of shared responsibilities. Private investors in Latin America have grown to work with state corporations in some instances very responsibly. A network of private operations has developed around this hemisphere. The network has apparently taught domestic investors that private foreign corporations are not necessarily bad, that they can in fact be vehicles for improved profitability and more rapid growth, and that in joint ventures it is the local investor who has the advantage of more rapid and perhaps more effective technology transfer and of access to markets, to market expertise, to financial resources of different kinds, and to trading patterns that he might not otherwise have had.

In fact, even during the period of deterioration in some countries where the private sector might have disappeared completely, it has not. It has shown a flexibility and a durability that reflect the changing relationship between the domestic private sector and the foreign private sector, as well as a changing accommodation with state-owned corporations.

But we must not lose sight of the improving quality of life in Latin America. People concerned about wage levels must also be aware of the public services that are now provided. The very roads on which peasants walk these days are greatly improved; the water that is available, even if people have to draw it from a common well and carry it to their homes, is nevertheless municipal water. Health services have progressed during this time. Thus, our crisis today is a crisis of confidence more than anything else.

We have seen the flight of money. It has been estimated that between 1974 and 1982 approximately $50 billion worth of private money left Latin America. Another estimate indicates that of the increase of $245 billion in borrowing by the five principal debtor countries in Latin America between 1978 and 1982, approximately one-third was devoted to the purchase of foreign assets by the private sector in Latin America. We have also seen the phenomenon of the spiritual émigré: a person who may still reside in Latin America but who in fact has now centered his interests on other parts of the world.

One of the things the private sector can do most effectively, I believe, is restore confidence. The private sector alone, of course, cannot restore confidence. It has to work with changing political administrations in Latin America. Approximately 60 percent of fixed investment in Latin America is still privately owned. Although some erosion has occurred, that figure is still very large.

We cannot assume that state enterprises will die, be eliminated, or be destatized. Some of them are very large. Some of them are very important politically. Some of them are very well run, as a matter of fact. The ground rules under which all the productive sectors of Latin America operate—the state-owned corporations as well as domestically owned and foreign-owned corporations—can be changed, however, so that the public sector does not have such an unequal access to resources within the country.

That unequal access to resources led to a great many inefficiencies in the past. Providing more equal access to contracts with the state, to domestic financing, to reserves, and to funds for foreign transactions will help eliminate the inequality between state and private sector. We will then see more competition in the long run, as we have seen in some countries. Consequently, we will have better creation of jobs and a quicker revival of growth.

In most countries competition has in fact led to more rapid growth, as instances in specific countries illustrate. For the private sector to be effective we must, as I said, change the ground rules, after very frank discussion among the concerned parties. That discussion has begun in the dialogue with the IMF around the hemisphere. Private corporations will have to become increasingly involved. Latin American multinational corporations will have to be increasingly involved. Clearly, one of the reasons that domestic private investors in Latin America are less suspicious of the foreign investors is that now very large, privately owned Latin American corporations compete with European, Japanese, and North American ones. As their level of activity has risen and their size has grown, they have become more self-confident. Therefore, the prospects for legitimate competition among joint ventures, foreign corporations, and large domestic corporations are much better than in the past.

Another area of private sector activity in Latin America certainly needs to be mobilized and in some way included within the domestic economies: what many people have called the informal economy. In some countries it is an illegal economy.

Peru is perhaps one of the better examples to use because some statistics are available. Establishing an enterprise in most countries in Latin America is quite difficult. For example, it may take six hours in Florida to establish a corporation, whereas in Peru it takes that many months. In addition, the process is very expensive and is therefore inhibiting. Because people of small means find it legally complicated to form themselves into corporations and very difficult to acquire capital in the traditional way, they have established an illicit economy.

Again, Peru is a very good example; some estimates suggest that $4 billion worth of gross domestic product has been produced by this illicit economy in the past five years. This figure is very high and thus very difficult to prove. More work is being done. However, we do know that the illicit economy in Peru produces over half the domestic production of certain items like shoes and shirts, and it includes even an auto assembly plant. These people are operating at interest rates well over 100 percent, borrowing their money weekly to finance this kind of business. If they can do what they are doing today under those conditions, we can only imagine how well they would do if they were able to work within the broader domestic economy.

It used to be said that a cultural bar prevented entrepreneurship from working in Latin America. I have often heard it said that the Indian civilization does not permit this activity. The vitality of these parallel economies, however, demonstrates exactly the opposite: entrepreneurship is not only possible but is already one of the driving forces in the revival of economic activity in Latin America.

On the other hand, the attitude of many Latin American elites does constitute an obstacle to consolidating this parallel economy into the larger economy in Latin America. One of the distinctions between the economic establishment in the United States and that in most countries in Latin America is that here we attempt to co-opt the best in our society and bring it into the establishment. The establishment undertakes certain responsibilities as well as enjoying certain privileges, of course. Our establishment, however, is not hereditary.

In contrast, in Latin America, the status of the elite has tended to be hereditary up until very recently in most countries. For that parallel economy to be consolidated into the national economy, to realize the real potential that has developed during the past twenty years through improvement in public services and education, the Latin American establishment must open itself to newcomers.

To fulfill one of the responsibilities of interdependence, the private sector in this hemisphere must work to promote the inclusion of the most valuable human resources into an effort to revive the economies. Societies must become more open to intellect. Returning to my original point, I believe that a revival of growth may lead to a better distribution of income and eventually to the support of participatory political structures.

I see a clear relationship among market economy, democratic government, and the protection of human rights. Countries with democratic or participatory governments and market economies are far more protective of human rights than are others, in fact. I am not certain which of these factors comes first, but they appear to work in concert. Clearly, all must be encouraged.

Perhaps I have come close to an interventionist's view at some points, for example, when I stressed the importance of new talent. My remarks could be interpreted as an endorsement of political intervention in the economy. How far does U.S. responsibility for such political interventions extend within this interdependent relationship? Within the structure of interdependency should we insist upon this kind of political accommodation?

In our discussion of intervention we must acknowledge that what has always been seen as intervention from North to South is now shifting. Increasingly, intervention will move South to North. For that reason, it behooves us to be far more careful in our interactions with our neighbors in this hemisphere.

As the Hispanic population of the United States grows, it will increase its political importance, as has occurred with earlier waves of immigration into the United States. I see a qualitative difference between this wave of immigration and earlier ones, however. Although not yet as large a percentage of the population as were some of the earlier groups of immigrants, Hispanics are becoming politically active very rapidly. Unless we work hard to make the relations between our country and the other countries of this hemisphere easier during these next generations, we may see played out in the polity of the United States problems that we used to consider international problems. The people who come here from Latin America bring with them a very vibrant sense of home, which they do not lose very quickly. Within several generations the ties with the old country are not lost.

For example, the pressure for a bilingual society in the United States again represents both an opportunity and a problem for us. Although I am bilingual, I think it is a bad idea to have two official languages if we can avoid it. Yet the pressure builds. Conceivably, within a number of years, people will vote in two national elections. This type of political linking has never before occurred in this hemisphere, and that too is likely to push us toward new forms of interdependency.

Economic interdependence can be handled best within the private sector because it does not rise to the level of sovereign concern. We must be more active within the private sector, muting volatile issues as early as possible so that we avoid knotty questions of sovereignty.

Over time, I think the United States will loosen its tight links and identity with Europe and will draw increasingly closer socially, economically, and politically to the other countries of this hemisphere. Ultimately, I see this hemisphere interdependent as "an American people."

Discussion

QUESTION: When you addressed the point that cultural identity can conflict with appropriate economic strategy, I tried to think of an example. Would Chilean copper be such a case? During the administration of Eduardo Frei there was a movement toward joint ownership, foreign and national, and then with the presidency of Salvador Allende there was very quickly a nationalization of copper.

Did this represent a move in the direction of cultural identity without sensitivity to appropriate economic strategies?

MR. MARKS: Clearly nationalization reflected Chile's urge to control in the belief that Chile should be altogether sovereign. But I think it was also very closely related to the economic theory of the Allende government: that is, the state should own, first, all the resources and then fairly rapidly should acquire manufacturing operations as well.

QUESTION: Could you explain how pervasive the illegal or entrepreneurial businesses are, and what their ownership base is?

MR. MARKS: That is a fascinating subject. First, in talking about the private sector in this hemisphere, we need to adjust our definition somewhat and not accept the pejorative connotation of that term. In the past when Latin Americans have used the words "private sector," they have referred to large corporations, large landowners, and foreign investors. The private sector, however, ought to include everybody who does not work for the state—the person who shines shoes on the street, the gentleman who pushes a cart around the city sharpening knives, to cite two common examples. And there are many others between one who shines shoes and one who owns a very large corporation.

Today the small entrepreneurs are clearly part of the private sector, although in the past they have not been seen as part of the private sector. In the past they have been seen as a serious problem: something must be done for them. We must facilitate what they are already doing. As entrepreneurs, they are creating employment at a far lower cost than anyone else can.

Recent studies of Peru and Brazil have shown that when money has been made available through special channels to these people, a job can be created for about $1,500. That is small in comparison with the cost of creating a new job in large-scale industry, for example.

The problem these people run into most frequently, however, is working capital. They have no assets to offer a bank to borrow money. It is expensive to lend money to people that small. Because the paper work is expensive, the banks have attempted to avoid these loans as far as possible. Consequently, these people have borrowed money from others in the street and have paid an exorbitant rate of interest. Without those exorbitant rates of interest, imagine how much more rapidly they could be creating capital and more and more jobs.

The task of getting money to them is the most important consideration. How can we do it? When we contended with this problem in the United States many years ago, we found it to be quite difficult. According to the concept of supervised agricultural credit (which did not become a reality in this country until the New Deal), a farmer does not need a big farm to offer as collateral; if his planting program and marketing program are not appropriate, we should not lend him money because he will go bankrupt. The farm will be repossessed. Whereas if the farmer who only rents land has a very good program worked out in terms of crop and market cycles, we should lend him money. But that is a judgmental process, which requires time and is consequently expensive.

Many organizations today are attempting to promote the growth of this informal sector. An organization called Accion, for instance, is supported by a number of U.S. corporations specifically to make small loans of $500 or $1,000. The loans provide a subsidy, in effect, to a bank to make the money available without a whole new superstructure of lending. The organization pays the banker the cost of making this kind of a loan to the person, not necessarily guaranteeing the loan except in some cases.

I do not see any easy way to handle this particular problem. Creating a new bank in any one of the developing countries to handle the problem does not seem feasible. I think it will have to be handled by these ad hoc groups, organizations like Accion.

QUESTION: Doesn't this private economy benefit the middle class as opposed to the elite, as stated earlier? Is it also a proof that indigenous businesses can and will flourish in countries over time if the environment permits? And is it not also true, that instead of just redistributing wealth, that economy creates new wealth?

MR. MARKS: Very definitely. And this form of economic activity does not benefit the elite. Because each one of these people buys some kind of raw material for his product, it has a multiplier value, which can be enormous. It is unrecognized today, however, and excluded from the calculation of gross domestic product in most of these countries.

QUESTION: Earlier you mentioned a rational plan for Bolivia that would bring about a great deal of development and stability; cultural conditions, you said, prevented that from working out as planned.

What were the cultural conditions that prevented development? If you went back to implement the plan, how would you change it to accord with the culture?

MR. MARKS: One of the failures of that stabilization program was the heavy emphasis on foodstuffs for Bolivia in the short term. The United States was shipping flour, sugar, and a number of other foodstuffs. These shipments of commodities did not kill Bolivian agriculture, but they had a stultifying effect for perhaps twenty years on Bolivian agriculture. When that foodstuff went into Bolivia, it immediately filled the entire distribution network. The local wheat farmers, for example, could not sell their product at all and went out of business. For a period of time these shipments destabilized agriculture more than ever in Bolivia.

People in the United States felt a humanitarian concern to be as helpful as possible at the time. In the long run the efforts backfired. As an aside, hardships that to us seem horrendous often do not seem as bad to people who have lived with them all their lives. Now, I am not suggesting that people should continue to live with such hardships, I am just suggesting that their tolerance is considerably greater than we imagine and that sometimes the ameliorative programs we have proposed are quite damaging in the long run. Sometimes we try to proceed faster than is advisable.

In Bolivia, we also failed to take into consideration, in that program and in others, the degree of corruption possible in the distribution of products. Much of the product flew out of Bolivia into Chile and Brazil, where it was resold at much higher prices. The profit, of course, did not go into the state treasury.

COMMENT: Before the Kissinger Commission, I argued that a very important element in the program ought to be the encouragement of economic activism, particularly the entrepreneurs in the small business sector. I based my argument on the grounds that in the church preaching and literature there was almost nothing encouraging economic activism. Much of the literature concerns the relations of church and state and political activism but contains almost nothing on economic activism. The same holds true in the literary traditions of Latin America and to some extent in the legal traditions.

We need a lot of corporate encouragement. In El Salvador, whose population had doubled since the 1950s, not all the land reform in the world could provide enough employment. People will have to be resourceful in generating employment. For example, almost no bicycles are visible, and it seems to me that somebody should manufacture bicycles. But even if we could start nudging the leaders toward economic activism, we have almost no tradition to support it.

MR. MARKS: I think you are perfectly right in your criticism. I contend that this is something that the private sector, in the broadest definition, should be doing. For example, those of us engaged in business in this hemisphere should be very concerned about changes in Latin American laws that would allow the creation of foundations and private universities similar to those in the United States. There are not very many good private universities in Latin America, and there should be more. They can only be created, however, if it is possible for funds to be transferred easily from the profit-making sector into the foundations and universities. Today that is very difficult to do in Latin America.

If I were making suggestions to Latin American governments today, I would recommend that they change tax laws to facilitate the kind of giving possible and even attractive to wealthy people in the United States. It would have a multiplier effect in education and in the economic area. But that is very difficult to do and has been very slow moving.

QUESTION: How much of an obstacle to that kind of entrepreneurship is the victim psychology of dependency theory? This theory holds that there is a great conspiracy to keep people down, that somehow they are not in control of their fate. This conviction operates not simply with the poor but with elites as well. Is victim psychology as much a part of the moral-cultural horizon as seemed to be indicated earlier? That is not the kind of thing that can be changed by reforming tax laws. How does that psychology get turned around to create circumstances for economic growth?

MR. MARKS: That problem is more an intellectual one today. I see evidence in these parallel economies that in most of the countries of Latin America people are freeing themselves from the psychology of dependency. To begin with, they are at the lowest level of the economy, and they are not aware of the relationship between their domestic economy and the United States and Europe. They are concerned only about the economy within a ten-block area.

Now, fortunately perhaps, their world view is very restricted. They are concerned with opportunity within that ten-block area. I think that view ought to be promoted. With a change in viewpoint, development is likely to occur more frequently and in more areas.

In historical terms the reason Latin American development is different from ours is that the guild structure survived longer in Spain than it did in Northern Europe. The Spanish economic structures transplanted in the Spanish colonies were very different from the economic structures of North America. In North America, we have believed that the state should derive great benefit from private endeavor by taxing it. The state does not put many obstacles in its path but taxes it later. From the very beginning in Latin America everything had to be patented; everything had to be approved. A businessman still has to go through an incredible process of agreement with the state before he can actually do anything in the economic sphere. That terrible press of bureaucratic regimentation has got to be removed, although it is difficult because of entrenched bureaucracy in most of those countries. The bureaucracy feels a very strong social responsibility, which we may very well criticize and doubt, but they do feel it.

QUESTION: Although this is no doubt out of your area, what do you think about the role of the church in Latin America? Is it very influential? Is there any structured dialogue between the hierarchy and business leaders? Are the statements made by Latin American bishops at Puebla at all influential in the moral-cultural world?

MR. MARKS: I think that the political importance of the church is exaggerated. By becoming too strong an advocate in a particular direction, the church, unfortunately, diminished its importance. In a sense it gave up a position of arbiter, which it formerly had enjoyed, by becoming too strong an advocate. Perhaps that was important to do for other reasons, but I think something was lost in having taken that very strong advocacy position.

Today the hierarchy seems to be moving back toward the position of arbiter, consciously toward a position of greater, if not authority, certainly influence. It is attempting to exercise the influence that, in fact, it gave up for a time. I think that the church as an institution should exercise responsibility in Latin America as an arbiter. It has a role to play there that can be very important in facilitating the structural change now occurring. I think it is necessary, however, for the church to drop some of the economic baggage of the past. The view of the church toward economic activity continues to be different from ours, certainly.

The point of view of the Catholic church in the United States about economic activity seems to be very different from that of Catholics in most countries in Latin America. To promote economic activity, the church in Latin America must change some of its stances.

I must say, too, that I believe the question of population growth in Latin America is a very important consideration. In my view it will be impossible to maintain economic growth proportionate to the existing rate of growth of population in this hemisphere. In economic terms it appears impossible to keep up, with Mexico the worst example of that problem between now and the

185

end of this century. I believe that we have only begun to see the real strength of that problem.

COMMENT: On the subject of the elite in Latin America, I suggest that in addition to the cultural and attitudinal aspects already mentioned there is an important structural aspect. This has to do with the concentration of economic power and the way the banking system is set up in many of these countries; banks function not only as banks do in this country or in Western Europe but also own enterprises in the financial, industrial, agricultural, and commercial sectors. In them is concentrated a great deal of power. To have access to trade, a person must belong to one of these groups.

The solution, then, goes beyond changing attitudes and necessitates breaking up the structures. This seems to have been the case in Mexico, in Chile, and to a lesser degree in Colombia and Venezuela. What about Peru? Maybe you could enlighten us a bit.

MR. MARKS: In Peru, of course, the banks were nationalized, but before the nationalization they were not such large owners of other corporations as they were in other countries. Mexico is an interesting case. The enormous concentration of economic power in the banks, provided by the ownership of other facilities, was in effect a new position of state. When the Mexican government called for the Mexicanization of industries, we had a very large operation in Mexico, and we wanted to Mexicanize by selling stock. We were among the first to work on that, but the Mexican government refused to allow us to sell stock because, it reasoned, while we would reduce our economic interest in the firm, we would still maintain our control because the large number of stockholders would not have any real influence over the direction of the corporation. We had to sell to a single Mexican investment firm, to a bank, or to a tightly held group. That concentration of economic power in the Mexican banks occurred over a relatively short time.

Your basic point, however, is very important: access to credit must be democratized. That has been one of the vitally important motors of development in the United States. The first land bank in the United States existed before 1800, for example. The mechanics may need to be different from one country to another, but you are perfectly right that access to credit must be democratized.

A NOTE ON THE BOOK

*This book was edited by Dana Lane
and Janet Schilling of the
Publications Staff of the American Enterprise Institute.
The cover was designed by Karen Laub-Novak.
The typeface used for the text of this book is Times Roman,
designed by Stanley Morison.
The type was set by
Hendricks-Miller Typographic Company, of Washington, D.C.
Edwards Brothers Incorporated of Lillington, North Carolina,
printed and bound the book,
using permanent, acid-free paper made by the Glatfelter Company.*

SELECTED AEI PUBLICATIONS

AEI ASSOCIATES PROGRAM